MAC

The Wind Beneath My Wings

Sherry Hobbs

Black Rose Writing | Texas

©2023 by Sherry Hobbs
All rights reserved. No part of this book may be reproduced, stored in a retrieval system or transmitted in any form or by any means without the prior written permission of the publishers, except by a reviewer who may quote brief passages in a review to be printed in a newspaper, magazine or journal.

The author grants the final approval for this literary material.

First printing

Some names and identifying details have been changed to protect the privacy of individuals.

ISBN: 978-1-68513-241-5
PUBLISHED BY BLACK ROSE WRITING
www.blackrosewriting.com

Printed in the United States of America
Suggested Retail Price (SRP) $23.95

Mac is printed in Palatino Linotype

*As a planet-friendly publisher, Black Rose Writing does its best to eliminate unnecessary waste to reduce paper usage and energy costs, while never compromising the reading experience. As a result, the final word count vs. page count may not meet common expectations.

Praise for
MAC

"An incredible memoir of one of the first B24 and B29 bomber pilots. Author Hobbs, his daughter, has skillfully woven a tapestry with detailed research about a hero full of bravery, compassion, and love for his family, his squadron and his country."
–J. Ivanel Johnson, author of the *JUST (e)STATE* mysteries

"For those who have read biographies and histories of World II, the reader will find in Sherry Hobbs' biography of her father, Colonel Harold McNeese, known as Mac, an unusual and personal perspective. Not only did Ms. Hobbs' memory and love for her father color his biography, but it well-reflects the gentle man known as Mac."
–Iris Hattersley, author of *Lucky Thirteen*

"Far more than a wonderful telling of the life of a B24 bomber pilot, this book is chock full of detail and research into WWII. A must read for any who fancy aviator war stories."
–Richard Johnson, World War II Enthusiast

"This book is a triumph."
–*MJV Literary*

I dedicate this book to my father, Col. Harold G. McNeese, one of the first men to fly the new B-24 bomber and, later, the newer B-29 bombers in WWII. It is also a story about a man who lived his life with honor, integrity, and a hefty dose of humor.

I also dedicate it to all the men and women who served their country in WWII, particularly those in the 307th Bombardment Group in the 13th Air Force and the 39th Bombardment Group in the 20th Air Force with whom my father served during two tours—first on Guadalcanal and then in Guam. The incredible bravery these men showed is astounding. These young men risked their lives every time they flew in these new and unproven planes. They were more likely to die in accidents than by enemy fire.

I would like to honor three other fathers in my family who also served in WWII:

My uncle, 1st Lt. Robert "Bob" Godfrey McNeese. Mac's brother served in the army and took part in the Alaska Aleutian Islands Campaign against the Japanese.

Roby Hobbs Jr., my father-in-law, was a Navy Seabee who served in several battalions in the South Pacific, building the vital runways and air bases needed by all the branches of service and the Allies throughout the war. He took part in the Northern Solomon Islands Campaign.

My brother-in-law's father, Lizardo Lee Cordova, took part in the North African Campaign serving as a tank radio operator with the Western Task Force, commanded by Lt. Gen. George S. Patton. When Patton took over the armored command, the U.S. could push the Germans east.

Finally, I dedicate this to my darling husband, Michael, whose progressive dementia didn't allow him to understand what I was doing. He knew, however, that I was incredibly busy, and so rarely and cautiously interrupted me at the computer to ask for help to put clothes in the washer or find the batteries for his hearing aids. I love you, Mike.

Foreword

Imagine you are a teenager or young adult and that in the fourteen months following the Japanese attack on Pearl Harbor, you are a soldier in our Army Air Corps, newly trained and deployed. After a long journey, you have arrived at your unit's destination. It is an island with which you are not familiar, named Guadalcanal.

In briefings, you have been informed of a plethora of tropical diseases, also new to you. Some are transmitted by the many insects, particularly mosquitoes. As you are just twelve degrees latitude from the equator, your stay will be both hot and humid. What you didn't know until your arrival and the ensuing weeks was that your air base would be bombed nightly, a flood would destroy your camp, that the closest English-speaking people, other than your brothers-in-arms, are over 1,400 miles away, and that though your squadron will be intercepted by scores of Japanese fighters, most of your combat missions would be flown without any fighter escort. Relatedly, the personnel loss rates for your unit would range as high as 50 percent, and many of these men were your friends.

You are an airman, attached to the 13th Air Force, 307th Bombardment Group (Heavy), assigned to a nine-man crew, flying a B-24D model *Liberator* four-engine bomber. You are so forward deployed, your aircraft are in Japanese-controlled airspace soon after your takeoff. Should the need arise to bail out, you will likely be strafed and killed. Should you survive a crash or ditching and be captured, you will be tortured for information and beheaded or otherwise executed. The 13th Air Force will become known as "The Jungle Air Force," and by the following year, your 307th BG will become known as the "Long Rangers," following multiple, record-setting, long-distance combat missions.

As your unit moves "up the slot" in the Solomon Islands, your airbase will follow. By the end of World War II, your airbase will have moved ten times. Though significant, your targets will be as unfamiliar as these airbases under your boots—Wake Island, Bougainville, Shortland Harbor, Kahili, Munda, Rabaul, and many others. To this day, most Americans would find it difficult to locate these targets on a map without a navigational aid. Despite the aforementioned conditions and hazards, you are a proud member of this original echelon of airmen in the Southwest Pacific Area (SWPA) Theater and eager to bring the war to these Japanese strongholds.

The author, through this labor of love, has woven a historical perspective of her family's history, the international events preceding World War II, the 307th Bombardment Group history, and her father's service with this unit. Harold G. McNeese's (Mac's) non-combat experiences are shared through multiple letters home and give an insightful view of the day-to-day life of an airman in the SWPA. Her thorough account is a tribute to her father and these largely unheralded men who served us so well in this remote corner of the world during the initial stages of our U.S. Army Air Corps war in the Pacific from 1942 through 1943.

As Mac would make a career in the military, he would return to the Central Pacific Theater in 1944, flying the B-29 *Superfortress* with the 20th Air Force's 39th Bombardment Group, 62nd Bombardment Squadron. The author also provides an account of this deployment and Mac's and their family's experiences during the Korean War and Vietnam. Collectively, the personal and technical information within this work provide a rare glimpse into an air corps, then air force officer and his family's experience over two decades beginning in 1941, lives well lived in service to our country.

Jim McCabe, Historian
307th Bomb Group (H) Association
Pearl Harbor Day 2022

MAC

Prelude

September 6, 1947

    Impatiently rapping a pen on a clipboard, the tiny, blonde woman stood in a doorway wearing a starched, white uniform with a white cap. "Col. McNeese?" she said. She looked around the room as a sea of anxious faces turned to her gaze. Raising the timbre of her voice, she repeated, "Col. McNeese?"

    "I'm over here," Mac said as he snuffed out his cigarette in the circular, metal ashtray and hurried toward her. Col. Harold Graham McNeese was in the waiting room of the Los Angeles Hospital. Nervous fathers packed the large room with gray walls as they sat, paced, chain-smoked, and waited for their name to be called.

    "You can go in now to see your wife and new baby daughter. They're in Room 307," she said. "They are both doing fine. Your wife had a bit of a time as the baby was born breech, but we sedated her to keep her out of pain. Just go through those double doors, sir, and make a left."

    "Thank you." Mac quickly pushed through the doors and disappeared down the hallway. The room, marked 307, was ajar. He strode toward the hospital bed, kissed Jerrie, then turned his sparkling, green eyes to gaze down at me. Mother smiled, holding me as I lay on her chest.

    "She's beautiful, just perfect," he said as he reached down and carefully cradled me in his arms. He seemed to glow with pride. My eyes could not yet focus, but his chestnut-brown hair bristled in a military crew cut that framed his oval face. It was Saturday, and Mac dressed in black slacks and a starched, white shirt with the sleeves rolled up over his elbows. A pack of cigarettes peeked from his shirt pocket, and a tight smile formed on his lips. Taking in a deep breath, he raised himself up an inch or two, so ready for fatherhood. Mac was incredibly relieved that we both survived the ordeal of a breech childbirth. I had entered this world feet first, ready to charge through life, my father's daughter.

Of course, I had no inkling of what my father's life was like prior to my entry into this world. What happened in the preceding twenty-nine years that brought him to this moment? How could I have known that just two years before my birth, this man, who now held me so gently in his arms, had returned from war a hero—a pilot who flew eighty-three combat missions before the war ended?

As the years passed and I grew up, I learned to love this man who was my father—tender, loving, and fair, always encouraging me to read, to learn, and to spread my wings. But I wanted to understand how he became the man he was, a man of conscience, courage, and integrity.

I discovered little about his early life pre me until I was an adult. When prompted, during visits, he told me fascinating stories about his early days as a young man in the U.S. Merchant Marine and as a brash, young pilot in WWII. In my forties, I skimmed two books written by men who served with him in the brand-new 307th Bombardment Group, reading the pages where his name appeared, but gave it only a momentary thought. I was too busy with my own life.

It wasn't until I opened a cardboard box of memorabilia I received after my father died and I retired that the significance of his life, in its totality, struck me. Opening this unassuming, brown box was like opening a time capsule. Tossed in a heap, like so many objects thrown in a junk drawer, were commendations, photos, documents, and letters he wrote home during WWII. His matter-of-fact account of his first combat mission from Guadalcanal, when his plane went down in flames, stunned me.

I poured through the treasure trove of items, and at once, I wanted to learn more about my dad's early life and his post-war assignments and accomplishments. When I finally closed the lid of the box, I felt compelled and honored to tell the incredible story of this remarkable man and the people, events, and circumstances that shaped his character and life. I discovered he formed the traits he exhibited as an adult early in childhood. As William Wordsworth so succinctly and poetically reminded us, "The child is the father of the man."

Part 1

Chapter 1
The Dogfight

Looking out through the windshield, Mac could see miles ahead of him. The skies were an azure blue, and not a cloud was visible. Far below them, the green-tinted ocean rolled monotonously to their left.

The planes moved into formation positions. Turning his head to his left, Mac could clearly see the copilot in the plane next to them, about one hundred feet away. The distance was a delicate balance of tight, defensive firepower and the difficulty pilots faced flying in formation. Not close enough to collide, but not so far away that a single flak burst between two planes *could* severely damage both aircraft. Unlike the Japanese, American heavy bombers flew in formation because this was the most effective tactic against enemy gunfire and fighter defense. There was safety in numbers. Getting into formation required a good deal of time and effort, adding up to an hour of flying time. It also increased the possibility of pilot fatigue and used up a sizable percentage of valuable fuel, but the procedure was essential. Mac was flying in the number three position as wingman to the lead plane in a six-plane formation.

The only object he could see was the plane just ahead, center right. He glanced over at his copilot, Van, who sat to the right of him. He was tense and engaged. With the clear weather, the visibility now at 14,000 feet was excellent. Even with headphones on, the monotonous growl of the four engines on the B-24 *Liberator* sounded like angry lions protecting their prey. The six B-24 bombers, now in formation, collected their twelve escort fighters. Four P-38s and eight P-40s surrounded the six planes, and together, they continued on course up the channel. The islands on either side were Japanese occupied.

Mac turned his head back to the windshield in front of him. Even with the noise of the engines, it felt calm. The air was still, but knowing what lie ahead, he could feel his skin prickle with electricity. The hairs on his arms stood up, and his palms were wet with sweat. This was what he had waited for, had trained for, had dreamed about since he had taken his first flying lesson two years before. He felt neither nervous nor afraid; he was pumped too full of adrenaline.

Mac checked his watch. They were about a half hour from their target. The bomb bay doors opened as the formation turned in unison toward Shortland Harbor, at the northwest end of the Solomon Islands, where the Japanese Navy had erected a seaplane base. Inside the plane, no chatter was heard. The crew was enmeshed in their own thoughts. Outside the plane, the stillness felt like a hurricane was approaching, with chaos and disaster swirling ahead of them. It could have been just an ordinary, beautiful day to fly, but they were on their way to drop bombs that would explode on ships with people inside the ships who would die. Enemies to be sure, but people just the same. The enemy would undoubtedly return fire from the ground and from the air. It was February 13, 1943, and this just might be the last day of their lives.

The bombardiers in the six planes carefully set their Norden Bombsights with the altitude and wind speed. They looked through the device's telescope for an aiming mark below them and set that as well. Command had instructed the five trailing bombardiers to release their bombs as soon as the lead bombardier discharged his, to blanket their targets.

As they neared the harbor, the once-clear skies suddenly darkened—not with clouds, but with planes that filled the airspace like a swarm of angry wasps headed straight toward them. Fifty Japanese *Zeros*, already airborne and awaiting their arrival, met them with intense machine gunfire. Nothing the young crews had done in training had prepared them for this.

Suddenly, bullets were flying into the plane, pinging them and creating points of light through the aluminum metal fuselage. Rapid rat-a-tat sounds of machine gunfire from the swiveling guns within the body of their own plane were deafening. The waist and tail gunners returned fire through the openings as they swung the guns around on their turrets, firing at the enemy planes. The noise of gunfire hitting the outside of the *Liberator* and piercing the body all around them sounded like a sudden, violent rainstorm had caught them while they were trapped under a tin roof. But they were all too busy trying to stay alive to acknowledge fear, even to themselves.

They passed the corner of Fauro Island and entered the Shortland Harbor area at 12:50 in the afternoon. Mac could see scattered Japanese shipping below and a large transport ship with about 10,000 tons of cargo lying about a mile off Bougainville Island. These were their targets.

He watched as the plane ahead of him, piloted by Lt. Russell W. Rowe of the 424th BS, released its bombs. One of them malfunctioned, and the second fell impotently into the ocean. Then suddenly, while still over the target, enemy fire struck the plane, and it burst into flames, disintegrating in front of them. Besides the nine regular crew members, there was a U.S. Navy photographer on board as an observer.

Gunfire then hit a second plane piloted by Lt. George A. Trager, also in the 424th BS, just after reaching the target. Mac couldn't see if they had been able to drop their bombs or not, but Lt. Trager began a slow glide toward the sea. Mac and Van watched helplessly as that plane also burst into flames and crashed from about five hundred feet in the air. Two bombers, two crews, obliterated seconds apart.

Because of operational difficulties, the first fighter escort of twelve planes shrank to six even before they reached the target and had to turn back. The Japanese shot down the three that made it to the target, leaving only three fighters to protect the remaining four B-24 bombers and their crews. Everyone was firing at the *Zeros* while bullets came at them from all directions. The seven planes were desperately outgunned and outmanned.

Seeing the lead plane go down in flames, Don, Mac's bombardier, checked his bombsight once again. He then waited until the target was directly in his crosshairs and pressed the button, releasing the plane's payload. The fuses had a forty-five-second delay, which ensured that the bombs didn't blow up in the plane's nose. Black smoke and sooty, burning hydrocarbons boiled up all around them. Suddenly, Don yelled, "Bombs away!" The *Liberator* gave a gentle lurch up and was 4,000 pounds lighter as the bombs fell away from the plane. The four individual and two racks of bombs sank a Japanese cruiser and two other vessels below them in the harbor, like hitting sitting ducks in a pond.

Stationed in the extreme front of the plane, bombardiers doubled as front gunners or nose gunners, firing the gun on the front turret on the way to the target and after releasing the bombs. Don immediately took his position at the machine gun and began blasting at the enemy planes that were shooting back at them.

The navigator, 2nd Lt. Les Carroll, who operated the radio and radar, sat behind the pilots facing the outside of the plane and now doubled as a waist gunner. He stood at an open bay window, firing furiously at the *Zeros* as they swooped in for the kill. The flight engineer, Staff Sgt. Bill Adams, who sat behind the pilots next to Les, controlled the upper gun turret, which was located right behind the cockpit, in front of the wing.

Four crew members manned waist guns, a retractable lower ball turret, and a tail gun turret in the plane's tail. They did as much damage to the *Zeros* as they could muster. The rat-a-tat sounds of thousands of rounds of machine gunfire, from within and from outside, filled the cabin with bullets, riddling the plane. It felt as if they were trapped inside a large, metal barrel while a firing squad shot relentlessly into it.

The three trailing B-24s released their bombs seconds after Mac's plane released theirs. Then in unison, the four planes made a left turn, climbed to 15,000 feet (about half the cruising altitude of a commercial jet), turned away from their target, and headed back to base. Suddenly, bullets hit Mac's number one engine, and it caught fire as they passed over Fauro Island; then the wing burst into flames. Unable to keep up with the squadron, he dropped out of formation and headed out to sea, chased by thirty or forty *Zero*s and twelve to fifteen float planes now attacking him like leopards pursuing a wounded antelope.

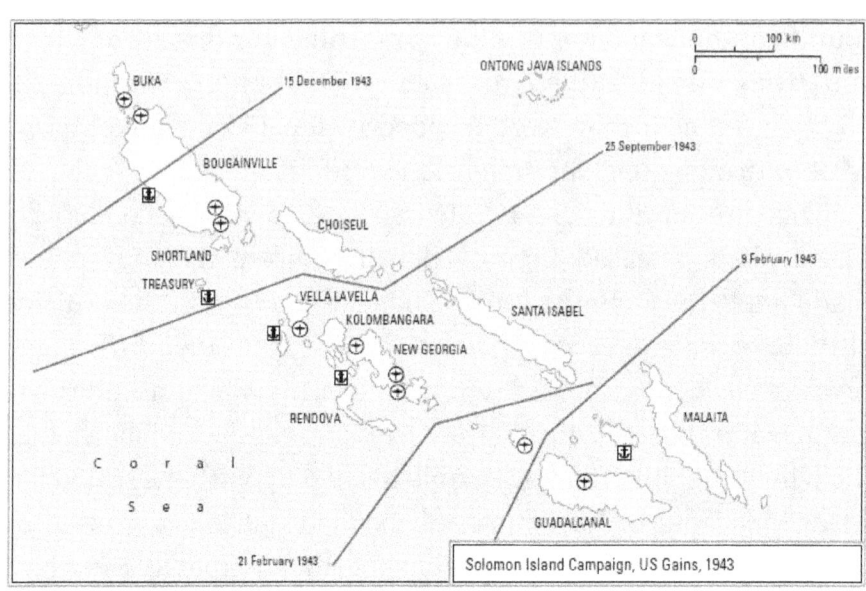

The Slot

Bombs Away headed "up the slot"

Chapter 2
Harold G. McNeese "Mac"—The Early Years

The Scotch-Irish McNeese clan had emigrated to the U.S. from Scotland generations before Mac's birth and had settled in what was then Oklahoma territory. His grandfather, William G. McNeese, was a pharmacist who owned drug stores in Marlow and Mangum, Oklahoma in the mid-to-late 1800s. He was called Doc, and he was the closest thing there was to a medical doctor in those parts, treating the many ailments of the residents in those towns.

But Doc was, by all accounts, a heavy drinker and an unrepentant womanizer. His wife, Mary Mangum, the daughter of the town's founder, was a brilliant woman in her own right with an independent streak. A woman of means, she invested in oil rights and property, and after saving enough money, she filed for divorce and moved to Texas with her two young sons, Harold and James, in tow. There she opened a booming retail business.

The two boys thrived, and when Harold graduated from the University of Texas, he moved to Chicago, Illinois to attend law school. He took classes at night and worked in a law firm during the day, where he met and married Margaret Godfrey, the daughter of a prominent Chicago family. Their first son, Harold Graham McNeese, who was called Mac, was born on April 15, 1918, the year WWI ended.

Harold had already discovered that he was not cut out to be a lawyer when he met a gentleman who owned a roofing business.

"I can use a bright, young man like you," he said, and hired him on the spot. With an outstanding sales record, the owner of the firm quickly promoted Harold to sales manager and sent him off to various cities in the Midwest to open offices and hire and train the growing sales force. This, of course, meant frequent moves for the young family and would begin a pattern of relocation and change of environment for Mac that he grew to relish.

Harold, although successful in the roofing business, was, like his mother, an entrepreneur at heart and dreamed of moving back to Texas and starting his own business. Black-and-white silent films had become extremely popular since their debut in 1905 in Pittsburgh, Pennsylvania, and movie theaters had popped up all over the country. But in the ensuing fifteen years, many had grown shabby, falling into disrepair. Now, the country was on the cusp of the decade of the Roaring Twenties, and people were in the mood for fun and entertainment, which included going to the movies.

"I've got some money saved, and I've been thinking you are right about investing in movie theaters," Harold said to his mother on a phone call one day when Mac was about a year old.

"Come back down to Texas, son," his mother told him. "Oil's a gushin' and crops are bustin' out of the ground. Business is booming here, and there's plenty of opportunity. Oilers, farmers, manufacturers … everyone's got money to burn, and they're dyin' for entertainment. There are a lot of small towns with older theaters that need fixin' up. You could buy them for a song, gussy them up a bit, and resell 'em for a tidy profit."

The Roaring Twenties was indeed an exciting time in which to live, particularly in Texas. In the aftermath of WWI, there was a no-holds-barred feeling of freedom. Prohibition was the law of the land, but speakeasies proliferated. Jazz and dancing rose in popularity. A feeling of great vitality swept through the country—and most of the world. America had become urbanized. There was so much recent technology. With mass production, automobiles, telephones, radio, and electrical appliances were widely available and used by millions of people in the Western world. Mass-market advertising companies, a new industry, pushed to increase consumer demand. They focused on celebrities, especially sports heroes and movie stars, as people rushed to fill movie theaters and gigantic sports stadiums.[1]

With his mother's encouragement and urging, Harold quit his management job in the Midwest and moved his family south to the growing, business-friendly state of Texas, intent on making his fortune. Making the first of many moves throughout Texas, they landed in Henrietta, where Mac's brother, Bob, was born the year after they arrived.

Harold moved his young family from one small, dusty Texas town to another, buying up old theaters and renovating them. He replaced worn seats, painted the walls, put in new movie machines, new screens, and rubber carpeting. He owned theaters in Victoria, Catello, Alvin, Mexia, and Kenedy, among other cities, and the family prospered for the next seven years.

Then 'talkies' burst on the cinematic scene in 1927, and the costs of converting theaters to sound became prohibitive. Recorded sound was not on the film itself but accompanied it on a separate wax disc that the projectionist had to synchronize with the film. They played the sound on a turntable physically coupled to the projector motor while they flashed the film up on the screen.[2]

Harold sold all the theaters and moved the family once again, this time to Dallas where he became manager of the Theater

---

[1] Wikipedia. "The Roaring Twenties."
[2] WarnerBros.com. Website.

Owners Association. Then, lured away by a lucrative job offer, he moved the family one final time to San Antonio to be the sales promotion manager of San Antonio Power and Light Company. His future looked bright.

It was also a good time and place for young boys to grow up. The state of Texas was full of adventure for exuberant boys. They rode ponies, swam in creeks, and played cowboys and Indians. The McNeese family's peripatetic lifestyle surely fed into Mac's need for change, exploration, and adventure. He had an innate curiosity about the world, and he thrived on the many moves.

Mac's mother, Margaret, doted on her boys and lavished them with love and praise, instilling them with great self-confidence in their abilities to succeed in life. No doubt, their successful and competent paternal grandmother also played an influential role in their development, although she described the boys as "quite a handful." Both were bright, rambunctious, and possessed a sense of humor and quick wit. A devoted yet no-nonsense nurse named Quilla was hired to keep a close watch over the rowdy duo.

Mac was always serious about school, however, and seemingly excelled at everything he did. His brother, Bob, recalled that he and Mac attended a one-room schoolhouse and were seated according to I.Q. determined by intelligence tests that were routinely administered to schoolchildren in the 1920s. He said Mac sat in the front row, and he was stuck in the back between a Mexican boy who spoke no English and an unfortunate lad with a harelip, whom no one could understand. This story is suspect because of Bob's great sense of humor, but Mac was undoubtedly at the head of the class.

At a time in history when most people never left the city in which they were born, Mac's father took risks and chased opportunity wherever it led. Luckily, wanderlust was in Mac's blood and thrill-seeking in his DNA. He thrived on this nomadic lifestyle, enjoying the change of environment and the chance to learn new things that the moves always promised. He was also a voracious reader and read everything he could get his hands on, but he particularly loved adventure stories. Mac grew up reading books by Ernest Hemingway, Jack London, and Rudyard Kipling. His curiosity fueled his desire to learn everything he could about life and the world around him. He saw humor in the human condition and laughed often, enjoying or telling a good joke.

The 1920s were a heady time in America and most of the world. People were enjoying life. Mac's first decade of childhood was idyllic. Then global and personal tragedy struck their world like a one-two punch to the gut from a heavyweight boxer.

Harold Sr., Margaret, Mac and Bob

Mac and Bob in Texas

Chapter 3
Mac—The Teen Years

The decade of the Roaring Twenties was about to come to a screeching halt. It roared only in abject pain after 'Black Tuesday'—October 29, 1929—when Wall Street crashed, plunging the world into the abyss that would be called the Great Depression. This dark period in history lasted until 1939, another full decade, when only another war would end it. As exhilarating and joyous as the 1920s had been, the 1930s were as dismal and dark as a coal mine.

Mac was eleven years old when the Great Depression began. With the crash of Wall Street, personal income, revenue from taxes, profits, and prices dropped, while international trade fell by over 50 percent. Almost a quarter of Americans were suddenly out of work. There was certainly no disposable income for entertainment. Movie theaters languished as productions decreased and audiences shrank.[3]

The Great Depression affected regions and states in diverse ways. In Texas, where the McNeeses were living, cities instituted austerity programs, fired married women, cut teachers' salaries, reduced appropriations for public education, ended some urban services, and froze employee salaries.[4] It hit farmers in Texas and throughout the Southern Plains especially hard. During WWI,

---
[3] https://dp.la/exhibitions/the-show.
[4] Docest.com. "Texas and the Great Depression."

the demand for wheat from Europe increased, which encouraged farmers in the U.S. to plow up millions of acres of native grassland to plant wheat, corn, and other row crops. But when the United States entered the Great Depression, wheat prices plummeted by 60 percent.

What started in New York quickly spread around the globe, creating a worldwide economic disaster of major proportions. Like a tetherball swinging around a pole, the Great Depression spun quickly, devastating the economies of rich and poor countries alike.[5] Cities everywhere suffered, especially those dependent on heavy industry. Construction came to an abrupt halt in many countries. Farmers and rural communities suffered as crop prices fell everywhere, but few industries or professions were unscathed as people had little money to pay doctors, lawyers, or shopkeepers. Eventually, most nations faced extreme unemployment and deflation. This created poverty and hunger around the globe. The world faced a dire existence.

• • •

Then, Mother Nature piled on. In 1931, many Southern and Midwestern states, including Texas, experienced a severe drought across the region. As the lack of rain caused crops to die, wind carried dust from the over-plowed and over-grazed lands. Dust caused many people to be stricken with dust pneumonia and die in the years that followed. Drought and dust storms intensified in what was later called the Dust Bowl. Without rain, huge, thick, black dust storms emanated from eroded fields that destroyed entire farmlands and homes, sickening the populace. Like a buzzard picking apart a dead carcass, the Dust Bowl made the effects of the Great Depression exponentially worse for people in the Southern Plains. Millions of Texans who had

---

[5] Frank, Robert H., and Ben S. Bernanke. 2007. *Principles of Macroeconomics*. 98. 3rd ed. Boston: McGraw-Hill/Irwin.
[6] https://www.weatheringtexas.com/the-dust-bowl/.

farmed for generations—along with another one and a half million folks from Nebraska, Kansas, Colorado, New Mexico, Oklahoma, Arkansas, and Missouri—abandoned their land and made their way to California in search of a better life.[6]

Three years after the start of the Great Depression, Harold Sr. fell ill. "Your father is sick, Harold. You need to do your best in school. If the Lord takes him, I'm counting on you to be the man in the family."

Harold Sr. died of dust bowl pneumonia when he was only forty-two years old. Mac was fourteen. His mother, Margaret, now widowed and apparently penniless, had no job prospects and had nothing to sustain the family. She decided to leave Texas. She was a nervous, dependent woman by nature and had relied on the men in her life to take care of her.

"We're moving back to Chicago," Margaret told her boys shortly after her husband's death. "I can't afford to stay here any longer. The dust is intolerable, and we will all die if we stay." They packed what they could and made their way north to Illinois.

For a while, Mac and Bob bounced around, sleeping on the couches of various relatives in Chicago until the family landed permanently with Margaret's sister, Jeanne, her husband, Freeman Bradford, and their son, Bill.

Their cousin recalled, "My first memory of Mac was when my sheltered life as an only child in suburban Chicago was shattered by the arrival of two cousins from Texas: Mac and his brother, Bob. Their father had died, and they were going to live with us. I was eight, Bob was eleven, and Mac was fourteen. With six years' difference in our age, Mac and I did not become close buddies. Instead, he became my older brother, a teacher, a pillar of support, a disciplinarian, and above all, an example whose accomplishments I could brag about."

Mac, suddenly thrust into the role of man of the family, was now a budding teenager, and as the elder son, he shouldered his responsibilities eagerly. He worked every day after school, bringing his paycheck home while maintaining a straight A average and excelling in athletics. His was the last generation in which the roles of men and women were so clearly defined.

For Mac, there was no confusion. Men needed to be brave and strong, work hard, and take care of their women and children. A woman's role was that of a wife, mother, and homemaker. Her job was to cook the meals, take care of the home, and raise the children. In return, her husband would provide, cherish, and revere her. This was how Margaret raised Mac, and at fourteen, he fervently believed this to be the true nature of men and women. He felt an enormous responsibility resting on his young shoulders and was incredibly accountable to the people who depended on him. He saw his role as provider and protector of family and country, and he never let either down.

Mac graduated from high school with honors in 1936 and enrolled in college at Northwestern University. After finishing his first year, he took a break from studies to see the world. He was intrepid. So, at age twenty, he joined the United States Merchant Marine as an able-bodied seaman and spent the next two years working on a cargo ship and soaking up exotic, far-flung locales in Asia and China, always sending money home to help support his widowed mother. Mac saw the world as a conundrum—how seemingly geographically vast, yet tiny and intertwined it was. People intrigued and interested him.

When I was a teenager, Mac regaled me with tales of his sea travels to various ports, including Shanghai. He was a marvelous storyteller. In the 1930s, this port city in eastern China was a dangerous den of iniquity where once, while drinking in an unsavory bar by the docks with fellow sailors, he was almost 'shanghaied.' Kidnapped and drugged, his captors threw him in a cart and took him to an unknown location to be held for ransom, which was a common risk to sailors in Shanghai in those days. With his gift of storytelling, I sat spellbound, the adventure shadowy and mysterious. Through grit, wit, and trickery, he escaped and ran through a labyrinth of narrow streets and alleys to get back to his ship while being chased by his pursuers like a wily roadrunner fleeing coyotes nipping at his heels.

By 1939, Mac returned to Chicago after his tour with the U.S. Merchant Marine, intent on finishing college. But on September 1, Germany, led by the dictator Adolph Hitler, invaded Poland, triggering WWII, and that event forever changed Mac's life plan. Indeed, it would alter the lives of millions of people. He knew it was only a matter of time before the United States became actively involved in the war, and he intended to be ready.

Mac wanted adventure and excitement. He also wanted the respect that came with heroics and duty to country. He enrolled in DePaul University's preliminary army air course to become a pilot and graduated as their highest-ranking student.

Mac at 14

Merchant Marine

Chapter 4
Japan Joins the Axis—1940

While Europe and the United States laser-focused on Hitler and his trampling and occupation of countries, on the other side of the world, Japan was busy plotting its own version of colonialism for Asia and the South Pacific, extending its political and economic access, power, and control over other militarily weaker countries.

There were two leaders of Japan during the time of World War II: Emperor Hirohito and Gen. Hideki Tojo. Hirohito took over at a time of democratic sentiment, but like Germany, his country had turned toward ultra-nationalism and militarism, and, to some extent, Hirohito became marginalized. The much more powerful Tojo, a general of the Imperial Japanese Army, was the prime minister and pushed Japan to become a totalitarian, one-party state.[7]

Japan had already started on an aggressive colonial expansion at the turn of the twentieth century. As an island nation, they may have felt somewhat isolated from the rest of the world and thought they could continue to expand their sphere of influence while the West was preoccupied with Hitler. They had previously forced their way into China during two

---

[7] van Wolferen, Karel. 1989. *The Enigma of Japanese Power: People and Politics in a Stateless Nation.* 351.
1st ed. New York: Knopf.

successive wars: the Russo-Japanese War from 1904 to 1905 and WWI from 1914 to 1918. Japan wanted the resources of other countries and felt that they could just take them with impunity. When the Great Depression began in the 1930s, the country solved their economic problems by invading and occupying Manchuria. In July 1937, Japan instigated another war with China and captured and took over the city of Nanking in a six-week reign of terror, committing mass killings of at least 200,000 people and countless rapes. This time, their aggression got outside attention.

Tensions between the U.S. and Japan had been gradually building for almost a decade during the Great Depression. The United States had territories and economic interests in the Far East they wanted to protect, and Japan was moving to occupy these countries. Because of the atrocities committed in Nanking, and to hurt them financially, the United States began passing economic sanctions against the Japanese Empire, which included trade embargoes on aircraft exports, oil, and scrap metal and gave economic support to the Chinese forces battling Japan. And then, just to rub dirt into the festering wound, the U.S. froze Japanese assets in the U.S. A hostile and furious Japan resulted.

At first, Tokyo and the United States tried to work things out diplomatically, but the U.S.'s unwillingness to remove the economic sanctions outraged the Japanese people. As diplomatic negotiations with Japan broke down, President Franklin D. Roosevelt and his advisers knew that an imminent attack on the U.S. was quite probable. In fact, political hawks in both countries had talked openly about going to war with each other for years.

While the war in Europe was underway in 1939, President Roosevelt ordered the U.S. Pacific Fleet to move from California to Pearl Harbor, in Oahu, Hawaii, in anticipation of a war with Japan. By May 1940, the U.S. had made Pearl Harbor the principal base for its Pacific Fleet. Japan saw this move as an aggression and a direct threat to them, which only increased tensions between the two countries.

Along with its hostilities in China, on September 22, 1940, Japan invaded French Indochina and occupied Vietnam, Malay, Indonesia, and Thailand, all of which provided the lion's share of the world's rubber production. They then turned to Germany and Italy and signed the Tripartite Pact in September 1940, allying themselves with the two fascist regimes at war with England and the subjugated and powerless France. The pact assured mutual united help if any of the signatories suffered an attack by any nation not already involved in the war, such as the U.S. or the Soviet Union predominantly. Japan was now joined with Germany and Italy as part of the Axis Powers, and trouble continued to brew and turn bitter, like a pot of coffee left too long on the burner.

In October 1941, buoyed by their alliance with the Axis Powers, the Japanese Cabinet met to consider war plans. "In the event that there is no prospect of our demands being met by the first ten days of October through the diplomatic negotiations, we will immediately decide to commence hostilities against the United States, Britain, and the French," they declared. Their demands included a free hand to continue with their conquest of China and Southeast Asia with no buildup of U.S. or British military forces in the region, and to be assured of the cooperation of the West as they usurped goods from occupied countries. Knowing this was an unrealistic expectation—and one to which neither the U.S. nor Great Britain would agree—the empire of Japan began making plans to go to war.

Japan knew the United States was a world power and would defend that status against their own comparatively smaller nation, so they figured a surprise attack was their best chance of success. Japan wanted a limited war: sneak in and decimate the U.S. Navy battleships before anyone knew what was happening, then move out swiftly. This would allow Japan time to capture islands in the Pacific and build an extensive empire free of American interference, while the U.S. was busy scrambling to rebuild its fleet. By the time Americans were ready for action, they theorized, Japan's defense perimeter would be so strong with added battleships that the United States wouldn't have the will or the means to fight its way across the Pacific.[8]

Japan also thought the people of the United States were soft, with no appetite for another war, and would quickly surrender after a swift and devastating blow, wiping out their navy. They couldn't have been more wrong.

---

[8] Citino, Rob, Senior Historian. *TIME* magazine.

Chapter 5
The U.S. Readies for War

The first world war ended in 1918, the year Mac was born. When he reached the age of majority, he had not known war, but it was still fresh in the minds of his parents' generation. It had been a devastating, senseless—as virtually all wars are—loss of millions of lives.

WWI was one of the bloodiest conflicts in the history of the human race. The deaths that directly resulted from that war are about 50–56 million people (about twice the population of Texas), while deaths from famine and disease claimed another 19–28 million people (about the population of Texas). Of the total deaths, 21–25 million were military, while civilians who died in the war were 50–55 million. Another war so soon after the 'Great War' was unthinkable, and the U.S. was not preparing for another one.[9]

There was no separate branch of the military for airpower following WWI. As John Frisbee describes in *Air and Space Forces* magazine, when WWI began in 1914, none of the European countries even had airplanes that were designed for military use. Their aircraft were unarmed, had a top speed of about sixty-five miles an hour, and at first were used only for observing enemy troop movements. Four years later, at the end of the war, both

---

[9] www.worldatlas.com/articles/wwii-casualties-by-country.html.

the Allies and the Central Powers had thousands of armed pursuit, bomber, attack, and observation aircraft. The speed of pursuits had increased to 130 miles an hour, and the British, French, Italians, Germans, and Russians had developed multi-engine bombers with a wingspan of one hundred feet.

However, immediately following WWI, Americans had no appetite for setting up a new military service for airpower. Most people believed, as did the army, that the most important function of airpower was defensive. The United States had moved toward isolationism and would remain stubbornly of that mindset, much to the consternation of Winston Churchill, until the attack on Pearl Harbor. America had no known enemies after WWI, and the world was happily at peace. The U.S. military actually forbade men to plan for, or even discuss, offensive operations. Beyond that, American bombing planes of the 1920s and early 1930s had such short range and limited bomb-carrying capacity that a decisive bombing campaign against targets far behind enemy lines appeared to be technically impossible.[10]

By June 1941, however, with the U.S. on the brink of war, the mood had changed. Army generals now viewed airpower as a vital part of warfare. However, their view was that airplanes were still primarily defensive, limited to the battlefield and its immediate rear areas. They also believed that the field army should control airpower, which initially hampered the creation of a separate branch of the military. With war now imminent, the two conflicting air commands—GHQ Air Force and the Army Air Corps—streamlined into one called unit, namely, the United States Army Air Forces (USAAF). This was the successor to the previous United States Army Air Corps and is the direct predecessor of a separate branch, the United States Air Force, later established in 1947.

---

[10] Frisbee, John L. 1983. "The GHQ Air Force." *AIR & SPACE FORCES* magazine.

For the first time, airpower was being talked about by many former WWI pilots as having the potential to win a war offensively. If bombers could target military installations rather than incurring the bloody battles of armies on the ground, perhaps pilots could win wars more quickly and more humanely. In July 1941, a new unit called the Air War Plans Division (AWPD) coordinated planning efforts with the already-established War Plans Division (WPD), tasked with making long-term plans for war. This new unit was to provide President Franklin D. Roosevelt with "overall production requirements required to defeat our potential enemies through airpower."[11]

The first problem that the AWPD had to tackle was that the current bombers left over from WWI were obsolete, and they didn't have the range to fly long distances before refueling. This was critical with a war in the Pacific that seemed imminent. An entirely new bomber had to be engineered and manufactured when WWII began. This new plane would need to fly faster, higher, and for longer distances than current bombers could do. Engineers went to work designing this new bomber.

The second problem was reaching accuracy in bombing. During World War I, they used what was called the Course Setting Bombsight, which was composed of a slide rule-type instrument that was used to calculate the effects of the wind on the bomber based on simple vector arithmetic. The bombardier used a slide rule to calculate the effects of the wind, then dialed the speed and direction into the bombsight. This would move the sights to show the direction the plane should fly to take it directly over the target with any crosswind considered. However, the accuracy of the wind measurement was always limited, and errors in setting the equipment or making the calculations were common. In addition, the bombsight was attached to the plane itself and moved as the plane moved, so it was never steady.[12]

---

[11] "Records of the Army Air Forces [AAF]". *National Archives*. 15 August 2016. Retrieved 15 June 2019.
[12] Wikipedia. "The Norden Bombsight."

A new bombsight had been in the works for ten years. And although not a secret, practically no one outside the military had even seen a picture of the device called the Norden Bombsight until 1944, and its design remained a closely guarded secret.

Once the Norden Bombsight was ready, the members of the AWPD submitted their plan called 'Air War Plans Division One.' This proposal went beyond offering basic production requirements and provided, instead, a comprehensive air plan to defeat the Axis powers.[1] The plan, AWPD-1, completed in nine days, emphasized using heavy bombers to carry out precision bombing attacks as the primary method of defeating Germany and her allies. It also included a list of strategic targets that would decimate the German Army, including electrical power plants, aluminum plants, aircraft assembly plants, and synthetic oil refineries.

A year later, after the United States became directly involved in World War II, AWPD delivered a second plan—AWPD-42— which slightly changed the earlier plan to incorporate lessons learned from eight months of the war in Europe and to include the war in the Pacific.[13]

The newly named Army Air Forces now rushed to engineer and build a new bomber and put Norden into every one that would roll off the assembly line in 1942. This newly designed aircraft was called the B-24 *Liberator*. Men would now have to be trained to fly, operate, and maintain this new plane. The USAAF set plans in motion.

• • •

The rest of the American military was racing to prepare as well. Since World War I had ended over twenty years before, the U.S. Army and Navy suddenly found themselves involved in war again, unprepared for many critical requirements. America had not strengthened or enhanced any of their armed services, as

---

[13] *AIR & SPACE POWER JOURNAL* staff. "Air War Plans Division 1: The Air Plan That Defeated Hitler."

Europe had done. They were under-supplied with everything—equipment, guns, tanks, and ships. But most of all, they needed its young men to fight.

In 1939, the U.S. Army only had 174,000 soldiers, including the Army Air Corps. Although a draft had first taken place during the Civil War, this was the first time in history that men were called in a time of peace. All males between the ages of nineteen and fifty-seven were required to register with their local draft board, though the government limited the number to only 900,000 men for training, and they had to serve for only twelve months.

With imminent war on the horizon, millions of men would now have to be inducted, housed, fed, and trained. At its peak over the next five years, the U.S. Army ballooned to over eight million men and women in uniform, plus an additional 3.4 million in the navy. The United States had not yet entered the war, but the military was gearing up in anticipation of the almost assured inevitability.

Chapter 6
Pearl Harbor—December 7, 1941

As the war in Europe raged on throughout 1941, the president of the United States, Franklin D. Roosevelt, was in regular communication with England's prime minister. Winston Churchill was convinced that they could not win the war without the U.S.'s direct involvement, but it was not a political fight Roosevelt could take on easily with Congress and the American people. He was reluctant to involve America militarily in what many considered Europe's war. Most people in the United States simply thought the problems of Europe would stay on that continent and the Europeans would soon get the situation resolved. However, after two years, the U.S. could no longer continue to coach and call plays from the sidelines. A new enemy was about to bring the war directly to America's shores. The United States would soon become a major player involved in a world war on two separate fronts.[14]

• • •

By the summer of 1941, the negotiations between the U.S. and Japan had broken down, and Japan's Adm. Isoroku Yamamoto spent months plotting a secret and surprise attack to destroy the

---

[14] "Justin Ives." Owlcation. July 19, 2022. https://www.owlcation.com.

American Pacific Fleet in Hawaii. His aim was to crush the morale in the U.S. Navy so that they could not stop his forces as they began their advance against territories—many of them American—in the South Pacific.

Despite knowing that war with Japan was a strong possibility, the United States had not increased security at its most important U.S. naval base, Pearl Harbor, and the Japanese caught the U.S. napping. They were sitting ducks anchored in the middle of a huge barrel of water.

A large force of Japanese submarines left Japan first. Five carried midget subs to scout around the Hawaiian Islands so that they could torpedo any American warships that might try to escape the harbor during the attack. Then, under cover of darkness, all six of Japan's first-line aircraft carriers set out on this deadly mission. On board the carriers were over 420 planes. These six ships made up the most powerful carrier task force ever assembled. The Pearl Harbor strike force included speedy battleships, cruisers, and destroyers, with tankers to fuel the ships and the aircraft carriers as they slowly traveled the 4,000 miles across the Pacific Ocean to Hawaii. It was a stunningly gigantic armada on a deadly mission.

Then, just before dawn on December 7, 1941, 180 Japanese aircraft, including torpedo planes, bombers, and fighters, launched from their carrier ships and headed south to Oahu, Hawaii. This was the first launch. The submarines had already birthed the midget subs, which were now cast loose like young calves from their mothers, stealthily heading to the harbor's narrow entrance channel, all in the blackness of night.

As the sun rose on a beautiful, warm, Hawaiian Sunday morning, palm trees swayed in the gentle breeze. It was a serene setting. The navy had given many military personnel passes to attend religious services off base. Everything seemed tranquil on this beautiful island and the quiet harbor. No one suspected a sneak attack.

At 7:02 a.m., two U.S. radar operators on the main island of Oahu, Hawaii spotted large groups of planes in flight, headed toward the island from the north. The officers in charge instructed them to issue no warning because they were expecting a fleet of B-17s from the U.S. Consequently, they sounded no alarm. But of course, these planes were not the B-17s they were expecting. Almost an hour later, at 7:55 a.m., Japanese bombers arrived at Oahu, resulting in an attack that came as a devastating and deadly surprise to U.S. Navy personnel on ships anchored in the harbor.

As the bombs dropped with extraordinarily little defense, they made much of the Pacific Fleet useless. Five of eight battleships, three destroyers, and seven other ships sank or suffered severe damage, and bombs obliterated over 200 planes. The enemy killed a stunning 2,400 Americans and wounded 1,200 more. It was indeed a devastating attack on the U.S. Navy.

While the bombing of Pearl Harbor may have initially looked like a major win for Japan, the attack had, in fact, failed in its aim to annihilate the U.S. Pacific Fleet. Their bombers had missed oil tanks, ammunition sites, dry docks, and repair depots. Some historians maintain that this was one of the biggest errors the Japanese made. The U.S. could immediately begin repairs on the ships rather than being forced to delay for months. However, much more importantly, not a single U.S. aircraft carrier was in the harbor at the time of the attack. Fortuitously for the U.S., all three Pacific Fleet carriers had been out at sea on training maneuvers and were left intact to exact their revenge six months later at the Battle of Midway.[15]

---

[15] Danforth, Bruce. August 27, 2015. "Why Japan Attacked Pearl Harbor."

Chapter 7
The U.S. Joins the Allies

The day after Japan bombed Pearl Harbor, President Roosevelt stood before a joint session of Congress and somberly declared, "Yesterday, December 7, 1941—a date that will live in infamy—the United States of America was suddenly and deliberately attacked by naval and air forces of the Empire of Japan." He asked Congress to approve a resolution declaring war on Japan, which was almost unanimously approved by both Houses of Congress, with one pacifist dissenter. True to the agreement of the Tripartite Pact, to support Japan, Germany and Italy declared war on the United States four days later. This led to the U.S. joining the Allies in the fight in Europe. The United States was now officially at war with Japan and, by treaty agreement, with the Axis powers in Europe.

One week after Pearl Harbor, Mac, like many other young, American men, proudly answered his country's call to serve.

"I enlisted in the Army Air Forces, Mother," Mac said as he walked into the kitchen. His mother was at the sink and turned to face her son, her mouth forming a wide oval. "They've ordered me to report to Lindbergh Field in San Diego next week for primary training. I fly out on Saturday."

Margaret walked to the kitchen table, sat down hard on the chair, and put her soft, fleshy hands on her chin. Tears welled up in her eyes.

"I knew you and Bob were going to get caught up in this god-awful war," she said as she wiped her hands on her apron, "and now it's done. But please, son, don't fly to San Diego. Flying is so dangerous. I'll be worried sick. Take the train; it's so much safer."

"Flying to San Diego is dangerous, Mother?" Mac said. "I am going to San Diego to become a pursuit pilot. I'll be flying planes in combat. People will shoot at me. That will be dangerous. Flying from Chicago to San Diego is not."

"I know what you are determined to do," she said, pressing one hand nervously into the other. "Just please take the train. I don't know the pilot on that plane to San Diego, and I will feel so much better knowing you are safely on the ground."

Unable to make his mother see the absurdity of the situation, Mac finally relented. To appease her, in mid-December, he took the train from Chicago to San Diego. Somewhere in Texas, the train hit a cow that had wandered on the tracks and derailed, injuring passengers and, of course, poor old Nellie. *So much for the safety of ground travel*, Mac chuckled to himself. He always loved a good irony.

Mac wanted to fly pursuit planes, later called fighter planes, but fate, or more precisely the army, would put him on a different path. It was a path that suited him just fine, as it turned out. He soon learned that he'd be flying a brand-new plane—a bomber that was still being developed that would fly faster, higher, and farther than any plane in existence. He would join a group of men who would be the first to learn to pilot this new plane. Mac was now a twenty-three-year-old man, mature, responsible, and incredibly driven. He would go wherever the Army Air Forces needed him. The training on these new planes, which were still being assembled, would take another six months, half a year, before they considered him and this new bomber group ready for combat. But ready they would be.

With the bombing of Pearl Harbor, 40 percent of new recruits in all branches of the military, like Mac, volunteered to serve. Young men who would normally have been pursuing school, jobs, and starting families responded enthusiastically to their country's call. Like second stringers finally called into the big game, the young men of America signed up in droves. This was no longer a war 'over there.' Japan had attacked America without provocation.

The powerful, collective, gut-wrenching feeling of being suddenly and viciously assaulted was a huge motivator for action. It was also a rallying cry, uniting young men in a common cause and brotherhood. But unlike Mac, who had moved often as a child and traveled the world as a Merchant Marine, most of these young men had never put as much as a toe outside the confines of their city, town, or whistle-stop, let alone traveled the far reaches of Europe, Asia, or the islands of the South Pacific. But they were more than enthusiastic; they were gung ho and hungry for revenge.

Signing up men and swelling the ranks of soldiers was probably the simple part for the services, but housing, feeding, and training all these new recruits was an altogether unique challenge. Preparing millions of raw civilians for immediate war certainly must have been one of the most daunting and ambitious tasks the U.S. military had ever undertaken. All branches of the service responded.

The Army Air Forces, in particular, was paltry, and most of the combat planes from the WWI era were, of course, obsolete. New planes were still being designed and built in a flurry. Bases and camps had to be created from scratch or expanded, and men had to be trained to fly, navigate, and use the new bombsight and machine guns once the planes materialized. Others had to learn how to maintain and service these new planes and their equipment. All this needed to happen in a matter of months from an organization known more for its ingrained, plodding, tortoise-like structure than its ability to move like a herd of gazelles. But move, they did.

After the United States entered the war on the side of the Allies, President Franklin Roosevelt and British Prime Minister Winston Churchill met and agreed upon a strategy to first eliminate the European threat, which was indeed dire, before fully concentrating on defeating Japan. This became known as the Europe First or Germany First strategy. Although Japan was a serious threat, the Allied leaders decided they could contain them in the Pacific region, and the U.S.'s recovering navy could keep them busy fighting a delaying action. The Nazis, on the other hand, had wreaked havoc and destruction across Europe and even portions of Africa. In a somewhat surprising turn of events, the United States went from being attacked by the Japanese to attacking the Axis powers in Europe in a matter of days.

Per the Europe First policy, the U.S. sent all the resources that were on hand, including the few existing bomber groups with older model planes and most of their available military personnel, to Europe to fight Hitler. A brand-new bombardment group needed to be created, not only to learn to fly this new plane, but to protect the Pacific Northwest and Hawaii from another attack. The military wanted to concentrate as many planes as possible in that area of the United States. But this new group, with its new, long-range bomber, would primarily fly in the South Pacific to fight Japan.

• • •

The Army Air Forces created the 307th Bombardment Group in February 1942, two months after the Japanese attack on Pearl Harbor, and it was to be stationed at Geiger Field, in Spokane, Washington. The first actual assembly of men took place on

April 15, 1942, with a nucleus of only five soldiers, and quickly grew to include one officer and 500 recruits.

Ephrata, Washington, which is between Seattle and Spokane, was the first of many homes for the 307th BG. The location selected was a dry riverbed with one runway that commercial airlines had used as an emergency landing strip. The first duty of the newly enlisted men was to create and build the camp. They hacked bushes and cleared the scrub, rocks, and dirt, raised tents, and camp 307th was soon blooming like a dandelion weed in the middle of a desert.

Amid the clouds of dust, a gaggle of seven shacks and several tents rose like a phoenix from the ashes. Each tent had five or six cots, and at first, there was only one shower house with eight sprinklers that dripped freezing water. There were four kitchens but no mess hall, so the men sat on the ground in the open, dust and all.[16]

While the camp was being erected, the men who would make up the air echelon—the pilots, navigators, flight engineers, bombardiers, radio operators, and gunners—were still training in flight schools around the country. Mac was now at Luke Air Force Base in Arizona for six weeks of basic training, then sent for flight training at Lemoore Field in Lemoore, California. He trained on the Ryan PT-21/22 *Recruit*. This was a tandem, two-seater primary trainer developed by Ryan Aeronautical just the year before in San Diego.

Mac loved this colorful, fun plane. In his article *Ryan PT-21/22 'Recruit,'* J.K. Caldwell says, "Its Art Deco lines gives the feel of a 1930s sci-fi rocket. It is impossible to fly this machine without feeling the thrill of adventure." Soaring above the earth like a bird, with the wind in his hair, was what the young pilot knew it would be—freeing, breathtaking, exciting. Mac graduated June 23, 1942, from the Army Air Advanced Flying School at Luke Field in Glendale, Arizona as an aviation cadet,

---

[16] Britt, Sam S., Jr. 1990. The Long Rangers: A Diary of the 307th Bombardment Group (H).

and was then ordered to report to the Army Air Base in Salt Lake City to await further assignment. The wait was killing him. He was ready and eager to get going, but there was nothing he could do until he received orders to go somewhere.

Chapter 8
Japan Occupies the South Pacific—1942

Seven years before, in 1935, after finishing his term as chief of staff, the army assigned Gen. Douglas MacArthur the job of creating an armed force for the Philippines, which had become a commonwealth of the United States that year and later gained independence in 1946.

Two years later, MacArthur resigned from the military when the army ordered him to return to duty in the United States, reporting that he had not finished his mission in the Philippines and that he would stay on. He wanted to increase the size and capability of the Philippine Army. He remained there and served as a civilian adviser to President Manuel Quezon, who had appointed him field marshal of the Philippines. Five months before the Japanese bombed Pearl Harbor, however, the army recalled MacArthur to active duty, and he returned to the U.S. The Philippine Army was not fully ready. His famous vow to the Filipino people—"I shall return …"—was a promise he kept, though it was two and a half more years before he could fulfill it.

Within hours of bombing Pearl Harbor, Japanese planes attacked Hong Kong, and three days later, Japanese troops landed on Luzon, the Philippine's largest island. Within a month, they had captured Manila, the capital, and forced the outnumbered American and Filipino defenders of Luzon to retreat to the Bataan Peninsula west of Manila.

In March, with the Philippines now in Japanese hands, the army ordered Gen. MacArthur to Australia to command Allied Forces in the Southwest Pacific Theater. Japan quickly destroyed America's meager airpower on the islands. Because the U.S. had sent all available servicemen to Europe, MacArthur had not been able to get reinforcements and supplies, and he could do nothing more than bide his time in Australia.

The combined U.S.-Filipino Army was now pushed back to Bataan. They fought hard for the next three months and held out against the Japanese, despite a lack of naval and air support. Finally, on April 9th, with his forces severely crippled by starvation and disease, U.S. Gen. Edward King Jr. surrendered his approximately 75,000 troops at Bataan.

The Japanese forced their weakened prisoners to make a grueling, sixty-five-mile march to prison camps from Mariveles, on the southern end of the Bataan Peninsula, to San Fernando in what would later be called the Bataan Death March. Divided into groups of approximately one hundred, they forced the men to march in suffocating heat for five days to complete the trek. It was a debilitating, arduous journey that left thousands of troops dead because of the brutality of their captors. The Japanese starved, beat, and bayoneted those who were too weak to walk any farther, then left them by the roadside to die. They shipped the survivors by train to prisoner-of-war camps, where thousands more died from disease, mistreatment, and starvation.[17]

In the next four months, like a one-sided game of checkers, the Japanese jumped on and occupied Wake Island, the Gilbert Islands, Guam in the Marianas, Singapore, the Malay Peninsula,

---

[17] History.com editors. "Bataan Death March."

the Dutch East Indies, New Britain, and New Ireland. Because they had little opposition, they were relentless in their raids on countries throughout the South Pacific. Their appetite for territory was like a hungry whale, mouth opened wide, scooping up islands like schools of fish.

The attacks on British Empire possessions in the Pacific brought the United Kingdom, Australia, and New Zealand into the growing conflict in the South Pacific. The Japanese sought to decimate the U.S. and British Royal Navies, seize their island possessions rich in natural resources, and get strategic military bases to defend their now far-flung and burgeoning empire.

In the words of the Japanese Navy's Combined Fleet Secret Order Number One, dated November 1, 1941, the goals of the initial Japanese campaigns in the impending war were to "[sap] British and American strength from the Netherlands Indies and the Philippines, [and] to establish a policy of autonomous self-sufficiency and economic independence." They easily carried out these first strategic objectives in the first six months of the war.

A secondary Japanese goal was to set up an effective defensive perimeter from British India on the west, through the Dutch East Indies on the south, and to build island bases in the south and central Pacific as its southeastern line of defense. Anchoring its defensive positions in the South Pacific were the major Japanese army and naval bases on Rabaul, New Guinea, which they had captured from the Australians in January 1942, building a secure perimeter around their island of Japan.

In March and April, Japanese forces also occupied and began constructing airfields on Buka in northern Bougainville, as well as a large naval base and airfield at Kahili in southern Bougainville.[18] Bougainville, New Guinea sits at the north end of the Solomon Islands. The Japanese were marching forward and were, so far, weakly opposed. America was still primarily engaged in Europe, and the Army Air Forces was busy building and training its new bomber group in Ephrata, Washington.

In the South Pacific, the Allies tried to push back on the Japanese aggression, but as the list of military naval defeats and reversals for the puny Australian, British, American, and Dutch military and naval forces mounted, a feeling of depression swept over the general populace of Australia with the very real fear the Japanese would invade them at any moment. It didn't look good.[18]

By April 1942, just four months after Pearl Harbor and many other countries, the Japanese were now examining the possibility of capturing Port Moresby in New Guinea and Tulagi in the Southeastern Solomon Islands, along with New Caledonia, Fiji, and Samoa. You could practically lob a tennis ball from Port Moresby to Northern Australia, and its potential capture was of major concern to the Allies, particularly Australia.

The object of the plan for the Japanese was to continue to extend and strengthen their defensive perimeter and cut the lines of communication between Australia and the United States. The occupation of Port Moresby, New Guinea—*if* they could do it—would not only cut off the eastern sea approaches to Darwin on the north coast of Australia, but it would provide the Imperial Japanese Navy with a secure operating base on Australia's northern doorstep. This made the Australians extremely nervous indeed.

In May 1942, Japan made their big move. They swooped in and occupied Tulagi in the Southern Solomons, and then launched an invasion force from their large naval base on Rabaul, trying to capture and occupy Port Moresby. This

---

[18] Bergerud, Eric M. 1997. *Touched with Fire: The Land War in the South Pacific*. Penguin.

ultimately resulted in the successful—for the Allies—Naval Battle of the Coral Sea along the northeast coast of Australia. It involved the U.S. and Australia's naval and air forces, successfully pushing Japan back and out of that area. The Japanese retreated from Port Moresby for the time being, and the sigh of relief from Australians could almost be heard halfway around the world in California.

Chapter 9
The 307th Bombardment Group Is Activated in July 1942

Clearly, though, the war in the Southwest Pacific needed air support as soon as possible. As the Army Air Forces scrambled to develop this new bomber, personnel were constantly arriving at the camp in Ephrata, which continued to enlarge to accommodate them. For a while, it seemed to the men that all they were doing was moving tents. But by July 1942, most of the radio operators, flight engineers, and gunners had arrived and were immersed in training at the camp.

The pilots, bombardiers, and navigators were either still in training or awaiting orders around the country and would not show until several weeks later. When Mac had first received orders to report to Ephrata, Washington to join the nascent 307th Bombardment Group, there was, at first, a pang of disappointment as he had dreamed of flying fighters or what was then called pursuit aircraft. Who could blame him? It didn't sound like the excitement he had envisioned.

Bombers had been such an insignificant part of winning the First World War. Germany, Italy, England, France, and Russia had all used strategic bombings in WWI to hit cities to demoralize the local population. This caused air raid warnings and the building of shelters where civilians took cover. But because of the technology available at the time, they could not accurately target a military installation or anything else. It wasn't until the end of WWI that they even developed bombsights. Before then, crew members tossed bombs out of planes by hand. So, flying a bomber probably didn't sound particularly exciting, but Mac would soon change his mind.

The flight echelons had not yet arrived at Ephrata, so they could assign no planes or flying crews until they showed up, and no one—at least the ordinary grunts—knew what type of plane the brass would eventually provide. The ground crews began maintenance and operation training on the only bomber available, the B-17. Engineers developed this bomber in the 1930s after WWI and it was a good workhorse, but it didn't have the range for flying long distances over the Pacific Ocean. Few people in Ephrata knew at the time that a brand-new heavy bomber was getting ready to roll off the assembly line in San Diego and would soon head their way.

By the end of June, the U.S.-based B-24 *Liberators* entered combat service when the first four planes arrived. Factory workers were still assembling the rest. With the camp ready and some planes delivered, Mac flew to Ephrata to join the other pilots, all recently commissioned second lieutenants and aircrew, and begin training on the new bomber.

By July 11th, all assigned pilots had arrived at the base, and the trainers divided the 307th into four squadrons: 370th, 371st, 372nd, and 424th. With all the flight personnel now at Ephrata, they could assign actual crews. Mac and his crew would be in the 424th Squadron. His crew members included 2nd Lt. Harvey 'Van' Vanderslice, copilot, 2nd Lt. Donald Declercque, bombardier, 2nd Lt. Lesley Carroll, navigator, Staff Sgt. William Adams, assistant engineer, Robert Smith, radio operator, Roy Lund, engineer, Lawrence Averitt, assistant radio operator, and John Sargent, tail gunner.

Together as a flight crew, they began three months of flight training, flying at both high and low altitudes, navigation flights, practice bombing missions, and formation flying. Flying with such physical closeness and necessary teamwork, friendships developed quickly. In combat, these crews would need to rely on each other and run like a perfectly oiled machine with all parts working in sync.

Eventually, ten more *Liberators* arrived and were divided between the four squadrons. But due to mechanical failures, and the fact that spare parts were scarce, it forced them to ground planes frequently, so training was maddeningly slow. A war was raging, and men were itching to get up and away.

Part of the frustration of the snail's pace of training was that there was so much for everyone to learn: training in combat intelligence, gunnery, navigation, first and second pilot training, and aerial engineering. As Sam Britt recalled, the term training schedules turned out to be an oxymoron since there was no way they could keep any type of schedule. The planes needed frequent repair, and the military expected these new recruits to maintain and fly these extremely complicated aircraft. A shortage of planes for training also required that the men work in shifts, and crews had to fly around the clock. According to those chosen few of the 307th BG, it was exhausting, yet exhilarating.[19]

---

[19] Britt, Sam S., Jr. 1990. *The Long Rangers: A Diary of the 307th Bombardment Group (H)*.

Chapter 10
B-24 Liberators—A New Bomber

The B-24 *Liberators*, the plane that Mac and the other pilots at Ephrata were now learning to fly, were four-engine, heavy bombers, meaning they could carry and drop the heaviest payload of bombs. B-24s had the longest-range takeoff to landing of their era. This was vitally important when flying over the Pacific, where solid places to land and refuel were scarce.

Mac quickly got over his disappointment at not being assigned as a pursuit pilot and embraced the idea of being among a handful of men selected to fly this exciting new bomber. However, when the planes first arrived in Ephrata, there were a lot of complaints by some crew members, for several reasons. Compared to the B-17 that they were familiar with, the B-24 looked ugly and ungainly. Gunners who were not actively engaged in firing their guns had nowhere to sit, except on the bare, metal floor. It was also colder, and spot heaters didn't work well as drafts seemed to be everywhere. Designers, it appeared, had added all the equipment to the B-24 as an afterthought, while with the B-17, they built everything in.

When wearing full gear, moving around the B-24 was awkward, causing jarring collisions with aircraft structures and installed equipment. Designers had not even considered how to get in and out of the plane. They left it up to the crew to decide whether to enter through the bomb bay or through the nose wheel compartment, as there was no designated entry door. Claustrophobia was also a major concern.[20]

To fulfill the requests of the Army Air Forces, the *Liberators* were hastily mass-produced. Before the war, factories in the United States were producing automobiles, large and small appliances, and children's toys. A month after the attack on Pearl Harbor, President Roosevelt set up the War Production Board, whose purpose was to convert the factories of peacetime industries into manufacturing plants for weapons and military equipment. Every American automaker turned its workforce and facilities to military production. The assembly lines were in place and the workers were eager to do the job, but they were producing a new product they were unfamiliar with, and pressure was on to produce it quickly. With a new airplane, this amounted to a lot of haste in manufacturing, which meant a lot of bugs needed to be worked out in the field. Some of these defects would come at the cost of many lives because there was no time to do proper beta testing.[20]

From the very start, the B-24 had a higher accident rate than the B-17, which gave it the reputation of being a 'widow-maker.' In 1943 alone, 850 Army Air Forces crewmen were killed in 298 B-24 accidents. Not in combat, in *accidents*, which were all too common in the rush to develop them. It was later found that the lightweight construction, designed to increase range, and the location of fuel tanks in the upper fuselage, also made the planes extremely vulnerable to battle damage.

The *Liberator* was notorious among American aircrews for its nasty tendency to catch fire after being hit. This also happened during fuel transfers because the cabin would fill up with gasoline fumes and the bomb bay doors would have to be cracked open to clear the fumes. Though smoking was a customary practice in those days, few men smoked in the planes, as fire was a constant threat. If not for the feeling of invincibility

---

[20] Walker, Samuel I. 1984. *Up the Slot*.

that young men seem to have, many rational people would probably not have flown in these new planes. They were almost as unpredictable and prone to destruction as a soapbox car made by a twelve-year-old.

Cabins weren't pressurized or heated, and at altitudes over 10,000 feet (about the height of Mount St. Helens), crew members had to wear oxygen masks. It exposed them to temperatures that could reach 50 degrees below zero. Their sheepskin jackets helped give the crew some level of protection from the cold, but it was still frigid.

Engineers attribute the differences in creature comforts between the B-17 and the B-24 to the fact that the development of the B-24 occurred during wartime, where quantity was more important than quality. They had to modify these planes continually on demanding, urgent schedules as crews discovered defects. The B-17 was developed during the leisure of peacetime, which allowed time for adequate testing before going into service.

Someone initially nicknamed the *Liberators* the 'Flying Boxcar' because the plane was a boxy-looking, inelegant creation. It looked ungainly and awkward on the ground. The specially designed wing needed for a long-range bomber, called the Davis wing, sat high on the fuselage. This wing offered 15 percent less drag than ordinary wings. (Drag is the force that pushes planes backward and slows them down as they fly.) With less drag, planes can achieve faster speeds with the same amount of forward thrust as they had before. The *Liberator* was also dangerous to ditch or belly land, since the fuselage tended to break apart because of the position of the Davis wing when it hit any surface without the cushioning of rubber wheels. In the early days, it was apparently also not uncommon to see a B-24 falling from the sky with its wings folded upward like a butterfly.

Eventually, the military cleared the B-24 to fly at such high weight limits that takeoffs became dicey, even with full power on all four engines. Flight stability was dubious, and escape from a downed plane was extremely difficult once the pilot and copilot let go of the controls and tried to scramble out. Using yet another moniker, crews renamed the B-24 the 'Flying Coffin' as it had only one actual exit, which was near the tail of the plane. This made it difficult, if not impossible, for the flight crew to escape a crippled B-24.[21]

The *Liberator* carried a crew of seven to ten men, and ten 50-caliber machine guns that were mounted in the nose, top and bottom of the fuselage, and tail, plus 6,000 to 8,000 pounds (about the weight of an elephant) of general-purpose bombs. Engineers designed them specifically to travel the long distances needed in the South Pacific. Many B-24 missions were round trips of 1,500 to 2,000 miles (about twice the distance from Florida to New York City) over water.

But it was extremely demanding to fly, even for a fully qualified pilot, and these pilots were, mostly, all rookies. Before he arrived in Ephrata, Mac had completed just 223 hours (about one and a half weeks) of flight time, all on single-engine planes. The other new pilots had similar records. The *Liberator*, or *Miss Liberator* as they sometimes referred to it, was a complicated machine to operate, leading to prolonged pilot training programs and, occasionally, severe attrition of pilots willing to fly them.

As one pilot described the *Liberator*, it was a total contradiction in terms. "Human-like. The B-24 is rugged and yet sensitive, crude looking and yet beautiful, clumsy and yet clean-lined. She is, at all times, temperamental. No two B-24s are alike. For weeks, she can be gay and healthy, the engines sing and zoom, then without warning, she can become unruly, her instrument register wrong, her controls become sluggish, her engines spit oil. One plane can hungrily lap up gas, another sips it ladylike, another can tear away and fly faster than her sisters, while still another can only snail along. One plane is wing weighted; another is tail heavy. A B-24[21] has her moods. She needs attention; at times the attention of a squawking baby, at others, she gaily bounces along, cat-purring with contentment."[22]

In Ephrata, the 307th BG, with all new pilots and all new crews, prepared to fly these all-new, volatile, prone-to-accident planes under the most difficult of circumstances—combat—with ground anti-aircraft firing up and enemy planes shooting at them from all sides. The courage and dedication shown by these men is astounding.

B-24 Waist Gunner in action

---

[21] Hickman, Kennedy. "World War II: Consolidated B-24 Liberator." August 26, 2020. ThoughtCo.thoughtco.com/consolidated-b-24-liberator-2361515.
[22] 307th Bombardment Group (HV). 1945.
We'll Say Goodbye: Story of the "Long Rangers"—307th Bombardment Group (HV).

B-24 Cockpit

B-24 Top Turret Gunner

Chapter 11
The Battle of Midway—June 1942

The year before the Japanese bombed Pearl Harbor, the U.S. Navy had built a military base on Wake Island, about 1,100 miles (about the distance from Florida to New York City) southwest of Midway, which was also a U.S. possession. Within hours after the attack on Pearl Harbor, the Japanese flew thirty-six medium bombers from the Marshall Islands to Wake Island and attacked the base, destroying eight of the twelve Wildcats on the ground and sinking a U.S. cargo ship. The four planes patrolling in the air did not see the incoming Japanese bombers because of poor visibility caused by severe weather, but the next day, they shot down two of the Japanese bombers.

Then a second Japanese invasion occurred on December 23, 1941, and after a full night and morning of fighting, they forced the remaining Wake Island Marines to surrender. The Japanese now occupied Wake Island. Next, they wanted Midway as well.

In June 1942, the month before Mac and the other pilots began training in Ephrata, the Japanese tried to lure the American aircraft carriers they had missed in Pearl Harbor into a trap so they could destroy them and then occupy Midway Island directly west of Hawaii. They aptly named this little atoll as it lies midway between Asia and North America. It is at the extreme northwest end of the Hawaiian Island chain but is still about 1,300 miles (about half the width of the United States) from Oahu—about the flight distance from Houston, Texas to Washington, DC—and just at the end of the range of the B-24s.

So, Midway was not especially important in the larger scheme of Japan's plans, but the Japanese felt the Americans would defend it vigorously as a vital outpost of Pearl Harbor. In doing so, the Japanese thought they could lure the American aircraft carriers in and then decimate the ones that showed up to defend it.[23] Their ambitious plan also included preparation for further attacks against Fiji, Samoa, and Hawaii. They were on the move to cripple the U.S. Navy and gobble up as much territory as they could.

The U.S. did, in fact, consider Midway vital, as the establishment of a U.S. submarine base on Midway would extend the radius of submarines based in Pearl Harbor, allowing them to refuel and reprovision. Besides serving as a seaplane base, airstrips on Midway would also serve as a staging point for bomber attacks on Japanese-occupied Wake Island.

American cryptographers decoded the Japanese plans and learned the date and location of the upcoming attack on Midway, thwarting their scheme to capture the island. The U.S. Navy was not only ready but able to prepare its own ambush on the unsuspecting Japanese.

With the decoded plans, the U.S. Navy defeated the attacking fleet of the Imperial Japanese Navy, inflicting devastating damage to it at what was called the Battle of Midway. They sunk four of the six carriers that had been part of the attack on Pearl Harbor six months earlier, as well as a heavy cruiser. The U.S. lost only one carrier and one destroyer. This was a crippling setback to the Japanese Navy and a sweet retribution for the United States. Historian John Keegan called it, "The most stunning and decisive blow in the history of naval warfare."

---

[23] Willmott, H. P. 1983. *The Barrier and the Javelin: Japanese and Allied Strategies, February to June 1942*. Annapolis, Maryland: Naval Institute Press.

After Midway, Japan's ability to replace its losses in aircraft carriers and well-trained pilots and maintenance crews became insufficient to keep up with mounting casualties. Military historians widely agree that the Battle of Midway, and the exhausting, subsequent pummeling in the Solomon Islands, were the turning points in the Pacific War.

• • •

Headed to the South Pacific to carry out said pummeling, the budding 307th BG would not learn their destination for another four months, and it would be six months before they were deployed there. However, it would only be five months before Mac, his crew, and twenty-six other bombers flew their first mission to bomb the Japanese-occupied Wake Island, staged from newly reclaimed Midway Island.

Readying for Midway

Chapter 12
Coast Watchers of the South Pacific

After the Battle of Midway and the Battle of the Coral Sea off Australia's coast, the navies of the Allies continued to advance toward Japan. Japanese control of the Solomon Islands was a sharp threat to the Allies' extended position and certainly to the safety of the Australian and New Zealand people. Besides the military forces, however, a civilian organization was helping to defeat the Japanese.

Unlike France, where underground resistance groups took an assertive, confrontational approach to the Nazis, supplying not only intelligence to the Allies but stockpiling weapons and killing members of the SS—Hitler's henchmen—coast watchers and native islanders in the Pacific Islands had a more passive role. They, too, were of tremendous assistance to the war effort, but the nature of the Pacific War called for an entirely different tactic.

Coast watchers were civilians of the Australian Coast Watcher Organization, a service that a naval officer in Western Australia formed after World War I. He created this association of volunteers to report on any unusual or suspicious happenings along Australia's 23,000 miles of mostly isolated coastline. The members came from all levels of society. They were outback police, workers on remote cattle and sheep ranches, post and telegraph operators, sailors, and missionaries, among others, who all reported to the Naval Intelligence Division in Melbourne, Australia.

When war broke out in Europe in 1939, the Coast Watcher Organization quickly expanded beyond Australia to the South Pacific islands under Australian control—Papua New Guinea, New Britain, New Ireland, Bougainville, the Admiralties, the Trobriands, and, by arrangement with the British, to their Solomon Islands Protectorate. There were coast watchers on each of those islands.

Like the Australian coast watchers, the island members were a diverse group—district officers and other government officials, planters, trade store owners, missionaries, captains of trading ships, pearling luggers, even gold prospectors, all keeping a close watch on the coasts of their island for enemy activity and approach.

By the time the Japanese arrived in the South Pacific, the islands in the vast area of sea to Australia's north and east, both large and small, an extensive network of coast watchers dotted the area. This stealth group of undercover sleuths, known simply as coast watchers, wore no uniforms and had no distinguishing badge or insignia. The Australian Navy gave these men military rank or commissioned them in the Solomon Islands Defense Force, hoping, if captured, their military status would save them from execution as spies.

Lt. Cmdr. Eric Feldt, based in Townsville, Queensland, led the Australian Coast Watch during WWII, which became important in monitoring Japanese activity in the roughly one thousand islands that make up the Solomon Islands. Feldt codenamed his organization 'Ferdinand,' from the popular children's book about a bull, *The Story of Ferdinand*. "Ferdinand," he explained, "did not fight but sat under a tree and just smelled the flowers." The name was his way of reminding his coast watchers that it was not their job to get involved and draw attention to themselves, but to sit quietly and unobtrusively, watching, gathering information, then relaying it to the naval authorities. Like their namesake, Ferdinand, however, they could fight if they were stung.[24]

Operating behind Japanese lines, with no direct confrontation, these dedicated men not only supplied valuable intelligence that may have changed the course of history at Guadalcanal, but they rescued many sailors and downed fliers.[25]

Coast watchers could not have been nearly as effective as they were without the support of the brave and stalwart local natives. About 400 Melanesians served with the coast watchers, another 680 with the Solomon Islands Protectorate Defense Force, and about 3,200 served as laborers who also watched and reported Japanese activity embedded in the enemy's camp like undercover moles engaged in espionage.

---

[24] Wikipedia
[25] Martin, Michael. *Coastwatchers of the Solomons.*

Chapter 13
The Fight for Guadalcanal—1942

By the time the Americans received any sizable amount of equipment and men in the South Pacific, months into the war, the Japanese had claimed many island territories and were dangerously close to kicking in the door of Australia as a most unwanted intruder.

The Japanese had decided early on that they would need a large, well-trained, and well-equipped air force for a war in the Pacific, so their emphasis was now on taking island after island in the Solomons to form a chain of airfields. This was essential to their strategy and simplified their supply lines as well. These bases also needed to be near a usable harbor that could support ships bringing troops and supplies.

The first order of business for the Allied Forces, therefore, was to stop the enemy's advance in the South Pacific and to secure the Solomon Islands for themselves. The U.S. would need island bases and heavy bombers to do this.

Guadalcanal, at the tail end of the Solomon Islands, was a pre-war colonial possession of Great Britain, and with its proximity to Australia and New Zealand, it offered ideal locations for bases that could serve as supply routes between Australia and the United States. The principal aim of the U.S. during the first phase of the struggle for Guadalcanal was to prevent the enemy from building an air base there and then build one for themselves.

The Japanese occupied the smaller Tulagi Island, just north of Guadalcanal, in May 1942. Then on June 8th, they made their long-awaited move and landed troops on Guadalcanal's north coast. That was the only suitable invasion beach to land men and supplies because miles of coral reefs protected the south shores. In the following few days, Japanese ferried men and equipment ashore from destroyers anchored near the coast of Guadalcanal. As the Japanese constructed an airfield on the island, two eagle-eyed coast watchers watched silently and reported.

The Japanese were unaware that the Americans were also planning to create an air base for their fighters and the 307th Bombardment Group. While they were quietly building their base, their presence forced the coast watchers spying on them to move deeper into the jungle to avoid detection. But because the Japanese hired natives to help build the base, the coast watchers had their chance to infiltrate their scouts into the work gangs and gather vital intelligence. Besides the needed supply route, the goal of the Allies was getting close enough to attack Japan itself. Guadalcanal was the beginning. Guam and the atomic bomb were the end.[26]

The necessity of ejecting the enemy from its position and stopping the construction of the air base in Guadalcanal became increasingly clear to the Allies. The contest for the Solomons began when the 1st Marine Division landed on the beaches of Guadalcanal and Tulagi, starting a campaign that would continue for more than a year.

When the Japanese had almost finished the air base, the U.S. Marines struck, and the fighting was fierce and intense. The jungle environment of Guadalcanal forced the Marines to fight at very close quarters, a tough adjustment for U.S. Marines to make. Because of the density of the forests, the enemy's positions were usually not visible until attacking troops had closed within fifty feet of them. (Subsequent campaigns in the Pacific all

---

[26] Britt, Sam S., Jr. 1990. *The Long Rangers: A Diary of the 307th Bombardment Group (H)*.

presented similar conditions, as would Vietnam two decades later.)

The Japanese proved to be experts at using natural materials found in the jungle to build strong and well-concealed fortified positions. American units that thought they had discovered one or two machine-gun positions often found half a dozen or more secreted in brush and bunkers. Once Marines discovered a network of positions, the bunkers—some with reinforcing logs up to two feet in diameter—proved impermeable to all but direct hits by the largest caliber weapons. Nevertheless, the Marines did not hesitate to attack such positions and innovate effective techniques against them, including flamethrowers, to reach into narrow openings and flush out the enemy.

The greatest single factor reducing troop effectiveness on Guadalcanal, however, was disease, particularly malaria. For every man who became a casualty in combat, five fell to malaria. Scientists had not yet developed a vaccine for malaria, and tropical diseases would continue to degrade the efficiency of ground operations in those areas, as well as continue to threaten the lives of natives.

Then on July 31, 1942, while Mac and the men of the 307th BG were in the first month of their training in Ephrata, an eighty-ship American invasion force, carrying nearly 17,000 Marines, set out for the Solomon Islands to answer the question for the last time about who would control an air base on Guadalcanal. Incredibly, enemy patrol planes did not notice this huge armada during its week-long voyage down 'the slot'—the strip of water between the Solomon Islands.

The navy put the coast watchers on alert, and recently escaped native airstrip workers provided the Marines with priceless intelligence on the position of enemy troops and guns on Guadalcanal. Just before daybreak on Friday, August 7th, coast watchers woke up to the thunder of big guns. As dawn broke, everyone who could find high ground vantage points was rewarded with one of the more awe-inspiring sights of the Pacific War—American warships literally covered the sea between Guadalcanal and Tulagi. Allied Forces, predominantly U.S. Marines, had landed on Guadalcanal and easily seized the airfield from the Japanese military.

The landings on Guadalcanal went smoothly, in part because of the intelligence gathered by the coast watchers, and partly because the Japanese construction workers still building the airstrip didn't have the stomach for a fight. By nightfall on August 8th, the Allied troops secured Tulagi, and they later renamed the Japanese airfield under construction on Guadalcanal Henderson Field.

But the fight wasn't over as far as the Japanese were concerned. Now that the U.S. had it, the Japanese intended to retake it. The Marines worked feverishly to put up a defensive perimeter around the area to protect it, while Seabees labored day and night to complete the airfield the Japanese had begun. The U.S. Navy's 6th Construction Battalion followed the Marines into Guadalcanal on September 1st and became the first Seabees—organized and trained to build, to engage in the combination of fighting and building. They made the air base operational, and keeping it that way during months of fierce combat was their principal task.

There were, of course, coast watchers at strategic points around Guadalcanal, ready to warn of approaching danger. Added reinforcements over the next two months increased the number of U.S. troops at Lunga Point, where Henderson Air Base was located, to over 20,000 men. Protecting Henderson Field and securing Guadalcanal was critical to eventually winning the war.

• • •

The Marines had landed and seized the airfield quickly, but the battle for Henderson Field on Guadalcanal became the focal point for the wills of two warring nations. The Japanese, after being totally surprised by the Allied offensive, made several attempts between August and November to retake Henderson Field, and bloody battles ensued.

During the night of October 15th, the Japanese bombed U.S. naval ships just north of Guadalcanal from their warships, and five Japanese aircraft carriers were sitting ready for the right time to make their move. The U.S. had only one aircraft carrier in the area, the *Hornet*, which was obviously no match for that large of a task force. But the *Hornet* did sneak in close enough to Rekata Bay on Santa Isabel Island to launch a strike against the Japanese seaplane base, destroying twelve seaplanes.

By then, the Japanese had completed a new airstrip on the tip of southeastern Bougainville, New Guinea that they called Buin (and Americans called Kahili) from where they launched bombers attacking Henderson Field. The Allies desperately needed heavy bombers to retaliate and hit Kahili. Until they arrived, the enemy kept navy fighter planes at Henderson Airfield busy defending their turf.

On November 12, 1942, the Japanese organized a transport convoy to leave from Shortland Harbor in Bougainville and head south to Guadalcanal. The goal was to take 15,000 infantry troops and their equipment and try, once and for all, to retake the airfield. They assigned several Japanese warship forces to bombard Henderson Field, with the goal of destroying Allied planes that posed a threat to the convoy. Because of coast-watcher intelligence and intercepted messages, however, the Allies knew exactly where the convoy was headed and when. On the evening of the 13th, the coast watchers reported that the big Japanese convoy had left Shortland Harbor and was on its way south to Guadalcanal.

This valuable piece of intelligence allowed the American planes—B-17s from Espiritu Santo and dive bombers from the carrier *Enterprise*—that had joined Allied Forces to support the invasion of Guadalcanal in early August to drop bombs down at the transports like a torrential rainstorm. They sank six of the Japanese ships that were en route. Of the 15,000 Japanese troops that set out for Guadalcanal, only 2,000 arrived. The Japanese had no choice but to cancel the attack. Outmanned and outgunned, they turned and left with their tails between their legs.

• • •

Because the U.S. had navy planes that were now based at Henderson Field on the north end of Guadalcanal, the Japanese could not use large, slow transport ships to deliver troops and supplies to their soldiers fighting the Marines deep in the jungles of Guadalcanal. Instead, they had to utilize warships based at their naval base in Rabaul and in the Shortland Islands at the north end of the Solomons because these warships—mainly light cruisers or destroyers—could usually make the round trip down 'the slot' to Guadalcanal and back in a single night under the cover of darkness. This minimized their exposure to an air attack, but these smaller ships could not carry heavy equipment and supplies, such as heavy artillery, vehicles, much food, or ammunition, to Guadalcanal with them, so their troops became increasingly isolated.

After six months, which included three major land battles, seven large naval battles, and almost daily aerial battles, the victory finally culminated in the decisive Naval Battle of Guadalcanal in early November 1942, resulting in both sides losing many warships in two extremely destructive nighttime battles. The U.S. turned back attempts by the Japanese to bombard Henderson Field with battleships. Allied planes also sank most of the Japanese troop transports and prevented a majority of the Japanese soldiers and equipment from reaching Guadalcanal.

This battle was the last major attempt of three failed campaigns by the Japanese to seize control of the seas around Guadalcanal or to retake the island and air base. Thereafter, the U.S. Navy could resupply the U.S. forces at Guadalcanal when needed, including the delivery of two fresh divisions by late December 1942.

The inability to squash or retake Henderson Field doomed the Japanese effort to combat the Allied conquest of Guadalcanal and was another major turning point in the war. Allied success in the Solomon Islands' campaign prevented the Japanese from cutting Australia and New Zealand off from the United States as well. This vital campaign to secure Guadalcanal came at a heavy cost, as all battles do. The Allies lost approximately 7,100 men, 29 ships, and 615 aircraft. The Japanese lost 31,000 men, 38 ships, and 683 aircraft. But Henderson Field was securely in U.S. hands. By December, the Japanese abandoned all their efforts to retake Henderson Field and evacuated their remaining forces by February 7, 1943.[27]

The Marines had secured Henderson Field, and Mac and the 307th BG would arrive four days later to occupy their new base.

---

[27] Wikipedia. "Guadalcanal Campaign."

Chapter 14
The Natives of the Solomons and Chief Jacob Vouza

Mostly, the natives of Guadalcanal, and throughout the islands in the Solomons, lived their peaceful lives going about their business, unmindful and heedless of the war going on all around them. They subsisted on produce gathered from their communal gardens and the fish and other seafood they netted.

When the Allies arrived, they encouraged the natives to stay away from the Japanese, but that did not stop the Japanese from killing or capturing hundreds of natives. It was especially hard for them to stay out of the fray when Japanese landing parties looted their villages and pillaged their gardens, as happened one day when the Japanese sent eight men to set up their own coast watcher station on the south coast of Guadalcanal. This plundering infuriated the local villagers, who struck back several nights later, killing every Japanese soldier except one radio operator, who fled into the jungle, never to be seen again.

The Japanese showed their cruelty and practiced their belief that anyone not a Japanese was *Kichibu*, or 'beast.' When coast watchers saw isolated Japanese parties, they were frequently tempted to ambush them, but most of them refrained, as their job was to watch the enemy, not engage with it.

Even when cruelty was not involved, there was tension between natives and the Japanese. The occupiers paid extraordinarily little for the supplies they commandeered and the labor they demanded. They were unfriendly and often lived in such rough and squalid circumstances that the natives had little respect for them.

As with all coast watchers, the twenty-three coast watchers in the Solomon Islands relied heavily on the support of the local people, and Solomon Islanders were overwhelmingly loyal to them and to the Allies. This close association helped the coast watchers function effectively behind enemy lines.[28] Throughout the campaign in the South Pacific, natives risked their lives to rescue downed flyers and shipwrecked sailors, then often spent days of dangerous work getting them safely back to a coast watcher who could alert a rescue team.

The Guadalcanal campaign was the first major land offensive by ground troops of the Allied Forces against the Empire of Japan. All earlier offensive moves had been by sea or air. The Allies secured the air base, now called Henderson, and won at Guadalcanal with a good deal of help from the indigenous people and Chief Jacob Vutha, or Vouza, as he was called by the Americans. For the first time, the Allies needed scouting and intel help on the ground.

When the first American troopships of Marines had approached Guadalcanal on August 7, 1942, at the beginning of the Guadalcanal campaign, a trio of natives greeted them, including the chief of the island, who paddled out to the flagship in his outrigger at the mouth of the Tenaru River, offering his services and those of his people to the Americans.

He explained to the Marines that he had retired from the native constabulary as a sergeant major but had fled from his home when the Japanese had invaded his beloved Solomon Islands. Realizing his incredible value, a group of Marines

---

[28] Putz, Catherine. Managing editor. *THE DIPLOMAT*.

quickly whisked him to the command post. He shook the hand of Division Intelligence Officer Lt. Col. Edmund J. Buckley and proudly introduced himself as Sgt. Maj. Jacob Vouza.

At five foot ten, Vouza was a tall, muscular man—practically a giant among the mostly short natives. And he was in superbly good shape. He would easily walk forty or fifty miles to tend to the needs of the villages under his authority. The natives of his tribes were divided into three classes: the Salt Water Natives, who were the most progressive, the Water Pond Natives, and the Bush Natives, the most primitive.[29] He oversaw them all.

Vouza and the other native scouts became a tremendous asset to the Marines during the yearlong Guadalcanal campaign. The British had previously recruited and trained these select men for law enforcement purposes, and they worked closely with men like Captain Martin Clemens, an Australian coast watcher on Guadalcanal who spied on the Japanese. This dedicated group of native men provided the Marines with valuable information on enemy troop movements, while also guiding them through Guadalcanal's often tricky jungle terrain crossed by erratic rivers.

Among all the natives, though, Jacob Vouza became the favorite of the Marines, and later, the 307th BG when they arrived. They were all impressed by his keen scouting, information-gathering abilities, and affable nature. He quickly became 'one of the guys.'

One Marine gave the sergeant major a small American flag as a gift, which he treasured. However, this token of friendship nearly cost Vouza his life when the enemy found the flag in his loincloth and knew he was spying on them for the Americans. A Japanese patrol captured Vouza when he was on a scouting mission near the village of Volonavua. When they discovered the flag, they tied him to a tree with straw ropes, and the enemy

---

[29] 307th Bombardment Group (HV). 1945. *We'll Say Goodbye: Story of the "Long Rangers"—307th Bombardment Group (HV).*

soldiers delighted in clubbing him with their rifle butts. Still refusing to talk, they stabbed him in his arms, throat, shoulder, face, and stomach with bayonets and swords until he passed out from a loss of blood. Leaving him for dead, the Japanese vacated the area.

When this indomitable islander woke up, he gnawed his way through the ropes and made his way back to friendly lines, crawling on his hands and knees for almost four miles. He was weak from loss of blood and injuries and near death when Captain Clemens found him. The coast watcher, who could 'barely look at him' because of the severity of his wounds, took him immediately to an aid station. Before being treated, however, Vouza insisted on informing Clemens of the size and location of the Japanese forces approaching the Marine perimeter.[30]

Remarkably, this determined islander ultimately survived his horrendous ordeal and continued to lead other patrols throughout the remaining struggle for Guadalcanal—a loyal Allied soldier to the end. After the war, the U.S. presented him with the Silver Star and Legion of Merit for his exemplary bravery. In addition, Great Britain awarded him the George Medal and set up a scholarship fund in his name to aid underprivileged Solomon Island children in getting a better education. In 1979, Queen Elizabeth II knighted him for his exemplary bravery, and he became the Hon. Sgt. Maj. *Sir* Jacob Vouza.

Revisiting Guadalcanal years after the war, the Marine Raider Association placed a bronze plaque on a granite block, which read: "We dedicate to SERGEANT MAJOR JACOB VOUZA and his SOLOMON ISLAND SCOUTS for supreme intrepidity and valor in the face of the enemy during the struggle for Guadalcanal 1942–43."

---

[30] Vouza, Jacob C. https://military-history.fandom.com/wiki/ #cite_ref-5.

After Vouza died in 1984, the stone block with the bronze tablet became his headstone. The revered and admired scout and guide, who was willing to sacrifice his life for the Marines on Guadalcanal. Those who knew him and fought alongside him will remember always.

Chief Jacob Vouza

Chapter 15
The 307th Bombardment Group Prepares for Guadalcanal

During the last six months of the year, while the Marines were securing the Henderson Air Base on Guadalcanal, the first and second phases of training were being completed in Ephrata and orders were for the 307th BG to move to Sioux City, Iowa by October 1st for added training. Mac and his crew had completed just under 326 hours (about two weeks) of flight time in the new B-24 *Liberators*.

The move to Sioux City was apparently paradise compared to Ephrata, as there were actual barracks for all personnel and office space for all departments. This was an established army camp. There was a modern airport, concrete streets and walks, and wooden barracks, instead of tents in the middle of a sandy bog. In addition, Sioux City was large enough to absorb the now 1,500 young men of the 307th BG into their theaters, nightclubs, and restaurants. It seemed too good to be true … and it was. It only lasted a few weeks.

Training in Sioux City had an emphasis on gunnery, intelligence, night flying, and long-range navigation. Combat crews were all given a thorough physical examination, including pressure chamber tests, to determine their fitness for combat and high-altitude flying.

By the middle of October 1942, the 307th had organized and divided thirty-five combat crews within the four squadrons, who were working well together as teams. Mac's crew considered themselves great friends and comrades in arms, excited about their next duty assignment. Thirty-five brand-new B-24Ds, complete with all machine guns—including the nose guns and the very new Norden Bombsight—arrived at Sioux City. Finally, each of the crews now had their own plane. They named Mac's plane *Bombs Away*.[31]

The Norden Bombsight, installed in *Bombs Away* and in each of the *Liberators*, was top secret at the time—so secret that the bombardiers had to take a solemn oath never to divulge its workings. If the plane crashed, they were to destroy the bombsight immediately so it could not fall into enemy hands. They kept the device in a vault, and before every flight, the bombardier would carry it to the plane accompanied by two armed guards. Once in the plane, it sat on a platform, and a gyroscope stabilized it and kept it level, even when the plane bounced about in the wind. Using Norden's fifty-five-pound analog computer with a telescope and mirrors, the bombardier would enter the relevant data.

The sight combined an optical device, a gyroscope, and a computer. Earlier Norden designs of the gyrostabilizer corrected for the plane's drift, maintained altitude once set, and adjusted for aircraft control and speed changes. Dropping a bomb from a moving airplane and hitting a target thousands of feet below requires precise calculations. Sixty-four algorithms compensated for the thirty seconds it took for a bomb to hit its target: wind speed, altitude, speed of the plane, distance from the target, and multiple other factors, including air temperature and rotation of the earth. But it required the bombardier to make only three manual adjustments—for the bomb's weight, and the

---

[31] Walker, Samuel I. 1984. *Up the Slot*.

plane's altitude and speed—after which he would line up the target through the sight.[32]

After the computer calculated the trajectory, the pilot would switch on the autopilot and Norden would do the rest, dropping a bomb thousands of feet above a target sighted through the bombardier's telescope. The autopilot kept the plane on course, and the bombs released automatically, falling on the target below.[33]

With initial training almost completed and the planes ready, it didn't take long before the brass gave Mac and the rest of the flight crews the news that all four of the squadrons would leave soon, but where they would go was not part of the bulletin. The 'need to know' group did not yet include most of the 307th BG. They still hadn't even been told for which theater they would depart: Mediterranean, China, Burma, India (CBI), or the Pacific. Then on October 19th, Special Orders 67 directed their departure for Hamilton Field, California.

The four squadrons of the 307th BG—now each with their own shiny, new plane that had all the bells and whistles the Army Air Forces could provide—loaded up and flew to Hamilton Field. Each squadron now had twelve planes with twenty-four crew members, including ground personnel who were assigned to each plane. Nine men manned each plane. They still had not been told where their final destination would be, but since their orders were for California, it was pretty obvious that they were headed west and not east to Europe.

On Monday, October 24th, pilots, navigators, radio operators, and flight engineers from the four squadrons were all summoned to a briefing where they learned they would leave that night at 9:00 p.m. Operations Order 109 revealed their destination would be Hawaii. Flying nine hours, they would reach Hickam Field on Oahu just after daybreak the following

---

[32] Carl Norden Obituary prabook.com.
[33] https://ww2-history.fandom.com/wiki/Norden_Bombsight#cite_ref-Skylighters_Norden_1-0.

morning. They were as excited as men would be decades later to pilot Apollo 11 and walk on the moon. They were indeed pioneers in aviation history.

In final preparation, they held two valuable and fascinating training sessions that day for the engineers and navigators. The first was to learn about the function of a black box in the radio room and how to adjust it for ultimate performance. Like the Norden Bombsight, this black box was also top secret. It was called an IFF for Identification, Friend, or Foe. When the ground needed to identify a plane, they sent the IFF a signal. If the plane was American, it would respond to the signal. If the ground received no signal, then operators on the ground would assume that the plane was an enemy aircraft, and a fighter plane would respond accordingly, presumably blasting it out of the sky. It would have been difficult to overstate the importance of making sure someone adjusted the IFF to respond correctly. Engineers and navigators paid careful attention to this lesson.

The second part of their training was just as valuable. It involved special instructions on how to use a booster pump to transfer fuel from the bomb bay tanks to the wing tanks during flight. This was also fairly easy to grasp. Then one engineer asked the instructor an interesting question.

"What happens if the booster pump fails? Is there another way to get the fuel from the bomb bay to the wing tanks?" The instructor scratched his head.

"I've never heard of a booster pump failing, but after the regular training session, I'll demonstrate another way to pull gasoline from the bomb bay tanks for anyone who's interested." Staff Sgt. Dean J. Howell, the inquisitive, young flight engineer who had asked, was the only person to stay for the extra training. The information he learned would prove vital soon enough.

That night, as scheduled, Mac and the other B-24 flight crews left from Hamilton Field and took off for Oahu in the Hawaiian Islands. As the trainer had instructed Staff Sgt. Howell, the curious engineer, he began transferring fuel about an hour after takeoff. He used the booster pump to top off the four wing tanks and everything worked perfectly, just like the instructor had said it would. Then he switched number two and number three engines to use their fuel pumps to draw fuel from the bomb bay tanks. Again, everything worked perfectly, and the planes continued on their way to Hawaii.

Then, while still several hours out from Oahu, his pilot, who was monitoring the inter-plane frequency, suddenly shouted to his crew, "Hey, somebody's in trouble."

A pilot on another *Liberator* was explaining the problem in a tense voice. "The fuel supply in our wing tanks is low, and one engine has already quit. The bomb bay tanks are still full, but *the damn booster pump won't work.* We don't have enough fuel to reach Hawaii."

"Dean," the pilot called, "get on the radio and explain the workaround you learned this afternoon." After careful instruction by Dean on how to set the valves to use the engine fuel pumps, everyone waited several tense minutes. Finally, the other pilot's excited voice came over the radio.

"It's working! We've got the dead engine going again." If not for Dean's curious mind and foresight, those men might have died before they ever reached their base in Hawaii.[34]

Only thirty-four planes landed safely at Hickam Field. One plane and ten crew members from the 370th Bomb Squad, piloted by Lt. Robert H. Guskey, went down somewhere in the Pacific for an unknown reason.

---

[34] Walker, Samuel I. 1984. *Up the Slot.*

Chapter 16
The 307th Bombardment Group Reports to Hawaii

The 307th BG sent Mac and his crew, assigned to the 424th Squadron, to the base in Mokulē'ia on the north side of Oahu. They dispersed the other three squadrons—the 370th, 371st, and 372nd—to three other bases where training continued separately for all four of them.

Meanwhile, an old Norwegian freighter had been slowly transporting the rest of the 307th BG personnel—some 1,200 men—to its 'Pacific Paradise' in Oahu, docking on November 2, 1942. These young men, from mostly rural areas on the mainland, were excited about their new destination. They were going to Hawaii. But it turned out that Hawaii was not what the travel brochures advertised. When the 307th BG ground crews and other personnel docked, there were no wahines encircling their necks with flowered leis, no smiling, young men paddling out to meet the boats in their outriggers, diving for pennies in the crystal-blue waters. There were just big, ugly army trucks waiting to take them to their respective bases, like prison buses transporting convicts to a penitentiary.

The reason for the muted reception, they soon learned, was that within hours after the Japanese bombed Pearl Harbor, the U.S. had declared martial law in Hawaii. This meant that the military had taken temporary control of normal civilian functions. The islands were now under a curfew, with total blackouts from sundown to sunup strictly enforced. Like a ghost town, inhabitants had deserted every city, village, and outpost after 6:00 p.m.

The island was teeming with GIs and sailors now, but there was little Hawaiian aloha to be found. The male to female ratio was about 300 to 1 and, for obvious reasons, the locals were impersonal, suspicious, and unfriendly toward all members of the military. It was hard for GIs to even buy a drink on a day off. After waiting in long lines, locals pushed soldiers out of bars as soon as they bought their allotted rationed number of drinks. Under martial law, nightlife on the island was non-existent. Life was difficult for everyone, particularly the permanent residents.

Hawaii's proximity to Japan made it a prime strategic spot and put the islands at a unique risk of future attacks, but military officials doubted the loyalties of the island's many Japanese Americans. In the continental U.S., they forced people of Japanese descent into internment camps created hastily on the mainland. But it was not so cut-and-dried with the Hawaiian Islands, where 37 percent of residents of Hawaii were of Japanese descent, including 37,000 Osseo (Japanese-born people who were not eligible for citizenship) and 121,000 Japanese American citizens.

The war effort needed people working, and the military feared such a move might even stoke pro-Japanese sentiment. Besides, the logistics of imprisoning nearly 160,000 people in a territory that was small to begin with was insurmountable. And so, within hours of the December 7th attack, the Hawaiian Islands became one big internment facility by installing martial law.[35]

Except for children, the military fingerprinted every person on the island and issued identification papers they had to produce on demand. Hawaii was still a territory, not yet a state. The law that set up a territorial government in 1900 covered

[35] History.com.

Hawaiians with the basic protections of the U.S. Constitution, but martial law suspended all these under martial law.

To many Hawaiians, it must have felt like the Brown Shirts of the Nazis were in charge. Military and FBI agents rounded up suspected spies and 'suspicious persons,' and the army imposed a strict curfew. Habeas Corpus, which guaranteed recourse for unlawful detention or imprisonment, was suspended under martial law. The military took control of labor, and they temporarily even abolished trial by jury. They arrested over 2,000 people, most of Japanese descent, in the first forty-eight hours alone. The difference between the Gestapo and the U.S. Military was intentions and motivation for what appeared to be a power grab. Nazis were trying to isolate segments of the population for expulsion and extermination. The U.S. was trying to isolate people who might be in league with its enemies and harm the U.S. To the citizens of Hawaii, however, it probably felt remarkably similar. Fear, resentment, and anger toward the American troops must have been palpable.

And martial law was not so temporary. Hawaii would remain under military rule for almost three years.

Chapter 17
Final Training and Preparations for Guadalcanal

Shortly after landing in Hawaii, the flight crew added another unfamiliar word to their growing vocabulary: RADAR. The acronym stands for radio detection and ranging. This newly improved but not yet perfected device could detect solid objects miles away using radio waves, which worked in both dark and bright daylight.

They installed radar on all the B-24s, and the radio operators got a crash course on how it worked.[36] Radar is essentially a method of getting information. Radio waves are used to detect an object at a distance by transmitting a burst of radio energy and measuring the time it takes for the 'echo,' caused by hitting the object, to reflect back to the receiver. Operators can also identify the height and bearing—or direction of flight—of targets.

Initial operational performance was dismal, however. Barely 5 percent of the radar sets would work for an entire bombing flight. Plus, the operators were insufficiently trained because of the urgency of war, and the maintenance was inadequate. By the end of the war, through the improved radar systems and the demanding work by maintenance technicians, the radars were running reliably during the entire flight 95 percent of the time,

---

[36] Walker, Samuel I. 1984. *Up the Slot.*

and radar had proven itself to be a valuable technical tool for the future.

After radar education, phase two of training for the 307th BG in Hawaii was search and reconnaissance. The crews' primary jobs were to search the sea for enemy warships and to protect the islands from another potential invasion. But aside from the nine-hour flight to Oahu, the new crews had had little training in over-water flights. Flying over water is much like flying over land, except there are no visible points of reference on the ground … just miles and miles of rolling ocean that looks hypnotically the same. Where is the land, and can navigators find it before they run out of gas?

Today, a navigator simply punches coordinates into a GPS. But in 1942, that technology didn't exist. These men had to rely on the classic navigational tools: a map, a compass, a sextant, and some good, old-fashioned intuition. Navigators took about 500 hours (about 3 weeks) of ground instruction. They did another 100 hours of training in the air. At the end, they needed to plot a route with a course error no greater than eleven degrees, being no more than one minute off per hour of flight time. They also had to get within fifteen miles of an objective during a night flight. During World War II, some new navigation technology, like radio beacons, helped navigators direct their planes home safely.[37]

Because of this, a good navigator was worth his weight in gold and silver. A slight shift of wind that was undetected could send a plane miles off course. And when one ran out of fuel in the middle of the ocean, it was a genuine problem.

Danger was ever-present, even before the new 307th BG flew into combat. Accidents and equipment malfunctions in the new

---

[37] Hutchison, Harold C. *The Mighty History*.

plane were common. The first casualties in Hawaii occurred on November 10th, when Lt. Glynn C. Moore spun into the water off Kahuku Point. The squadron lost their second plane on November 29th, when Lt. Richard K. Bartholomew's crew of the 424th BS—Mac's squadron—took off in dangerous weather from Kahuku on a search mission. No one knew whether there was a mechanical problem or navigational error, but they flew directly into a mountain, and everyone on board perished.

Lt. James McClendon's crew of the 371st BS took off on December 16th and experienced an explosion and fire shortly after takeoff, which quickly enveloped the plane in flames. A new flight engineer had made a mistake in transferring fuel, which caused a large accumulation of gasoline in the bomb bay. When he opened the doors, a spark ignited the fuel. Only three men escaped alive. Lt. James G. Main, a new pilot along for orientation, was on the flight deck in the radio room at the time of the explosion. Severely burned, he managed to put on a parachute and rolled over the side through a gaping hole in the fuselage. Lt. Wendell A. Steele, the bombardier, and flight engineer Sgt. Robert W. Vaughn were in the tail and jumped through the camera hatch. The plane was perilously low for parachute jumps, and Steel's chute barely opened in time. When it finally did, he remembered swinging his feet and brushing the tops of tall sugar cane. Incredibly, that's how low he was when the chute finally blossomed. The others on board all perished in the crash.[38]

As fate sometimes decrees, two members of McClendon's regular crew weren't flying that day. Staff Sgts. William L. Pash and Robert L. Hopkins had been fooling around earlier in the day, pretending to disarm a Japanese soldier, and the safety was

---

[38] Britt, Sam S., Jr. 1990. *The Long Rangers: A Diary of the 307th Bombardment Group (H)*.

off the .45 automatic pistol. In the struggle for the gun, it went off, and a bullet hit Pash in the wrist. Part of the punishment for this dangerous horseplay was being grounded. Not being allowed to fly that day probably saved their lives.[39]

---

[39] Walker, Samuel I. 1984. *Up the Slot.*

Chapter 18
Wake Island—Mac's First Combat Mission, December 1942

Still doing reconnaissance from Hawaii, the 307th BG first encountered the enemy on Christmas Eve, 1942. Mac and his crew of eight men were among the twenty-seven B-24s that took off from Hawaii on December 22nd for an unknown-to-them mission. Mac now had just 600 hours (about 3 and a half weeks) of total flight time under his belt, and he and his crew had been flying together for only five months. Training was over; this would be their first combat mission.

Once they were airborne, the crews opened the secret orders and, for the first time, learned their destination. Their flight was to take them to Midway Island, now securely under U.S. control, for brief refueling and then on to Wake Island, their intended bombing target. Mechanics installed extra bomb bay tanks, and they painted the bottoms of the planes black to camouflage them against the night skies. Takeoff from Midway was at 4:30 in the afternoon, and they sighted Wake Island around seven hours later, just before midnight.

Under the cover of darkness, the twenty-seven bombers approached the island at 8,000 feet. After a steep glide down, they dropped to 4,000 feet for a run over the island. They assigned each crew member individual targets, with bunkers, barracks, runways, ammunition dumps, and fuel storage areas receiving the brunt of the attack. The lead plane dropped the bombs at 12:03 a.m. on December 24th.

A predominant part in the success of this mission was the element of surprise. U.S. bombing results were excellent, as the first three planes over the target received some illumination from the ground and, luckily, inaccurate anti-aircraft fire from below.

Crew member, Tech. Sgt. Carlyle Elrod, looked out through a waist window and described the experience. "As we approached Wake Island, we dived again and leveled out at 2,500 feet for the bomb run. Searchlights were stabbing and probing the sky; heavy anti-aircraft shells were bursting above the lights, and tracers from small arms fire formed an apex near our plane. I realized, for the first time in my life, that someone was trying to kill me."[40]

Four large fires started when the bombs hit the area, and one stick of incendiaries landed directly on the bunker and barracks area, setting fire to it all. They covered the entire target area below with smoke and fire after completing the bombing run. As the planes headed back, the fires lit the scene below like a giant reading lamp illuminating the extensive damage.

With the weather back on Midway rainy and miserable, crewmen awaiting the return of the *Liberators* didn't know how any of the pilots could find the landing strip when they returned. The skies were cloudy and gray, and visibility was zero. As they waited anxiously, they suddenly heard engines, faintly at first, and then louder and louder. Then, miraculously, it seemed, a B-24 broke out of the mist about 200 feet above them and landed with a perfect touchdown aligned with the runway. It completed its roll and taxied to a parking place, then stopped. Then another came into view, and another and another, all with the same precise result.

---

[40] Walker, Samuel I. 1984. *Up the Slot*.

Within an hour, twenty-seven *Liberators* were safely on the ground. This astounded the crewmen, awaiting their return. *How is this possible?* they wondered. Unbeknownst to them, a crack Midway radar team had been directing the planes and aligning them with the runway. For most observers on the ground, this was the first demonstration of the benefits of radar. All twenty-seven U.S. planes and personnel returned to Midway at 7:00 a.m. on December 24, 1942.

Because the flight took the crews across the International Date Line and back, they took off on Tuesday, bombed on Thursday, Christmas Eve, and landed back at Midway on Wednesday. Mac and his *Bombs Away* crew, along with the twenty-six other crews, then arrived back in Hawaii on Thursday, Christmas Eve, just in time for the celebration after the longest, over-water, mass raid of the war, having flown 2,240 miles (about twice the distance from Florida to New York City) round trip. The alcohol flowed, and the party lasted well into the night. The 307th BG soon became known as the Long Rangers.[41]

Following the Wake raid, a photo reconnaissance mission left for the island to take pictures for damage assessment. The plane flew out, but harsh weather prevented them from taking any photos. They couldn't see the ground. They tried again the following day, December 28th, and once again could not even find Wake Island somewhere below them through the dense mist and clouds, so they turned around and headed back to Midway.

Then, as they were only 600 miles away, the pilot, Capt. Anthony Benvenuto, notified Midway's control tower they were having engine trouble. Tragically, his last message read simply, "Can't make it." They found neither the plane nor any survivors after an intensive search.

A few days later, the 372nd BS lost another plane and flight crew when Lt. George F. Moznette Jr. crashed on takeoff, leaving

---

[41] Walker, Samuel I. 1984. *Up the Slot*.

the air base on Kauai. Also on board, as an observer, was Maj. Jonathan E. Coxwell.

Then, a most bizarre accident occurred. Maj. Elwood T. Lippincott, from the 371st BS, was practicing a new bombing technique with an observer on board who was standing between the pilot and copilot. As they pulled away after the bomb run, the G-force caused the observer's knees to buckle. Trying to steady himself, he reached up and grabbed the life raft handle. Maddeningly, many times when the life raft was supposed to release, it would fail. This time, unfortunately, it released, fell, and stuck on the right stabilizer, making it extremely difficult for Lippincott to control the plane. These planes were hard to fly under the best of circumstances, but this made it almost impossible. Unsure what he could do, and just to be on the safe side, Lippincott ordered the crew to bail out, which they did. He and the copilot then brought the plane in for a safe landing, saving the plane along with themselves. The other crew members who parachuted out also landed safely and were rescued.[42]

Following the loss of Capt. Benvenuto and his crew, they tried one more photographic mission of Wake Island. This time, to annoy the Japanese, they took along some bombs at the same time. The weather was favorable, and after taking pictures and completing the bomb runs, the formation re-formed, but suddenly five *Zeros* attacked them. There was minimal damage, but for the first time, the crew members noticed the fast rate of climb of these Japanese planes and their extreme maneuverability.

The Mitsubishi *Zeros* were like giant gnats, swooping down, attacking, and darting off again. This was Japan's dominant fighter. It was an agile aircraft that could climb quickly. But, built with a light airframe, they used neither armor nor self-sealing gas tanks in construction. This meant that, like most Japanese

---

[42] Walker, Samuel I. 1984. *Up the Slot*.

planes, the *Zero* was vulnerable to gunfire and explosion. As the war went on and metal shortages worsened, the fragility of Japanese aircraft became a bigger and bigger problem for the Empire.[43]

---

[43] Dennis, William G. *WWII HISTORY* magazine.

Chapter 19
The 307th Bombardment Group Arrives in Guadalcanal—February 1943

Now that the Marines had secured Guadalcanal and Henderson Air Base, the 307th BG was ready to move to their new home. Originally, they planned for all four of the squadrons to go to the South Pacific. However, someone in charge in Hawaii decided that two of the four, the 371st and 372nd, would stay on Oahu in case the Japanese planned another visit to Hawaii. They ordered Mac and crew, along with the rest of the 424th and the 370th BS, to Henderson Field on Guadalcanal.

This disappointed most of the men in the two squadrons staying in Hawaii. They felt left out of the action but had no choice. Of course, even though there was no enemy attacking them, the Hawaii-based groups were not without danger from the mechanical failures of the B-24. Two months later, shortly after takeoff on April 13th during a routine search mission, Lt. Stanley Schreiber lost an engine. Then, because of some unknown mechanical problem, he lost control of the plane as he tried to line up with the runway, and the right wing struck a building, crashing. Their navigator, 2nd Lt. Fred A. Coppack, survived the crash but died in the hospital. Cpl. Frank Covertine was the sole survivor.

Mac and his crew, along with twenty-three other *Liberators* and their crews, left Oahu and made their way to Guadalcanal. They arrived at their new base on February 11, 1943, just four days after the Marines had taken the island at the Battle of Guadalcanal. The 307th BG became the first heavy bomb group to be stationed in the Southwest Pacific, where they formed the advance echelon.

When the planes of the 370th and 424th BSs arrived, adding to the Navy SBD-scout planes, dive bombers, and TBF-torpedo bombers, Henderson Field was crowded. Now, with all branches, including U.S. Army, Navy, and Marines, represented in the Solomons, it seemed to many that there was no organization or liaison between the various Armed Forces units in the South Pacific Theater. Appointed Supreme Allied Commander Southwest Pacific Area (SWPA) on April 18, 1942, Gen. Douglas MacArthur was stationed in Australia. The U.S. Navy, under Adm. Chester Nimitz, had responsibility for the rest of the Pacific Ocean. This divided command had unfortunate consequences for the war itself, creating confusion and lack of coordination.

• • •

Most considered the stay on Guadalcanal to be the roughest period for the group of its overseas assignments. Ephrata must have seemed like a five-star hotel in comparison. And Hawaii? Well, Guadalcanal was not Hawaii, even with martial law imposed.

Living conditions at Henderson Field, as described by the men, were deplorable. Mud and dirt were ubiquitous, and mosquitoes—especially the female Anopheles mosquito that carries malaria—were as abundant as the mud and a lot more dangerous. The temperature averaged 85 degrees, day and night, with oppressive humidity. Diseases like malaria, dengue fever, elephantiasis, and typhus were constant threats and caused continual illnesses and deaths for many. To add insult to injury, the area included tarantulas and coral snakes. While it wasn't exactly Oz, they were definitely not in Kansas anymore.

Mac and his crew had little time to experience their new digs. Just two days after arriving at Henderson, on February 13th, six crews of the 424th Bomb Squadron, including Mac's, received the assignment to "keep pushing the Japs around." Still with 'propeller lag' after their long travel, their boots had barely gotten muddy. Considering the deplorable conditions of the camp, and the itch to go back into combat, when they scheduled his first mission from Guadalcanal so quickly, it must have thrilled Mac. It had been almost two months since the Christmas Eve Wake Island strike, and he was eager to make a second bombing raid. He was two months shy of his twenty-fifth birthday.

The goal of this mission was to stop the transportation of Japanese troops and supplies coming down 'the slot.' The Japanese had evacuated the last of their ground troops from Guadalcanal but still had plenty of troops on bases on nearby islands.

• • •

By 10:30 a.m., all six pilots had coaxed their engines into roaring to life, rolled out to the runway, and headed north to Shortland Harbor from their base at Henderson Field. The visibility was excellent, and the day was clear. The islands on either side of them dotted the landscape below as they flew north through 'the slot.' An escort of six Army Air Forces planes and six navy fighters joined the small strike force of six planes after they fell into formation. This would be a daring daylight raid for their first bombing mission in the Solomon Islands.

P-40 *Warhawks* single engine, single-man fighters were flying about a thousand feet above the *Liberators* to protect them against attacks from the nose, the weakest point on the original B-24D model bomber. Six P-38s, single-seated, fighter-bomber planes called *Lightning*, were above the P-40s. Certain peril awaited the eighteen planes flying in formation. The crews were prepared for a fight, but the enemy would have ample time to see them coming and would outnumber the small strike force.

Mac's crew had been flying together for six months and were close friends by then. These crews formed a fraternity like no other. Their lives depended on their good relationships, close communication, and careful coordination. They had to perform together like a symphony orchestra on opening night at Carnegie Hall.

Their target on this bright morning—Japanese shipping vessels in Shortland Harbor—was about 300 miles north of Henderson Field on a route that took them directly over other Japanese-occupied islands. It was a bold raid in broad daylight; there would be no sneaking up on the enemy. They could expect an aggressive and relentless defense by the Japanese.

Unlike the English, the U.S. bomb units during WWII gave up the security of night bombing for the greater accuracy and visibility of daytime attacks. It was a costly, deadly choice until fighter planes gained enough range to escort the bomber groups to their targets. But daylight bombing was unquestionably more effective and accurate than bombing at night, just a lot more dangerous. Even with fighter planes protecting them, the six, well-armed *Liberators* were still an exceedingly small combat team. Anti-aircraft guns from the ground and enemy plane fighters would most assuredly be there to greet them. This focused the men, and the mood was somber. Tension was palpable.

Soon after takeoff, all crew members went to their battle stations, preparing themselves for what lie ahead. All the islands up the Solomon Island chain north of Guadalcanal belonged to the Japanese, so they were at once in hostile territory. Tail gunners squeezed into their turrets. Navigators and bombardiers went to the nose where, besides their regular duties, they manned four flexible, .50-caliber machine guns. Flight engineers climbed into upper (top) turrets, and radio operators took control of the twin, .50-caliber waist guns on a circular track. After last-minute checks of their equipment, the engineers and first radio operators took their places at their respective guns. They were all poised, tense, and ready for action.

Shortly after passing the Russell Islands, the six planes climbed in unison to 13,000 feet. All the crew members were veterans of the earlier Wake Island mission, but this was only their second combat mission, and unlike the earlier one, this one was in broad daylight. There were no truly hardened combat veterans in the 307th BG, except for one man who remained back on Guadalcanal. He had been in the old 19th BG and had tangled with the Japanese many times when they finally forced the U.S. to surrender in the Philippines in May 1942.

These six flight crews, this group of fifty-four young airmen, so recently trained and so new to combat, were headed into battle for the first time since arriving at Henderson Field. Almost half of them would never return.

Chapter 20
Shot Down

Japanese gunfire had heavily damaged *Bombs Away*, but it was still flyable. The enemy followed closely, continuing to attack Mac and his crew for an hour and fifteen minutes without letting up. The three American escort fighters did a yeoman's job of protecting the remaining B-24s. After shooting down eight *Zeros*, the six planes headed back to Henderson Air Base. The *Zeros* followed Mac and the disabled plane as he led them farther and farther out to sea, knowing their short range and need to refuel would soon cause them to turn back.[44]

As Mac watched, Lt. Robert Rist, one of the P-38 pilots who had already destroyed three *Zeros*, circled back and made a dive into the swarm of *Zeros* that were surrounding Mac's crippled plane and coming in for the kill. Rist's heroism ended as the enemy shot him down in flames, spiraling into the ocean below.

With his cover gone, Mac put his damaged plane into a steep dive and headed north over the Pacific, trying to evade the enemy, still in hot pursuit. His diversionary course took them over the heaviest anti-aircraft positions directly below them. They almost flew over the enemy seaplane base at Faisi, which would have ended disastrously for Mac and his crew.

---

[44] Recorded army debriefing from Mac's own account.

Gunfire hit his number two engine, which burst into flames fifteen or twenty minutes after turning away from the formation. The plane could still fly with two engines out, but vacuum pumps and deicers tied to them would not. They were once again met with intense machine gunfire from the twelve to fifteen *Zeros* left that were flying alongside them, just out of range. They would swoop in like wasps, individually in quick succession from above, concentrating on the vulnerable nose and the tail of the plane. Although Mac didn't know it, the tail was completely unprotected, with no gunners in the plane's tail end. *Bombs Away* was now trailing fire from the left wing, and the body of the plane looked like a giant sieve as daylight streamed into the cavity.

He flew in a northeast course across the northwestern end of Choiseul Island, following the valleys, flying only fifty feet above the tree line. Five or six *Zeros* were still chasing and attacking them, but their passes were ineffective, kept away by the nose gunner, who continued firing furiously at them. Don shot one down, and they saw the second plane smoking.

With two engines dead, the propeller on the number three engine malfunctioned. Mac and Van attempted to change the angle of the blade—called 'feathering'—to stop it from spinning. This would decrease drag and slow the plane, but the attempt failed. They were now flying across the northeast shore of Choiseul. The only flight instruments still functioning were the altimeter and airspeed indicator, as well as the engine instruments, so it was impossible to evade the Japanese planes by taking cover in the nearby clouds. According to Mac's account later, because the controls were "very sloppy, they had probably shot away the rudder and trim tab cables," so he continued across Choiseul Island at an airspeed of 170 mph on a course of 45 degrees.

While still over the island, Wes came up on the flight deck. There were only two *Zeros* left attacking by this time. "Go check on the guys in the rear," Mac shouted over the din. "I can't communicate with them. We've lost radio connection, and I heard no gunfire from the back in a long time. See if they're okay."

Reporting back moments later, Wes shouted, incredulously, "There's no one in the rear, sir. Everyone's gone."

The four crew members had vanished. Apparently, ten or fifteen minutes earlier, just east of Fauro Island and just west of Choiseul, the engineer, radio operator, assistant radio operator, and tail gunner had all bailed out of the plane. They had apparently jumped through a large hole in the tail turret. The heat from the fire was intense in the back, and with no communication with the front of the plane, the four men must have thought they were going to crash and parachuted out when the airplane caught fire. Japanese fighters who had left the pursuit of the three B-24s strafed and killed them in their chutes, according to an eyewitness report. They attacked the men as they floated slowly down over the Pacific, as vulnerable as flies caught in a spider's web.

Mac continued out to sea on the same course of 45 degrees for fifty miles, losing the last of the *Zeros* forty miles out from land. Only two Japanese planes were left by then; eventually, they had to turn back to refuel. With number one and two engines out, Mac increased the power in the remaining two engines to 132 inches of mercury and 2,700 rpm to maintain airspeed and altitude of 100 feet over the water. But the plane was gradually losing altitude, and knowing that a water landing was inevitable, Mac turned the plane southeast on a course of 120 degrees for ten minutes, then headed in toward Choiseul Island on a course of 190 degrees.

"We're going to ditch in the ocean," Mac yelled over the roar of the engines. "We have to jettison as much heavy equipment as possible, including guns and ammo, to lighten the ship. Everyone," he ordered, "to the back, and throw out everything overboard that's not nailed down." They were minutes away from a treacherous attempt at landing amid undulating waves moving below them in this temperamental, new plane that tended to break apart in water landings.

Chapter 21
The Ditching—February 14, 1943

Bombs Away was headed straight down into the Pacific because the land was too far away to reach. There were two engines out, few controls left, and the wing a sheet of flames. When the last of the pursuing *Zeros* turned back, Mac focused his attention on landing the plane in the water. His remaining crew had tossed as much heavy equipment as possible overboard, and now, with the plane lighter, he pointed the nose down and stared at the ocean below, coming up fast to meet them. "Hold on," he yelled. "We're about to hit the water—hard."

It was a relatively calm ocean in a moderate swell when Mac ditched the plane. *Bombs Away* had no flaps or rudder control, and they hit the surface with flaps up, stalling at around 115 miles per hour. It felt like being in the middle of a crackling thunderstorm with the deafening noise of metal bending and breaking apart. The plane stopped in what seemed like only seconds, with its nose and part of the cockpit submerged underwater and the fuselage broken just behind the bomb bay.

When the plane stopped, Mac and Van quickly unbuckled their seat belts and looked for an exit. Holding his breath as the cockpit was filling fast, Mac pushed himself through the water. Placing his hands on either side of the metal-framed opening, he pulled hard, forcing his body outward and upward toward the light. He gasped for breath as he surfaced and looked around frantically for Van and the others. There was a momentary feeling of being totally alone in the middle of the vast ocean with nothing except a gigantic, aluminum, sinking bullet that would pull him down with it.

Seeing and hearing no one at first, he tried to go back into the plane to look for them, but he discovered that his harness and other debris were wrapped around his feet, entangling them. He struggled desperately to free himself from the strap caught around his ankles. Pushing down panic, he kicked off his shoes and slipped off the restricting harness. Fortunately, he had cut down his government-issued shoes, never liking the high tops, making them easy to discard.

Now barefoot, Mac quickly scrambled up on top of the plane and visually located each of the four remaining crew members— copilot, navigator, bombardier, and assistant engineer—who had all somehow exited the plane without entanglement. The three crew members who had gone to the rear of the aircraft to jettison equipment received minor cuts and concussions from being thrown about badly during the landing, but miraculously, no one was badly hurt. They had all scrambled out through waist windows and then had some trouble getting out from under the wing. Van, the copilot, had gone out through some aperture but later did not know which one. It happened all too fast.

By this time, the nose of the ship was completely underwater, and the plane had buckled right behind the wings but had not parted. Mac slid back into the water so that he and Van could grab the raft that was on top of the fuselage. There were two, five-man life rafts in the B-24s in compartments in the fuselage above the wings. They were mounted against spring-loaded plates with a latch, a pin, and a weight.

When a plane hits the water, the impact normally dislodges the pin, the doors of the compartment burst open, and the spring plate, attached by ropes, flings the rafts about one hundred feet out into the ocean. This force pulls a trigger mechanism, which causes the raft to inflate automatically. Once the plane has submerged below a certain depth, the ropes are then supposed to detach.

But since the rafts did not deploy as advertised, the men would not take their chances that the rafts would detach properly after the plane sank. Working as fast as they could, they struggled to cut the connecting rope with a small pocketknife, but it did not slice through the strands easily. Finally, the rope gave way, and with the raft inflated, the two of them climbed in and rowed over to pick up the three remaining crew members treading water nearby. On board the raft, they breathed a collective sigh of relief. This all happened in nanoseconds because the plane sank approximately five minutes after hitting the water.[45]

Before the aircraft disappeared beneath the surface, they picked up a flotation survival kit and an emergency medical kit that floated by in the water and tossed them into the raft before moving away. Unfortunately, in their haste to get out of the plane, they all emerged without the personal survival gear each of them usually carried. The kits were hanging on cartridge belts left in the plane with no time to retrieve them. Each kit contained a gun, a knife, additional medical supplies, and a canteen, all of which would have been immensely useful in the days and weeks to come. One small survival kit was all they had, and what the raft was supplied with: a gallon of water, eight K-rations, a signal mirror, a signal pistol with flares called a Very Pistol, fishhooks and line, a six-foot square of oilcloth, and chocolate bars.

Once they were in the raft, the first reaction of the crew was one of elation. They were alive, having survived the crash against tremendous odds. They applied first aid to everyone

---

[45] Mac's written account.

using the sulfanilamide from the first aid kit and then bandaged the severe wounds. Scrapes and cuts covered the bodies of all five men, but Bill had two deep cuts under one armpit and a wrist, and Wes had a nasty gash on his back. Don felt clammy, dizzy; he breathed rapidly and was confused, apparently suffering from shock.

Because of the extent of the others' injuries, Van, initially sick with vomiting and diarrhea from swallowing too much seawater, felt well enough to share the rowing with Mac for the first nine hours. The two of them then traded off with Don and Wes, who had recovered enough to take their turn at rowing. Rowing in rolling surf was an arduous job, as they'd landed in water approximately twenty to twenty-five miles off the northeastern shore of Choiseul Island, south of Bougainville, between Nanango Point and Ruingana.

Chapter 22
Land Ho

It took almost twenty hours of grueling, aching rowing to reach the enemy-occupied island of Choiseul. Mac looked at his watch, which had not only inexplicably survived the crash and taken a good dunking in the ocean, but it was keeping perfect time. They had traveled a little more than one mile per hour with rolling, treacherous waves. Exhausted, they pulled the raft up on the beach and quickly hid it in the brush. They then celebrated by sharing a can of tomato juice, one K-ration each, and slept the balance of the day and throughout the night.

Dawn shattered dreams of home and family when they awoke the next day, as their current reality came quickly into focus. They explored the immediate vicinity, searching for natives, who they had been told were almost always friendly to the Allies. They were hoping to get word to one of the Australian coast watchers that they had survived so that they could arrange a rescue.

Mac decided that he and Don would start out and first explore the coast in a southeast direction while the other three guarded the raft and supplies and watched for search planes. Hiking through the thick jungle vegetation, they made very slow progress. Because he was barefoot, Mac had to tread lightly and keep a watchful eye where he stepped, avoiding jungle entanglements, reptiles, and poisonous spiders.

After walking miles, they found no signs of human habitation anywhere, but they met lots of big lizards and crocodiles five to six feet long and hundreds of land crabs. The mosquitoes and flies, though plentiful enough, were not too nettlesome—they swatted them away as they trudged on. Discouraged about not finding any natives, Mac and Don returned to the other crew members and spent the balance of the day resting.

The following day, February 16th, they divided equally the remaining K-rations, which included cheese, candy, and fig bars, plus, they each ate one chocolate bar, reserving the rest. These were not your ordinary, run-of-the-mill chocolate bars; they were large blocks with six sections, fortified with vitamins, minerals, and proteins with instructions to eat one a day.

Some men stretched out their portion of K-rations for four days, while others ate their allotment within twenty-four hours, with the chocolate bars kept in reserve to be doled out daily. Naturally, the pig-outs coveted the hoarders' supplies, but everything was gone in such a brief time, it didn't create a serious morale problem. They were all hungry most of the time, and when the food was gone, they split the few cans of juice they found in the raft. Fortunately, drinking water was never a problem because it rained often. They used the six-foot oil cloth to collect the rainwater.

After eating their meager meal, Mac and Don, now joined by Van, set out this time to search in the opposite direction, northwest, along the shoreline. The only signs of life they found were some native names in English carved in tree trunks, but they had obviously made these markers some time before. They found no signs of recent human activity. Once again, the search proved fruitless in finding help, but about four miles out from the campsite, they crossed a freshwater stream. They would later return to it with their container.

When they got back to camp, one crew member, who had some dry matches, lit a fire. They made bouillon in an empty tomato juice can, which tasted delicious. Wanting to head south at night under the cover of darkness, they tried to launch the raft but were unsuccessful because the waves were so choppy. Discouraged, they went to sleep, soaking wet and cold, right where they were.

On February 17th, the third day ashore, the same three men returned to the freshwater stream and followed it for about six miles, hoping to find some sign of human habitation near the river. Progress was extremely slow and difficult through the dense jungle, and once again, they found no signs of human life, so they filled their gallon container with fresh water and returned to their makeshift campsite. Each man ate one more chocolate bar that evening.

Mac decided that staying in that spot any longer was not a good option. They needed to continue their trek south to Guadalcanal if they had any hope of being rescued or finding their way back to Henderson Field. Having found no one so far, and seeing no signs of anyone on the third night, they began the long journey homeward.

Just before nightfall, they stood shoulder to shoulder, covered by the dense bush, waiting for the sun to disappear behind the horizon. With the beach lit only by moonlight, Don and Bill climbed into the raft. Then, with much difficulty and multiple failed attempts, Mac and the other two crew members finally launched into the black ocean and jumped inside.

The five men rowed southeast along the shore for about eight hours, determined to go as far as they could under the blanket of darkness because they feared being spotted by a Japanese plane or ship when the sun rose. There was a favorable wind blowing, so they improvised a sail using two sticks and the oilcloth from the survival kit, and finally, just before dawn, they beached the raft and once again hid it in the brush.

As before, they first checked the immediate surrounding area for signs of natives, then ate one chocolate each and fell asleep in the raft for most of the day. That night, they took off again, using the sail, and rowed until dawn, continuing their routine of traveling by night and sleeping by day. The raft became their principal home, paddling it in the evening hours, steering by starlight, then beaching it and pulling it into the jungle during much of the daylight hours so they could sleep.

It elated the ravenous men to find coconut groves on day five, and for the rest of their journey, coconuts in various stages of growth sustained them. Bill was best at opening coconuts, while Van was best at climbing the palms, so they divided up the chores. They ate the hard meat of the large, ripe coconuts, drank the milk, and enjoyed the soft part of the green ones. The sprouts, which they frequently found growing off the coconuts lying on the ground, were surprisingly good. When peeled, they discovered they tasted a lot like celery.

Since they couldn't continue their journey south in the daylight, they spent most of their waking hours searching the jungle for natives. The brief list of daily activities now included shucking coconuts as well. They never tired of eating coconuts but craved at least one other food to supplement them. The only complaint they had with the coconuts was how difficult they were to husk and get to the meat and milk.

Eventually, they came across an abandoned village where they found two husking sticks, which worked very well for opening the coconuts. After jamming these thick, pointed sticks into the ground, they slammed the coconut down on them, making the hard, outer husk easy to peel off the nut. Frequently, they found coconuts lying on the ground, but when they couldn't, they shinnied up the tall trees and removed them by twisting the nuts until the vine broke. Hunger is a real motivator for learning new skills. It was slow, laborious work, and only two of them had the agility to climb the trees like desperate monkeys in search of lunch.

Chapter 23
Surviving in Enemy Territory

The five men were good friends when they started, but over time, the relationships became very strained. Mac speculated perhaps they had spent too much time together and knew each other too well, or maybe the stress of not knowing when or if they would be rescued weighed on them. When they had first boarded the raft, there was a general feeling of elation; they had survived the ditching with relatively minor injuries. They were alive. But after twenty hours of rowing and finally arriving on the island of Choiseul, mild depression replaced this feeling. They were cold, hungry, and dog tired in an unfriendly, dangerous territory with hundreds of miles between them and home base. These were young men, most still in their teens, with home and family halfway around the world. They wondered if they would ever see them again.

Depression deepened over the next several days. One crew member became completely uncommunicative, surly, and pessimistic about their chances of survival, causing everyone to slide further into hopelessness and depression.

"I'm leaving. I'm going on my own. You guys stay and die. Not me," he ranted.

"You won't find any friends in this location, and you'll only draw attention to the rest of us, which will endanger all of our lives," Mac told him. "If you defect, I promise you, I'll split your head open with a paddle the first chance I get." The rest of the crew supported Mac. "We are going to survive by pulling together, staying together, and keeping our wits about us. We must keep moving south toward Guadalcanal. If we find help along the way, all the better."

As they trudged along on the outskirts of the dense jungle, the only wildlife they now saw, and they were plentiful, were large, iguana-type lizards, four to five feet long. After dreaming about Betty Grable, the pin-up girl, one night, Mac awoke to find an enormous fellow sleeping next to him, cuddled up for warmth. Rattled and agitated, Mac leaped up, and the scaly beast slowly sauntered away into the brush, apparently feeling rebuffed and maybe a little miffed. Later, they learned that parts of the lizard are quite good to eat, but they had no way of killing and cooking them even if they had known that.

The survival kit included several fishhooks and a fishing line. They used insects and precious cheese as bait but couldn't tempt any fish to latch on to the hooks. After repeated attempts to catch fish in the ocean and streams, to no avail, they gave up trying and contented themselves with coconuts.

Navigating the ocean at night, they often saw six- to eight-foot sharks swimming near and around their rubber boat. On one occasion, one swam under the raft so close, they could feel the dorsal fin scraping the bottom, which was unnerving. They found they could disperse them by slapping the water hard with the flat side of the paddle, keeping them temporarily at bay.

When they reached the south end of Choiseul, they next needed to cross the Manning Strait to get to the west side of St. Isabel Island, so they rowed from one tiny island to the next tiny island. It took three or four more nights, and the last stretch took ten hours.

Traveling at night and resting by day, they continued southwest down the western shore of Santa Isabel, living entirely on coconuts for another five days. Then they discovered some fruit resembling small, wild, green plums on a bush and devoured them like ground squirrels finding nuts after a long winter's hibernation. They had tasted nothing in their lives so delicious.

Each night, they tried to advance a few miles down the coast toward the southern tip of Santa Isabel. The Japanese had a military base at Rekata Bay on the east side of the island, so they had to be constantly vigilant, as the enemy was not far away. They were inching closer to Guadalcanal, but it was arduous work, with only two paddlers rowing five men. Staying cautiously out of sight, they saw no Japanese soldiers or native patrols, but they knew they were nearby as they discovered evidence of them and heard them distantly in the jungle. They detected Japanese planes flying over every day, always able to recognize them by the annoying yet distinctive sounds of their desynchronized propellers.

Even in the tropics, the nights were chilly, and they longed for a lightweight blanket or jackets. They were wet most of the time because the continual process of beaching and launching in heavy surf frequently resulted in the raft capsizing and soaking them. This was distressing in the evenings without the sun to warm their bodies. For Mac, losing his shoes, which he had had to jettison when he became entangled getting out of the plane, was a serious handicap because sharp coral often cut his feet, but the oral medication and the saltwater helped the healing.

Having made some false starts following the shoreline of small inlets along the coast, the men kept on the outside of Barora Ite Island and Boro Island, with small islands and reefs between them and the ocean, making paddling easier, not having to battle the rough waves of the open sea. They would wait to row until about 1:00 a.m. and land at 7:30 a.m., always quickly pulling the raft into the jungle thicket to hide it before dawn broke.

The days now became monotonous, spent alternately resting, staying alert for company, and collecting and opening coconuts. But at least they were proceeding in the right direction toward their sanctuary in Guadalcanal, and not marooned on some island like Robinson Crusoe. Mac frequently reminded them they were making slow but steady progress. They seemed to move like sea turtles, migrating and foraging as they advanced closer to their nest.

One day, they looked up to see a U.S. Navy seaplane on Santa Isabel Island. The men attempted to signal it with the flare gun, but the plane was too high up and too far away to see them. On another occasion, they tried to signal a P-38 with mirrors, but again, without success. Then, on the night of February 25th and into the early morning of the 26th, they saw bomb explosions to the northwest and knew they were getting closer to occupied territory. Besides the Japanese base for both large airplanes and seaplanes on the other side of the island, most of the Japanese planes that attacked Guadalcanal from their bases in New Britain had to pass over the island of New Georgia, which was only 150 miles to the west of them. They felt a bit like the naked tail rats they saw scurrying in and out of the brush to avoid detection.

Chapter 24
The Rescue

Finally, on the nineteenth day out, they came upon another abandoned village with six or seven huts. They slept in that day, though still unable to protect their bodies from the bloodsucking mosquitoes.

That afternoon, the sound of strange voices awakened them. Alarmed, they jumped up to discover two native men and two children standing outside their hut, looking startled and very frightened. The four natives had certainly not expected to find anyone in the huts. Their eyes were wide, and they stood poised to run away, afraid they might be Japanese soldiers.

The Americans quickly allayed their fears, showing them proof they were not Japanese by producing American coins and a navigation watch with U.S. Army stamped on it. Finally, one native rewarded them with a big, toothy grin and introduced himself as Henry. After a bit of pointing and gesturing, and a couple of English words thrown in like a game of island charades, the airmen learned that this small party of four was away from the main village on a bit of a vacation, having a grand time, fishing and living off the land.

"Come," Henry finally gestured. "Follow." He pointed at a small canoe, and the four natives got in and beckoned the crew to follow them in the raft. Elated, the weary airmen happily jumped in their raft. Friendly natives had finally found them, and the hope of rescue was at the top of everybody's mind.

They rowed for about a half hour and then disembarked and trailed the rescuers to Henry's hut, hidden in a sheltered cove on the west side of Santa Isabel Island. There, he fed them their first proper meal in two and a half weeks—potatoes boiled in saltwater that contained leaves like spinach and chopped taro root. Filet mignon could not have tasted any better to their deprived palettes and empty stomachs, and they spent the evening happily gorging themselves on the epicurean potato soup. Their spirits lifted.

Luck was definitely on their side. While most of the natives were friendly toward the Allies, one thing all crews were fearful would happen was that they would be shot down near an island where cannibalism was rumored to still be practiced, and no one wanted to end up the main ingredient in airmen stew.

But even more realistic and probable was the fear of capture by the Japanese, who were ruthless in their torture, and the Japanese occupied many of these islands. The Japanese Imperial Marines had already proven their despicable reputation in the battle with the American First Marine Division, trying to recapture Guadalcanal the year before. They would take their machetes, cut open the stomachs of the wounded American Marines, and throw sand into the gaping wounds. This was a horrible, painful way to die from the slow infection that resulted. But thankfully, none of the fears that had occasionally haunted them were realized.

That night, they slept at Henry's camp and had breakfast again with boiled potatoes and taro root in the early morning hours. Then Henry's uncle and one boy took off in the small canoe to go to the main native hideaway to get and bring back a canoe large enough to accommodate all of them. While they waited with Henry all day at his hut, three other curious natives, who were also adept at island charades, visited them. It was most enjoyable and entertaining to have the company of other people knowing, too, that a rescue was near at hand. Everyone was in a jovial mood.

Then at midnight, the boy and his uncle returned, bringing with them a large canoe and six paddlers. They waited four hours, and at four o'clock in the morning, the five airmen jumped in the boat and took off for the hideaway with the expert rowers paddling northwest in and out of small islands for five more hours. Their course lay between Santa Isabel Island and Bero Island.

Finally, at nine o'clock in the morning, they arrived at a perfectly hidden hideaway and ate more boiled potatoes, which they had grown quite fond of by this time. The natives told them they had notified Corrigan, the Australian coast watcher on Santa Isabel, of their arrival and had prepared a hut for them with clean matting and blankets while they waited for word.

An hour later, a note sent by Corrigan arrived by runner that read to the effect that he had notified Lunga Pt.–Henderson Field of their presence, but because of poor radio reception, he had so far been unable to receive instructions about where they would pick up the men. No matter, the lost were found. It was now only a matter of time before someone would rescue them. How much time, they didn't seem to care. They were going home.

In the meantime, they conversed amiably and animatedly with the natives, who were not only friendly but declared they hated the Japanese. The crew members made gifts of their wings, silver coins, and Bill's ring to Edwardo Baku, chief of all Santa Isabel Island, who showed up to greet them.

They carried on a lively conversation, chatting with the chief through his half brother, Rufu Snufu, who spoke fluent pidgin English. Rufu Snufu himself was very curious about the war, asking many questions about when it would be over, who they thought was winning, and so on and so forth. The chief then assured Mac that he would kill any Japanese that fell into his hands, so great was his hatred of them.

Again, the natives treated them to a lunch of potato soup. This time it was creamier, enriched with coconut milk, and again some kind of leaf similar to spinach, taro root, and sugar cane. It was delicious.

Then the chief proudly showed them two testimonials from other downed flyers he had rescued, so they wrote one for him as well and all five men signed it, pleasing him immensely. Edwardo Baku beamed broadly, like a schoolboy receiving a gold star on his term paper, and added the testimonial to his growing collection.

At 2:00 p.m., the runner arrived again with a box of canned goods from the Australian coast watcher Corrigan, and more good news. The message from Corrigan said they were to put themselves completely in the hands of the runner, who was his number one boy and who would take them to a seaplane for the rescue, which was scheduled to arrive at 3:00 p.m. that afternoon—only an hour from then.

Fifteen minutes before the runner arrived, they looked up to see about twenty P-39s and P-40s circling overhead. They waved at them excitedly and later found out that the fighters were acting as cover for the seaplane that was about to rescue them. What a sight for sore eyes those planes were. The men cheered loudly, hooting and hollering as they followed the runner to an inland lake.

The entire village turned out to paddle the five survivors out to the plane, which they eagerly boarded like death-row prisoners suddenly exonerated and released from prison. They waved farewell, and thanks to their newfound friends, who surrounded the seaplane as they scrambled out of the raft, their rescuers hoisted them aboard the flying boat. As they settled into seats in the plane, the crew passed out more food, and the sound of the men's exuberant voices could be heard over the noise of the propellers.

Mac laid his head back and closed his eyes. He thought about his boyhood in Texas, and then his thoughts drifted to his home in Chicago. He had come a long way since leaving Illinois.

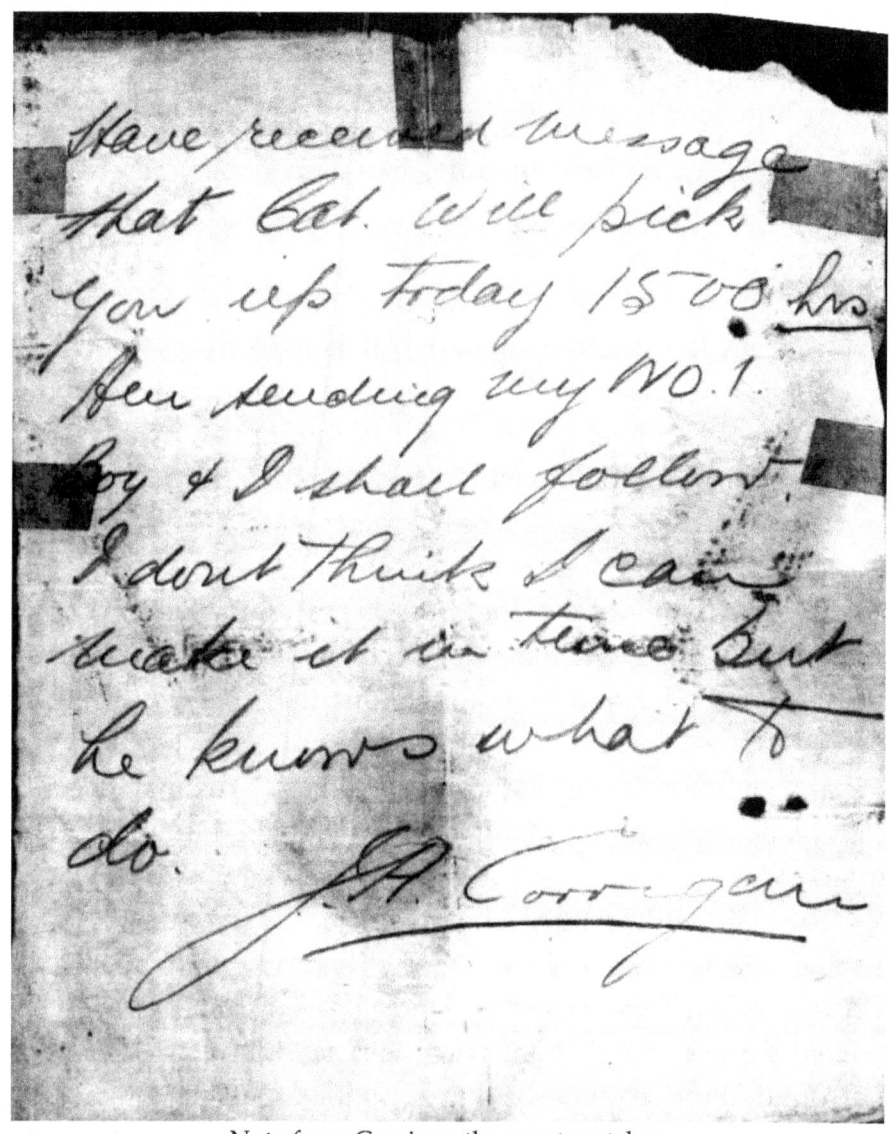

Note from Corrigan the coast watcher

The five survivors

Chapter 25
The Homecoming at Henderson Field

Cheers rang out as the five rescued survivors jumped out of the plane after landing at Henderson Airfield. It was like seeing ghosts return from the great beyond. Their fellow airmen had given them up for dead. No one had any hopes that anyone shot down on February 13th in the heart of enemy territory would ever return. Their survival was a huge morale booster to the rest of the troops, and Mac had firmly established his reputation as a leader who brought his crew home alive.

Leave to New Zealand was at once awarded to the five survivors. It was a sorely needed and mightily deserved rest, and they recuperated for almost a month. During this time, Mac wrote long letters to the parents of each of his four lost crew members, telling them of the last mission and detailing their bravery and service. He implored them not to give up hope of their sons being found alive. He told them they were wearing life jackets and jumped near land, so there was a good possibility they had survived. Mac had not known then that all four had been shot and killed as they floated down in their parachutes.

Below is a letter Mac wrote to the mother of Sgt. Lawrence C. Averitt, assistant radioman, who bailed out of the plane. He sent a similar one to the parents of the other three men: Robert Smith, radio; Roy Lund, engineer; and Elton Hartt, tail gunner. I do not know why John Sargent, Mac's original tail gunner from

Ephrata, was not on this flight. Perhaps a case of dengue fever saved his life.

• • •

March 7, 1943
Dear Mrs. Averitt,
It has been on my mind ever since our arrival back at our base to write the parents of each of the boys who were lost from my crew on our unfortunate mission of February 13. I feel that you will want to know the full story, so I will attempt to relate to you the details of our raid, leaving out only such information as might benefit the enemy.

Lawrence was, as you know, my assistant radio operator and an exceptionally good radioman. He had been with me since our first days at Ephrata, and I feel a deep, personal loss as he was not only an excellent operator but one of my best friends. He was extremely popular with all the men and officers, and was, in all respects, a fine combat crew member.

Our mission was an unusually disastrous one, and we lost a great many fine lads. It was a daylight bombing raid on enemy shipping, and we encountered exceptionally intense anti-aircraft fire and numerous enemy fighters. We were attacked long before we reached the target area, and Larry was at his station in the rear of the ship. He operated the ship's belly guns, where he was extremely accurate.

We were in formation at the time we were hit by an anti-aircraft shell, which put our no. 1 engine out of commission and set the left wing afire. Our radio had been previously put out of commission, so I had no contact with the men in the rear of the ship. Just previous to the explosion that set our ship afire, one of the other ships of the formation had gone down in flames, and this undoubtedly influenced the men and prompted their action in leaving the ship. All four men in the rear parachuted, believing the ship to be out of control and on fire. No one saw them go, so they undoubtedly delayed opening their chutes to avoid attracting attention from the Japanese fighters. This was a very smart thing to do and probably saved them all from being strafed.

Although our ship was badly damaged, I managed to elude most of the Jap Zeros after a running battle in which I lost another engine and part of my left wing. It was after we had left the Zeros behind that I sent my navigator back to ascertain the damage to the rear of the ship and to see if any of the boys had been wounded. I was dumbfounded to hear his report that the rear of the ship was deserted and can only surmise that the men left the ship, as I have described above.

It is my honest conviction that the four missing men, including Larry, my first radio operator, my first engineer, and tail gunner, are still alive. They were all wearing life vests and carried emergency equipment when they left the ship, and we were over land most of the time and never more than a few miles away at the most. Although they went down in enemy territory, there are miles of beach where there are no enemy installations at all. The natives are all friendly to the Allies and will aid any that they find as they did us. Even if they did not find natives, they would have no trouble sustaining themselves in the jungle and may eventually find their way back when they are discovered by the natives.

Of course, there is a possibility that they may have been captured by the Japanese and may be held prisoners.

It has not been my intention to build false hopes regarding the safety of Larry and the others. I only wished you to know the full details so that you may judge for yourself. They have a good chance, and we should not give up hope. Certainly, I do not intend to do so.

For the rest of the story, I might add that we were finally forced to make a water landing but were fortunate enough to get out of the ship into a life raft and make our way to shore. There were five of us left in the ship—four officers and one enlisted man, the assistant engineer. Fortunately, we were not injured and succeeded in making our way in the raft for nearly one hundred miles through the islands in the direction of our base. We were forced to paddle only at night to avoid detection by Japanese aircraft and lived entirely on coconuts for nineteen days. On the twentieth day, we were discovered by natives who contacted the authorities who arranged for our passage the remainder of the distance by plane.

We are going to rest for the next two weeks before going back into action, but believe me, we all feel that we owe the Japs a little extra something, and we intend to pay it with interest.

I hope someday to meet all of Larry's folks and would be proud to have you visit my home in Detroit. The address there, in case you should have occasion to visit my mother, is 492 Drexel Avenue. My mother is Mrs. Margaret Allison.

If there is any further information I can give you, or if I can ever be of assistance, please do not hesitate to write me.

Sincerely,
Harold G. McNeese
1st Lt. A.C.

• • •

Mac wrote the following letter to his own mother three days after his rescue:

March 7, 1943
Dearest Mother and Curt,

This is the first letter that I have been able to write to you in nearly three weeks, and not the least of my worries has been the thought that you will not have received any word from me. I regret terribly the fact that you had to receive the Missing in Action report from the War Department and saw to it that a radiogram was dispatched immediately on our arrival back at our base. I hate to make a liar out of the official records but feel free to say that I am very much alive and in the best of health.

It is really great to be back here among my friends and almost worth the experience. We have not done a thing since we arrived here but lie around and fatten up. Personally, I would not trade the experience for a good deal. It was not enjoyable but was certainly interesting. We are all leaving tomorrow for a two-week vacation in a large town some fifteen hundred miles distant. We are looking forward to it very much, as it will be our first contact with civilization since leaving our last base (in Hawaii).

I have just finished writing letters to each of the parents of the four boys who were lost from my crew. They were really a fine bunch, and I refuse to give up hope for them. I will be hard put to find another crew as good. They all bailed out without my knowledge, or they would be here with us today.

After they had bailed out, they left the ship almost defenseless, except for Don in the nose and Bill Adams in the upper turret, so the Zeros really made it hot for us. The ship was a sieve and part of my control cables were shot, so that I was very lucky to be able to land the ship without seriously injuring anyone. Outside of minor cuts and bruises, no one was hurt, for which I was thankful, as infections are so dangerous in this area. All we were able to get out of the ship was three days' rations and a medicine kit. We used the sulfanilamide powder in the kit to good advantage, and it healed the wounds in good shape.

After we had been hit, and I realized that the ship must soon go down, I headed directly out to sea to lose the Zeros, whose range is limited. I lost them fifty miles at sea, and after the last one had disappeared, I headed back to the nearest land. I had been nursing the ship as best I could from the time of our attack when one engine and part of our wing and control surfaces were shot away. We had gradually been losing altitude, and finally, it became necessary to land in the water. I had sent Don and Wes and Bill to the rear of the ship prior to the landing, with instructions to throw out all the loose equipment to lighten the ship as much as possible and to be ready for the crash landing.

After the landing, I was able to get the life raft out of the ship and picked up the other boys who were floating in the water. It took us nearly twenty hours to reach land, though we were only some twenty-five miles away. We beached our craft and stayed in the vicinity for three days searching for natives, practically all of whom are friendly to the Allies. However, we did not find any sign of life, so the third night started on our long journey homeward. From there on, the story becomes monotonous.

We rowed every night, steering by the stars, and by day searched for natives and coconuts. The coconut milk is very nourishing, and we never got sick of it, though we would have liked to supplement it. Nerves got a little ragged at times, but for the most part, we got along swell together—each man cooperated and no one shirked his part.

On the twentieth day, we were sleeping in an abandoned native hut when we heard voices and looked out on a native canoe containing two men and two children. The natives at first thought we were Japs and would not come near until we had convinced them that we were Americans. After that, they took us to their hut and fed us. One of them then went back to the main village to secure a large canoe with which to take us there. The food they gave us was yams and taro root boiled in saltwater, and believe me, they were delicious.

The natives treated us royally, and we made them gifts of our wings and some odd change we happened to have on us. They speak pidgin English, so we were able to make ourselves understood. They were able to get a message via runner to the nearest Allied outpost, who radioed our base of our positions. The next day, a PBY, accompanied by twenty fighters, picked us up.

After arriving back, I told the story to several foreign correspondents and to a delegation of generals and admirals—five generals and two admirals, to be exact. And had my picture taken with them. The rest of the boys had been taken to the mess hall, and I joined them later for a really delicious meal of cold ham sandwiches.

None of us ever had the slightest doubt that we would get back, though we had decided that we might have to row the entire distance. We covered nearly one hundred miles, though we probably rowed nearer one hundred and fifty, in a direct line for home, and by our own figuring would have made it in another three weeks as we had another 150 miles to go.

So much more I could say, but it will have to wait until after the war. Am writing you a V mail, as these letters are often delayed.
All my love to the folks. My regards to our friends,
Love,
Harold

Mac received a Purple Heart and Distinguished Service Cross for extraordinary heroism against an enemy in action on this mission. The DSC is the second highest medal the army bestows.

Telegram to Mac's mother

HEADQUARTERS USAFISPA
A.P.O. #502

19 May 1943

GENERAL ORDERS)
NO   120)

1. **AWARD OF THE DISTINGUISHED SERVICE CROSS (TO PERSONNEL MISSING IN ACTION**

By direction of the President, under the provisions of the Act of Congress approved July 9, 1918, (Bull. No. 43, W. D. 1918), the Distinguished Service Cross is awarded by the Commanding General, United States Army Forces in the South Pacific Area, to the following named officer missing in action:

HAROLD G. McNEESE, O-726442), First Lieutenant, United States Army Air Corps, for extraordinary heroism in the Solomon Islands area on February 13, 1943. While engaged in a daylight raid against an enemy base, Lieutenant McNeese piloted his heavy bombardment airplane through heavy anti-aircraft fire and opposition from enemy fighters with overwhelming numerical superiority. Before his ship had reached the target it had been hit and severely damaged and the left wing and outboard engine were aflame, but he held to the formation until the bomb release line was reached, and all bombs were dropped on the target area. The heat was then so severe that the occupants were unable to remain in the rear of the bomber, and the damaged craft and survivors were attacked by 12 Zero fighters. Lieutenant McNeese headed for open sea to force the assailants to break off the engagement as quickly as possible. One enemy craft was shot down in flames and at least one other was forced to break away, smoking badly before the fighters discontinued the attack. Lieutenant McNeese then headed for land, but the ship was in such condition that a water landing was unavoidable. Negotiating a successful landing of the badly crippled airplane, Lieutenant McNeese with the survivors after rowing for 18 hours, landed upon an enemy occupied island. Thereafter, he led the crew for 19 days through enemy waters. His utter disregard for his own safety and splendid leadership made possible the completion of the bombing run and the return of the surviving crew members to safety. Next of kin: Mrs. Margaret Allison, 16246 North Lawn, Detroit, Michigan.

****

By command of Lieutenant General HARMON

A. J. BARNETT,
Brigadier General, GSC
Chief of Staff.

WM A. LORD, JR.
Lt Col, Inf.
Actg Asst. Adj. Gen.

Distinguished Service Cross

Receiving the Distiguished Service Cross

Chapter 26
Guadalcanal—April 1943

Back from leave in Auckland, Mac and his flight engineer, Bill, whom he called his strong right arm, got right back in the saddle flying missions every other day. And flying combat missions was certainly more exciting and possibly less dangerous than staying on Guadalcanal. Jungle diseases and fatigue took their toll on the men, physically and mentally; it was a constant struggle to keep a positive focus on their important mission.

Years later, someone recalled that Guadalcanal was probably the only place you could stand knee-deep in mud and have dirt blown in your face. Added to that was a lack of drinking water, not enough fuel for the planes, and initially, no entertainment. There was only the beach. The stay was bleak for the young soldiers. The once-prevalent, head-hunting cannibals made for scary rumors and tales, and in case one needed something else to worry about, Japanese troops were still lurking on the island or nearby.

Like Ephrata, living quarters were tents but equipped now with mosquito netting. Even though it didn't seem like there were a lot of mosquitoes, they were abundant, and the ones that struck were very potent. There were plenty of cases of malaria and dengue fever among the airmen. To keep the little blood suckers abated, and to destroy as many as possible, the Americans hired natives to cut down the grass around their camp. The airmen said that the locals could wield a machete like a surgeon's scalpel and sang while they worked. One even sang the "Star-Spangled Banner." The Guadalcanal natives, it seems, were also savvy, capitalistic traders. At first, they sold a comb for a dollar. Then realizing they had the market cornered and that the demand outstripped the supply, they increased the price to five dollars.

The natives were also very fussy about their cigarettes and extremely loyal to certain brands. If a soldier loaded up on one brand to use for trading and then was moved to another island, he frequently couldn't give that brand away.

The food at Henderson Air Base was just as horrible as it had been in Ephrata, probably worse. Flight lunches were a can of Spam, a big Bermuda onion, and an unwrapped, unsliced loaf of dry bread—all tossed into a dirty, cardboard box. Most crew members did not eat on a flight but preferred to throw their food out over the target to show the Japanese that our food was almost as lethal as ours bombs.

For the small contingent of Army Air Forces personnel now in the Solomons, their channel of supply for planes and fresh recruits was almost nonexistent. It was a minor miracle that under these conditions, crews could get planes off the ground at all. In some areas, perforated, metal sheets called Marston matting that tore open tires had to be put down over the mud for planes to take off, making takeoffs and landings even more dangerous than they were already.

Flying a new plane like the *Liberator* had many drawbacks, but one of the biggest was that people at the supply depot had never seen a B-24 before, and the planes continually needed additional parts. Supplies had to come by air or sea, so replacements were extremely slow in arriving, and they were often the wrong ones. Besides plane parts, it was very difficult to get relief with a change of personnel because the European Theater was still the priority, and the men fighting the war in the

South Pacific could only limp along with whatever resources they could muster.

The first airfield built by Americans on Guadalcanal was Carney, located six miles from Henderson. They built it during the rainy season out of Marston matting on a mud foundation. It was never suitable for heavy bombers, but a lot of missions flew out of there anyway. They also did most of the repair work there, which involved hard labor, ingenuity, and long trips over rough roads. Some planes took a month to repair because of the shortage of parts, and they spent many man hours getting the planes back into commission. After they built Henderson, they mostly used Carney as an emergency air strip.

The men on Guadalcanal were certain that they were only as successful as they were initially because the Japanese were even more disorganized than they were.

Between the two squadrons of the 307th BG, Mac and the other pilots flew twenty-six missions in April 1943. Planes had to be shared because of damage and loss, and Mac picked up additional temporary crew members to fly with them. The men were glad to be a part of his crew as he now had a great reputation for being a skilled pilot with a cool head under pressure—someone who would bring his crew home alive.

Most of the bombing missions were against Japanese-held Kahili, Japan's main airfield on Bougainville at the north end of the Solomons, and ships in Bougainville's Shortland Harbor, the site of Mac's first ill-fated mission. The Kahili Airfield was at the south end of Bougainville and was one of the most important to the Japanese. For that reason, they fortified it well with a master radar searchlight, lots of anti-aircraft guns, other searchlights, and plenty of fighter planes. On one strike, over one hundred enemy fighter aircraft attacked one squadron of B-24s. As a result, losses were heavy on both sides.

As a major part of their war strategy, both the Japanese and the Allies needed air bases in the Solomon Islands, and the goal was to drive the other side out by bombing each other's air bases and troop and supply ships in the harbors. That's what both sides did, day in and day out. There were also sea searches and bombing missions for the 307th BG to Ballale, a small island in the Shortland Islands where the Japanese had built airstrips that were used as a forward airfield for Imperial Japanese Navy bombers and fighters and a couple of bombing missions on Munda Point Airfield on New Georgia and Numa Numa on the east coast of Bougainville, but Kahili Airfield was their primary target.

During April, the Japanese made only five bombing raids on U.S. air bases in the Guadalcanal area. On April 7th, they bombed U.S. air strips on Tulagi and Koli Point and sank a U.S. oiler, two destroyers, and a small tanker. Then, the enemy caused some damage when bombs hit a gasoline dump, and it caught fire during a raid on the night of April 16th, slightly damaging three navy scout planes. The enemy's last raid for the month came on April 18th, in which there were two consecutive attacks.

The first attack happened when eight enemy planes flew in late at night between 8:00 p.m. and 12:00 p.m. and dropped their bombs near the radar site, ammunition dump, and the beach, causing only slight damage. Sgt. Ira Anderson, in the 370th Squadron, remembered he was stretched out on his cot in his birthday suit when the alarm sounded. He had just returned to his tent from bathing in the Metapona River, and he hit the foxhole with nothing on but his shoes. The mosquitoes had a feast on this human buffet unexpectedly served up to them. He escaped the bombs and malaria but got dengue fever.

Just a single plane carried out the second enemy attack. It swooped down at four o'clock in the morning and set fire to a tent, damaging another navy scout plane. A P-70 then shot 'Charlie' down, the first known victim of an American, radar-controlled night fighter.

• • •

The last day of the month, they scheduled six of the 370th Squadron *Liberators* and six 424th Squadron *Liberators* to hit two Japanese airports on and around Bougainville—Kieta and Numa Numa—at dusk, but the mission didn't go as planned. Mac and his crew took off as scheduled with the other eleven planes. However, two of the 370th planes that were headed to Kieta developed mechanical problems on the way, so only four could reach their target and bomb the airport. Only three of the six 424th *Liberators* made it to the south tip of Bougainville, and with clouds obscuring the view, only one of those planes could reach and then bomb Numa Numa. The weather on the islands was always uncertain.

Mac and Capt. John Storer piloted the two planes that made it to the area but were unable to bomb it. Clouds obscured the island, so neither could find it, so they bombed the Japanese-occupied Kieta instead, igniting several fires. The leaping flames, secondary explosions, and towering smoke columns showed there was more on the ground at Kieta than simply an innocent village. They had hit the right military spot. Oddly, one Japanese fighter plane finally showed up and turned toward the bombers. Then, apparently thinking better of it, the plane disappeared back into the clouds without firing a shot.

Several more U.S. planes met with disaster in April related to mechanical failures of the B-24. Capt. Ralph F. Andrews of the 424th Squadron crashed on takeoff on a mission to Numa Numa, and Lt. Robert F. Miller of the 424th BS crashed in the ocean between Guadalcanal and New Florida Island while on a mission to bomb bases on Bougainville.

After these two crashes, officers in charge grounded all planes and subjected them to a thorough inspection. Maintenance had always been a problem because replacement parts were so hard to get, and to further complicate repairs, all work had to be done outdoors, regardless of the weather. Despite the difficulties, they said that the line mechanics worked miracles with what they had, but several major mechanical problems needed to be addressed before they could be called safe to fly.

While the two squadrons on Guadalcanal were engaged in heavy combat missions almost every other day, the two sister squadrons of the 307th BG, the 371st BS, and 372nd BS, which had remained in Hawaii, had been doing routine search missions for an enemy that was nowhere to be found. But the memory of the Pearl Harbor attack was too fresh in the minds of Hawaiian authorities, and they would not yet release the two Hawaii-based squadrons to go to the Southwest Pacific.

Finally, they assigned the 371st and 372nd BSs to operate against the enemy in the Gilbert Islands, about 2,400 miles southwest of Pearl Harbor. Two crews left Hawaii for Canton Island on April 17th. After refueling, they took off for Funafuti, the capital of Tuvalu in the Ellice Islands. Tiny Funafuti is only seven miles long and a maximum of 200 yards wide. One bomb shell could easily destroy it, but it was vastly important for the U.S. to hold on to because it would be the staging base for missions to Nauru and Tarawa farther south in the Gilbert Islands.

Nauru was important to the Japanese because they mined 98 percent of their phosphate there. But on this night, someone decided, rather hastily, that instead of bombing Nauru, they would bomb Tarawa, an island roughly shaped like a long, thin triangle, approximately two miles long. It is narrow, being only 800 yards wide at its widest point. But within a few months, this little piece of real estate would become the site of a bloody battle that would be pivotal to the Allies' advance to Japan.

Eight crews from the 372nd BS and four from the 371st BS left Funafuti on this mission to Tarawa just as an air raid sounded, and anti-aircraft prepared to go into action on the ground. The enemy missed the B-24s, but the heavy anti-aircraft fire kept them from doing much damage on Tarawa. All but two of the B-24s returned to Funafuti on time. One of those returned two hours later, and the other crash-landed in a lagoon nearby.

Immediately upon returning, they refueled the planes and reloaded bombs. The next day, despite the air raid sounding again, Japanese bombers killed or wounded several 372nd BS and 371st BS crew members. Most of the crews had not been to sleep for two days, and there were not enough pilots to relieve the exhausted ones. The survivors returned to their base in Hawaii the following day.

In May, while on a search mission for a downed plane, the 372nd BS lost previous squadron members who had been transferred to the 7th AF when Lt. Russell A. Phillips' plane went down in the ocean. His bombardier was Lt. Lou Zamperini, the 1936 Olympic runner who had earlier made headlines at Hitler's headquarters in Berlin by stealing the Swastika flag for a souvenir. He and the rest of the crew survived floating in the ocean for forty-two days, only to be picked up by the Japanese and taken prisoners. As depicted in the movie *Unbroken* made years later, the Japanese brutally tortured Zamperini when they discovered his identity as they tried to prove that their runners were superior to him.[46]

• • •

The following is a poignant letter sent to Mac from B. T. Carroll, the father of Lt. Wesley M. Carroll, the navigator (who suffered mental breakdowns during and after the ordeal at sea and was sent home on the recommendation of the Auckland Flight Board, who pronounced him "psychologically unfit for combat"). I

---

[46] Zamperini, Louis, and David Rensin. 2003. *Devil at My Heels: A Heroic Olympian's Astonishing Story of Survival as a Japanese POW in World War II.* William Morrow.

wish I had a copy of Mac's response to him. Knowing my dad, I have no doubt he was kind and supportive.

• • •

April 9, 1943
Dear Lt. McNeese,
We want to congratulate and thank you from the bottom of our hearts for your skill and bravery in landing your plane, saving our son, Wes, and the other boys with you. I read a portion of your letter to Mr. Adams, and I want to ask a favor of you. I want you to tell me just how Wesley made out under fire and in your 19 days in the jungle.
Now Lt., I don't expect you to write me a letter to make me feel good. I want his faults, and if he did not make good, I want you to tell me. We have only received one letter from him, and he told very little of what happened. You all must have had a nerve-racking experience. Thank God some of you came out alive, and we are praying for the others of your crew. Please don't spare my feelings in regard to Wes. Again, all I can say is thank you, and may God protect you and yours.
B. T. Carroll

Following are two letters Mac wrote home in April after he returned from Auckland, New Zealand and was back on Guadalcanal:

April 13, 1943
Dear Mother and Curt,
Here I am, back at the old stomping grounds after nearly a month's absence in Auckland. We enjoyed ourselves immensely, but it is good to be back. Our squadron has moved during our absence, and we are now engaged in putting up our camp. We have had to clear away the jungle and build our tent-houses, but fortunately, most of the hard work was done while we were gone. Had a bit of mail waiting for me when I returned. However, all of your letters were written the last of

February, so I can only hope that everything is o.k. by you folks. Two of the letters were from Bob telling of his transfer. I was glad to hear that, as he seemed to think it was a change for the better. Also received letters from Harriet. She has been an excellent correspondent, but I have not written her very often as it seems rather pointless. However, I did not mind you giving her my address.

I expect to be flying again in a few days and am really itching to get those throttles in my hand. I have really become a heavy bomber enthusiast, though there was a time I would have preferred pursuit.

Everyone has been kidding me about all the weight I put on in Auckland. Only 10 pounds, but it's in the wrong place!

Love,
Harold

Following is a letter home from Guadalcanal written by Mac at the end of that busy and rather disastrous month:

April 23, 1943
Dear Mother and Curt,
We have finally gotten a movie here for us and we really enjoy it. Tonight, we saw Damon Runyon's Big Street *with Henry Fonda and Lucille Ball. It was very good, but of course, the sound broke down during the most interesting parts. Flew up to our old base at 708 yesterday and found at least a dozen letters awaiting me there. Most of them from you, and I was certainly relieved to know that you are all right. One of the letters from Violet Bennet and one from Aunt Jeanne. We have our little stove and coffeepot operating at full throttle now, and we usually enjoy a cup of coffee before going to bed. Our camp is slowly taking shape now and is quite livable. We usually go down to the river for a swim during the day, and we really appreciate the luxury of a daily bath. I mailed you a letter a few days ago in which I enclosed some pictures that one of the boys took of us after we returned from our forced landing. These pictures were taken after we had had a good night's sleep and I had been given some shoes. You may also notice in*

the picture that I had my wristwatch on. It ran perfectly all during the trip home and is still keeping excellent time.

I wish that I could send you a picture of myself as I am after my return from Auckland. I am really fat and sassy and tip the scales at a mere 170 pounds. I am very glad that you did not send your letter regarding our accident to Bob. I imagine the old boy has enough to worry about without receiving any such news as that. Have not had a letter from the old boy since he made corporal but am delighted to hear it. Wish he was stationed near as I would sure like to get him on my combat crew. I have a brand-new ship now, and it's really a honey. Adams, my engineer, still has not returned from Auckland as he caught a cold there just before we left and had to stay there until he is completely recovered.

Am having quite a time thinking of things to say tonight, so you will have to excuse the potpourri character of this letter. Tell Aunt Grace when you write that I received my Reader's Digest okay and I certainly enjoy it. I bought a small library in Auckland but have just about finished them by this time.

Don is still sitting around doing nothing as they do not have any jobs open in the squadron at this time. I do not think they will send him home before the rest of us, but that wouldn't make him very mad. (Of course, it would infuriate the rest of us.)

No more for now, folks, but say hello to everyone for me and tell Jeanne that I am going to write her a letter very soon. Incidentally, my new address is 709 (APO). Sorry I didn't mention it before as it cost me several weeks of anxious waiting I would not otherwise have had. Alternate your next few letters with straight air mail and V-mail, Mother dear, and I will check on their relative time en route.

Love,
Harold

Mac wrote the following letter home the day after the Bougainville mission. Obviously, he could make no mention of it.

April 30, 1943
Dear Mother and Curt,

I was certainly glad to get so many letters from you the other day. They had been accumulating for two months at my old APO number.

Our camp is fixed up very nice now. Yesterday, we installed electric lights, so we don't have to go to bed at dusk. One of the boys got hold of a phonograph, and we all enjoy that. Radio reception is very poor except on short wave, but we listen to Tojo's Zero hour often. They have an English-speaking announcer, and it emanates from Tokyo. It's really better than Charlie McCarthy (though not intended that way). And they play American tunes. The announcer gets off some sly propaganda in this vein, "Boys, how would you like to be home sitting in your favorite chair sipping a cold beer?" We all agree that we'd like to do just that—after we've cleaned up the mess out here!

Love,
Harold

Chapter 27
Guadalcanal—May 1943

They desperately needed the two Hawaii squadrons in the Solomons. Finally, on May 8th, after the colonel in charge of the Guadalcanal-based squadrons had spent much effort and many months trying to convince the Hawaiian department commander, they were told they were to be stationed at the U.S. Naval Base in Espiritu Santo (now Vanuatu) south of the Solomon Islands.

When their ship carrying the ground crews arrived, it took less than a week to set up the camp, which was nicer than the one the other two squadrons had on Guadalcanal. They constructed this one with materials brought from Hawaii—they all had screened-in tents with a floor and offices and supply sheds. They laid coral roads, and they constructed an excellent theater. At least there was that.[47]

All of the bombing missions for the 307th BG were long, agonizingly stressful, and grueling: reach the target without getting shot down, bomb the target, then hightail it back to the base without getting shot down. Mac and the others flew an average of seven or eight hours on each mission, so normally, they flew every two days with a day of rest in between. Japanese

---

[47] Britt, Sam S., Jr. 1990. *The Long Rangers: A Diary of the 307th Bombardment Group (H)*.

bases in and around Bougainville—Kahili, Ballale, Shortland Harbor, and Numa Numa—continued to be the primary targets.

Weather in the Solomons was a major factor in planning successful bombing missions. The Norden Bombsight depended on the visual sighting of the target through the telescope. If there were clouds, the mission had to be aborted. The Norden also did not live up to the theoretical vision Carl Norden had in his laboratory of being able to hit a pickle barrel from 20,000 to 30,000 feet. It was a mechanical device, and just like the planes that flew them to their target, assembly workers had put them together hastily. As historian Stephen McFarland told Malcolm Gladwell in part in an interview, "When gears and pulleys are moving, they cause friction, and the slightest bit of friction means that your analog equivalent to those mathematical formulas has been messed up." Imagine in combat, McFarland goes on:

"People are shooting at you, and enemy aircraft are coming at you at closing speeds of five hundred, six hundred miles per hour, and all this horrible yelling and screaming and bombs and explosions going off and everything else—the bombardiers tended to pucker, if I can use that phrase. They would lean forward as they became more and more intent on trying to make sure the crosshairs stayed on the target. And when they did so, they actually changed the angle of vision through that telescope ... it was impossible."[48]

On May 6th, a mission of only four planes set out from Henderson Field. Kahili was the target for two, and Ballale the other two. But violent thunderstorms raged west and northwest from Choiseul Island, and the two crews headed to Kahili could see nothing outside the planes. The crude radar didn't provide enough detail to bomb without eyeballs on the targets, so they gave up and headed back to the base. The two planes headed for Ballale found some holes in the clouds and dropped five bombs over Fauro Island. Then the clouds cleared, and Ballale came

---

[48] Gladwell, Malcolm. 2021. *The Bomber Mafia*. Little, Brown and Company.

open momentarily. They dropped fifteen 100-pound bombs in two runs. A successful day's work.

The next day, the severe weather moved south and reached Guadalcanal. On May 7th and 8th, thunderstorms pounded the area. A torrential downpour continued, and by midafternoon, the rainfall from the mountains came roaring down the Metapona River in a flash flood that covered the campsite like a thick, muddy blanket. The deluge enveloped the area around the camp as the fast-moving river pushed under the tents, and the newly built 'Chapel in the Wildwood' collapsed. Water was waist deep. Men had to move 150 tents, piece by piece, to higher ground, and it took weeks to rebuild the camp. The flood was such a memorable event that the airmen of the 307th who lived through it divided the experience into two spans, like the Roman calendar: before the flood (BF) and after the flood (AF). This unexpected deluge obviously reduced the number of missions they could fly for the month to only eleven.

On the 14th, amid the chaos of mud-clearing and moving, the enemy dropped five bombs on Bloody Ridge, just south of Henderson Field, and five on a small ammunition dump, causing some damage, but everyone did a swan dive into a foxhole and covered their heads. One of the night fighters shot one Japanese plane down. 'Charlie's' best effort came five days later, on the night of May 19th and the early morning of the 20th, when eight Japanese bombers came over the campsite and dropped their loads. The explosions resulted in the death of six U.S. soldiers and injured fourteen others. They also destroyed the aid station, a small mailroom, and fourteen personnel tents. In retaliation, a P-38 night-fighter shot down two of the eight enemy bombers.

Combat experience had shown that the B-24 needed additional armament. The nose guns were flexible .50 caliber and did not cover a wide enough area, and it was difficult to hit any target without a stable platform. They needed turrets in the nose and belly. The ground crew at Carney heard that back in Hickam Field on Oahu, someone was experimenting with a tail turret transplanted to the nose of the planes and had worked out plans to install a retractable Sperry ball turret in the belly. The former Bendix turrets with remote control and sighting had proven impractical and needed to be removed. They needed the flexible, .50-caliber guns in the tail. With the relocation of the camp, May was a good time to rearm the planes. These major reconfigurations would need to be done in Hawaii, so, one by one, the planes went back.

On May 16th, the first plane left for a week's stay at Hickam in Hawaii to be retrofitted and rearmed. The 307th sent them back in dribbles so as not to deplete the squadrons and keep enough planes for combat, but these modifications made the *Liberator* a much more formidable force to enemy fighters and increased the respect the crews had for the bomber. She was still unpredictable and dangerous, but she was now definitely a lady to be reckoned with.[49]

Toward the third week of May, they increased the bombing altitude for B-24s from 7,000 feet up to 15,000 feet, a move that decreased the anti-aircraft fire damage by 50 percent because they were more difficult to reach. The higher altitude also made daylight raids easier, though some missions were still being flown at night.

On May 24th, three single Japanese planes flew over Guadalcanal and caused slight damage to equipment and wounded one man. There were six condition reds. Whenever men were killed or wounded, it was when they were in their tents and had not taken cover in a foxhole.

With the camp newly moved out of the mud, the end of May saw a concerted effort to spruce up the living area to boost morale. Some men planted a vegetable and flower garden, and

---

[49] 307th Bombardment Group (HV). 1945. *We'll Say Goodbye: Story of the "Long Rangers"—307th Bombardment Group (HV).*

some of these ingenious Americans made many kinds of creature comforts out of scrap, including a revolving barber chair out of an old airplane.

On the last day of the month, three planes from the 370th Squadron flew out and hit individual targets in the north Bougainville area, chalking up a fairly good month for the 307th considering the epic flooding event.

· · ·

Following are letters home from Hawaii where Mac's plane was being retrofitted:

May 6, 1943
Dear Mother & Curt,
Arrived today at our old base after a pretty long and tiresome trip. It is really marvelous to be back in civilization for a while, and we are really making up for lost time. I can't imagine how I ever thought this place monotonous. Certainly, I never imagined that I would enjoy a visit here this much. My business here should take about a week, after which we will go back again. Continue to write me at my regular address, as I will be back at work when you receive this letter.

I brought four men with me on the skeleton crew but continued to pick up passengers on the trip up—finally landed with fifteen men aboard. The boys are busy now lapping up beer as our supply at APO 709 is very inadequate.

If you can get Al Perraud's address, Mother, I would like to have it. My Regards to the Folks,
Love,
Harold

· · ·

He wrote this letter back on Guadalcanal with a newly appointed plane after a week in Hawaii:

May 12, 1943
Dear Mother and Curt,
Was sitting here in operations reading some intelligence bulletins when I noticed that our old, battered typewriter was not in use. So, to keep my hand in it, and also to let you know that everything is still o.k. by me, I will try to get this letter off to you.

We are set up pretty nice here in our new camp. We are pretty crowded, but nobody minds that. We were lucky enough to get mattresses for the cots, and this is indeed a luxury out here. The few nights we have slept here are the first time we have had mattresses since leaving the States. The food is very good, and in spite of the heat, we never miss the chow line. This morning, for example, we had hotcakes and syrup.

The letters we get here take a good long time to reach us. I received your letters about five weeks after they were written. Yesterday, I received a letter from a friend of mine in Africa written four months ago. It can't be helped, but it is hard trying to answer letters written so long ago. For example, this fellow, whom I knew in basic flight school, wanted to know how I like flying pursuit ships. (He knew that I went to Luke Field, a pursuit school.)

Received two letters yesterday from Bob. He seems to like his new outfit. Much better than the last one and tells me that he is in charge of a small-arms crew. This is a good job and the type of work that Bob would like. Although he says that he does not know when he will get back to the States. (He could not say even if he did.) I feel sure that his outfit will be relieved before very long.

Our outfit, too, will be relieved after a while, and there should be a thirty-day furlough when we get back.

We have movies here now, and we really enjoy them. They are usually interrupted by "Washing machine Charlie," the nickname we have for the Japanese bombers. However, "Charlie" has a healthy respect for our ack-ack and has to stay up so high that he is lucky to hit the island. The only value of his attacks is the nuisance value, and we really get peeved at him when he causes us to miss a show.

Don, Van, and the rest of the boys, with the exception of the combat crews, are still back at our old field. They have no ships and are practically reduced to a housekeeping squadron. I am flying with a fine crew now. They are boys I have picked out from other crews that are temporarily incapacitated due to sickness.

Be sure and let me know, Mother, as soon as you receive the money orders and checks that I sent home.

Give my regards to the Allisons, the Paulisons, and the Bradfords.

Love,

Harold

• • •

Below is an upbeat letter home before Mac leaves again for an unknown assignment back in Hawaii:

May 16, 1943

Dear Mother & Curt,

I received a letter yesterday from you and one from Grams. Both written April 26. Am sorry that Grams is going back as I know she was a lot of company for you.

Major Smith showed me your letter to him last night. It was certainly a swell one, Mother dear, though I suspect that you might be a bit prejudiced in my favor.

Glad to hear that Bill likes the army. Hope, for his sake, that he continues to do so.

Everything here is o.k. I am as healthy as a 4H clubber—plenty of good food and sleep.

I am going to take a little trip in a day or so and will be gone for a week to ten days. I will write to you at every available opportunity, but don't worry if you don't hear for a little while.

In your next letter, send me Bob's address as I have lost my address book. Also, give me any news you may have of the old boy. I hope that he will get home in a few weeks, and it is more than likely that he will.

By the time you receive this, I will be back here again. It is a very routine flight and will be pretty monotonous.

Hope that you both are well and that you like your job, Curt. Incidentally, in case I forgot, thanks again for your swell letter, Curt.

Love,
Harold

• • •

Mac's younger brother, Bob, then a corporal in the U.S. Army, was serving in a vastly different island environment — the Aleutian Islands of Alaska. From airfields at Adak, Dutch Harbor, and Fort Glenn, U.S. Navy pilots flew patrol bombers, fighter bombers, and observation aircraft on combat and reconnaissance missions over the Aleutians. The U.S. military had begun construction of forward-operating bases in the Aleutian Islands of Alaska in 1941, anticipating the spread of the war in Europe to the Pacific Theater.

On June 3rd and 4th, 1942, six months after the bombing of Pearl Harbor, Japanese pilots had bombed Fort Mears and the Dutch Harbor Naval Operating Base on Amaknak Island. Three days later, a small Japanese force occupied the islands of Attu and Kiska.

By 1943, American troops, including Mac's brother, Bob, were stationed throughout this very remote, 1,200-mile-long archipelago protecting the homeland. The U.S. feared that if the Japanese occupied these islands, they would use them as bases from which to carry out a full-scale aerial attack on the U.S. West Coast cities of Anchorage, Seattle, San Francisco, or Los Angeles.

Almost a year after the Japanese had landed and taken Kiska and Attu, the American and Canadian troops could finally recapture Attu in June 1943, with heavy damage on both sides. For nearly a year, the remoteness of the islands and the challenges of weather and terrain delayed a larger American and Canadian force sent to eject them.

The Japanese Army abandoned Kiska one month later. U.S. troops remained in the Aleutians until the end of the war in 1945. Because the Japanese launched the invasion of the Aleutians simultaneously with the Battle of Midway, and by the same commander—Adm. Isoroku Yamamoto—some military historians believe it was a diversionary or distracting attack meant to draw out the U.S. Pacific Fleet from Midway Atoll.[50]

---

[50] National Park Service. https://www.nps.gov.

The flood

The flood

Chapter 28
Guadalcanal—June 1943

While the two squadrons of B-24s from Guadalcanal were in Hawaii being rotated out for the upgrades and retrofits, Japanese air activity escalated. At the beginning of the month, the Japanese had an average of twenty fighters based at their Kahili Airfield. At the end of June, that number increased to thirty-seven, and during July, the Japanese had one hundred twenty fighters based there. Japanese troop replacements were coming in to cover their losses, and then some. Kahili Airfield was growing to the dismay of the U.S.

On the night of June 3rd, the Japanese bombed a Marine position on Guadalcanal, and on the night of the 16th, they hit the 25th division area, resulting in six deaths, four wounded, and the ignition of a fuel dump. The very next night, they hit an area called Fighter II, located roughly 1.5 miles west of Henderson Field, injuring eight people and damaging a good deal of equipment. Two nights later, they were back and hit the area opposite Henderson tower, injuring one person, crippling a seaplane, and riddling several tents.

The strategy put together by the Allies in mid-1943 was an aggressive plan. It called for amphibious assaults on certain Japanese-held islands and their bases as part of a drive north toward the Philippines, and eventually, the Japanese home islands themselves. If the Allies could set up their own bases around the major Japanese bases, they could isolate them. They believed this would be just as effective as destroying the enemy bases through direct bombing attacks, and far less costly to Allied Forces. If Japanese ships couldn't get troops and equipment in and out, they would be as impotent as a rabbit caught in a boa constrictor's coil, slowly being strangled.

Encircling their powerful naval base in Rabaul would nullify the Japanese threat from the Solomon Islands and the Bismarck Archipelago, which included New Britain, while a second prong of the Allied advance drove through the central Pacific via the Gilbert and Marshall Islands. As part of this assertive counteroffensive, the promised new 307th BG crews began arriving in June 1943. They sent many to Guadalcanal to receive their preliminary training-scheduled twenty-four missions: the usual shipping searches and strikes but with a growing number of daylight raids.

Unfortunately, casualties for the 307th BG were also unusually high. June was a deadly month with eight planes down and sixty-eight crew members killed. Compared to the enemy's loss of two planes shot down and three damaged, this was not a good kill ratio from our perspective. Japanese night fighters offered the toughest opposition of the month.

They had modified all the *Liberators* by the end of June, and they were back on Guadalcanal, ready to roll, soar, and destroy.

• • •

Following are three letters from Mac that were written from Hawaii, and one upon his return to Guadalcanal.

June 1, 1943
Dear Mother & Curt,
It was great to hear your voice the other night. The next best thing to seeing you both in person. Will be doing that, too, one of these days.

I remember, when I was going to sea, that the best part of going always was coming home again. Like beating yourself on the head because it feels so good when you stop. Next time I come home, I'm there to stay.

Am getting a little bored with this civilized life. The people here are fighting a tough war. Everything is hemmed in by restrictions. Farther south, we can't bother curfews, blackouts, and gas masks, and we can almost spit on the Japs from there.

Am anxious to know if you received my letter containing the bonds and money orders. Let me know when you get it.

Love,
Harold

• • •

His second letter home from Hawaii:

June 12, 1943
Dear Mother & Curt,
Another day on the rock has passed, and I am getting very impatient to get back to the outfit. We have enjoyed ourselves here, and the change has done us good, but we are just a little tired of fighting this "pineapple war." The sooner we get back down, the quicker we will get home, and that's what we are all looking forward to.

I should have a batch of mail awaiting me at 709, and it will be good to get that.

Have been feeling great and eating like a horse—all the fresh fruits and milk that don't get farther south.

Have met some very fine people here, and they have been pretty swell to us. Tomorrow, we are attending a banquet at which myself and the crew are guests of honor!

Give my regards to the family, and the Perkinses, and Mrs. DeClercque.

Love,

Harold

       •   •   •

Mac's third letter home from Hawaii:

Dear Mother & Curt,
Will be leaving here very shortly for our home base after 3 weeks here. This place has gotten on my nerves more than it ever did before. Curfews, restrictions, proper uniforms (with ties), high prices, newspapers (with stories about our ace saboteur, Lewis) all add up to complete boredom for yours truly. Liquor is almost impossible to get for transient officers, and the ratio of men to the girls is 300 to one.

Had considerable work done on the ship here. We call the ship "Omar, the Dent Maker." I test-hopped it this morning, and it is all set to go. Have met a great many fellows here on their way home. Boy, how we envy them. Sure hope they get Bob home pretty soon. I should be home in the fall.

Love,
Harold

       •   •   •

The following is Mac's letter home from Guadalcanal:

June 29, 1943
Dear Mother & Curt,
Today finds us pretty close to the old stamping grounds. At least we are on the same island and will probably leave tomorrow for the old base. A great many of the boys have been transferred to this base as it is a sort of rear echelon, which will relieve us from time to time.

It is all right to tell you now that I was back in Hawaii for the past three weeks. It is permissible to say where you have been, but not where you are or where you are going. We had a good time there, but toward the last, got a bit anxious to get back, especially after reading in the papers of the different raids our boys have been on. It will be good to see Don and the rest, as they are a fine bunch of fellows.

I have not had a letter from you since the first of the month but know that I will have several when I get back. I am very anxious to hear how everything is going on the home front. I certainly miss you all a lot and am looking forward to the day when we can come home. It will not be too far off, and I am hoping that I will be able to spend Christmas at home with you. I hope that Bob can get home pretty soon, too. It would certainly be great if we could both be there at that time.

One of the boys is waiting for me now to go to supper, so I must continue this later in the day. I will write from 709 as soon as I get there.

Say hello to all the folks and Bob for me.

Love,

Harold

Chapter 29
Guadalcanal—July 1943

Close to the spot where Mac had months earlier ditched the disabled plane *Bombs Away* and he and his surviving crew had made their way to shore in the raft, the Japanese landed 300 men on the northeastern part of Choiseul at the end of June. With coast watchers ever vigilant, four companies of American Marine Raiders landed to quell the situation until the Allies could drive the Japanese entirely from this group of islands.

Mac was back from Hawaii, and it was another particularly busy month in the air. The two squadrons flew sixteen bombing missions, plus one rescue mission and seven searches for missing planes and crews. They dropped 408.8 tons of bombs on the enemy.

The squadrons flew two search and rescue flights and eleven bombing missions in July—nearly one every other day. Mac's flight log shows nine were bombing Kahili-Bougainville, one shipping vessel, and one bombing on Munda. They were pounding the Japanese out of the Solomons and isolating their bases.

The military plan was to keep moving north to the next group of islands, closer and closer to Japan. The last stragglers from the Japanese Army on Guadalcanal had all but disappeared. They had been periodically active, coming out of the jungle to make random attacks on Australian coast watchers trying to eliminate them. Coast watchers were going off the air to protect their locations, but by the end of July, the Japanese had disappeared from Guadalcanal entirely.

After the successful Guadalcanal campaign, the Allies planned to advance through the Central Solomons up toward Bougainville with further operations in New Guinea as part of the effort to destroy or isolate the main Japanese base around Rabaul. The two 307th BG Squadrons sent nine B-24s each, including Mac and his crew, along with the 5th Bomb Group flying nine B-17s.

Mac, who still didn't have a permanent crew to fly with him, picked up six members from another crew he considered excellent, including Sam Walker as his radio operator. According to Sam, in his book *Up the Slot*, "We were carrying a special present, something new for the Japs. Our bomb load consisted of 500-pound demolition bombs, some fused to detonate on impact and some with delayed action fuses. The delayed action bombs were fused to explode at six, twelve, and thirty-six hours after impact. Our bomb experts assured us the delayed action bombs would also explode if the enemy tampered with them. We hoped this would keep them unsettled around Kahili Airfield for a long time."

The *Liberators* began taking off at 10:30 a.m. from Carney Field, six miles from Henderson. They assembled into formation over Iron Bottom Bay and headed 'up the slot' on the first daylight mission against southern Bougainville since Mac's ill-fated February 13th mission. This time, they had a much larger and stronger strike force accompanying them. The B-17s and seventy-two navy fighters joined the group over the Russell Islands. Both B-24 squadrons formed three rows of planes following the lead. One, then two behind, three behind them, and three more following.

The 424th Squadron led the formation with Col. Matheny flying as command pilot in the lead plane. Mac was the wingman now flying *Frenisi* just outside and behind the wing of Col. Matheny's aircraft in flight formation. Their sister B-24 Squadron trailed to the left of them, and the 5th Group's B-17s trailed to the right.

"Soon after passing the Russells," Sam recalled, "Capt. McNeese began a steady climb to our 24,000-foot attack altitude, and I went back to my gun position at the right waist. Doug Apple was flying the other waist gun that day and beat me to the back."

"Your gun's okay," he said. "I tested it."

"Thanks," I said, smiling, but I fired a couple of shots anyway. "Doug was right. The gun was in good shape. With nothing to do for the moment, I began looking at the formation—especially the fighters. The big *Lockheed Lightning* P-38s, flown by army pilots, were our high cover and flew from five to eight thousand feet above us. They were flying faster than we were and crisscrossed from one side of our formation to the other and back again, always with two planes together in the buddy system.

"Next were the dark-blue *Chance-Vought Corsair* F4Us with inverted gull wings. Navy and Marine pilots flew them and were only two to three thousand feet above our formation. The P-40 *Warhawks* and P-39 *Air Cobras* were at our same altitude and were to the right and left of our formation. Some of the P-39s were army pilots, and some carried Royal New Zealand Air Force colors. It was a stunning, formidable sight to behold. Before long, the P-38s were making vapor trails. The others followed, as the cold, moist air hit the hot engines. *We would not sneak up on anybody today*, I thought, as I watched the trail behind each engine.

"We swung to the right across the northern tip of Choiseul Island, and the P-39s and P-40s began dropping the disposable gas tanks they'd carried slung under their bellies. Soon we passed Bougainville's tip, made a ninety-degree left turn, and headed toward Kahili Airfield. So far, I hadn't seen a single Japanese fighter. I poked my head out the open window and looked as far ahead as I could. I still didn't see any enemy planes, and a solid layer of white, billowy clouds several thousand feet below completely obscured Kahili Airfield. How were we going to bomb through that, I wondered? We couldn't, was the answer. Since we couldn't see the target, Col. Matheny, the lead pilot, decided to save the bombs for a better day. There were a few anti-aircraft bursts we assumed came from warships in the harbor, but no enemy planes attacked or even came close to us. It was an intimidating show of force. As we headed home disappointed, we chalked it up to a good training mission."[51]

For one crew, however, piloted by Capt. Sam Gregory of the 370th BS, this was anything but a routine mission. According to his account, "A hole in the clouds opened up and showed the target as we were directly over it. Suddenly, the #4 engine cut out, and the cylinder head temperature shot to 245 degrees. I attempted various emergency procedures, but nothing worked.

"We dropped the bombs," he said, "and turned and headed back to home base. Then the other three engines began to alternately cut out, catching fire, then going out. Then the #3 engine caught fire and stayed ablaze. When I tried to bring it back, engine #1 went out completely as well. I wasn't able to keep up with the formation and couldn't contact the flight leader, so I dropped to 5,000 feet and ditched the plane just off the southern shore of Choiseul Island."

The sea was moderately rough, but Gregory made an excellent water landing. The nose of the *Liberator* broke as it hit the water, disintegrating and breaking the windshield, forcing it into the cockpit, tearing off half of the top of the canopy and demolishing the #6 bulkhead. It pinned Staff Sgt. Arthur J. McCurry under the ball turret as it spun around when the plane hit the water. The other gunner, who pushed him out of the left

---

[51] Walker, Samuel I. 1984. *Up the Slot.*

waist window and into the water, freed him. It surprised one of the other men to find that he had landed among the oxygen bottles on top of the bomb bay with a gun mount in one hand and a life raft under his other arm. The radio antenna caught and held him tight until fellow crew members could extricate him. The cabin filled with water in ten seconds. Sgts. William G. Hardin and David L. Cox hastily reentered the sinking plane and brought out first aid equipment, emergency flotation gear, and anything else they could quickly grab. Staff Sgt. David W. Timpe had no recollection of the landing. The first thing he remembered was sitting in the plane, submerged in water, and seeing light above him through the open escape hatch, which he quickly scrambled out of. Gregory and the bombardier, Lt. Harry Sterkel, also reentered the plane to get more emergency supplies. Then Hardin pushed the raft over, and they helped the injured board.

The plane sank in about fifteen minutes in the moderately rough ocean. They tied the two rafts together and rigged up two sails from a parachute they had retrieved from the plane. It was a rough sea, and intermittent rain was falling. Rafts kept filling with ocean and rainwater and required constant bailing, with some men using their shoes for scoops. The uninjured took turns rowing, and they reached a small island by early morning on July 2nd. Pulling the rafts into the brush, they tended to the wounded, and then they all slept as though someone had drugged them.

The next day, a fighter plane flew overhead, saw them, and reported their position. At about 10:30 that morning, they heard the welcome noise of a plane and sent up flares and tracer bullets. Three B-24s from their own squadron and a PBY seaplane spotted the flares. The seaplane landed, but the six- to eight-foot waves made the rescue difficult for the plane to get close enough to shore to pick up the men. The uninjured men carried the wounded to a quieter cove where they could finally launch a raft, get aboard the seaplane, and return to base. It was a harrowing ordeal, but they made it back alive.[52]

Five days later, Mac and the rest of the 424th BS set out on yet another mission to neutralize Kahili Airfield. The planes arrived at dusk, and they saw all bombs dropping in the target area, which started large fires in the plane dispersal and supply dump areas. But the return anti-aircraft fire from below was heavy and accurate and hit all the planes. Flames and puffy, black smoke emitted from one of the B-24's engines. Someone saw Lt. Don S. Hathaway's 424th BS bomber flying 5,000 feet below the formation after leaving the target and turned right up the southwest coast of Bougainville, gradually losing altitude. They never saw his plane or one other—including all crew members aboard—again. Lt. Joseph R. Littlepage, 370th BS, piloted this second lost B-24.

There was never time to grieve for lost friends or contemplate their own mortality. There was always another mission to embark on. The overriding emotion was revenge.

The next night, they were back at it again. Lt. Jack M. Cobb became lost and was low on fuel. One engine was dead. The radio compass was out when he called, but the radar was still working. He could see an island but could not pick up the radio beam. The pilot reached the ground station at Carney Field, sending SOS signals and asking for a bearing. Then he veered toward the island that he thought was Russell and followed the shoreline.

Abruptly, at 1:30 in the morning, the #1 engine stopped, but Cobb continued heading for the island. He had two engines out now. Deciding that a water landing was best, he selected a quiet lagoon in the middle of the island. As he approached, he turned the landing lights on, then quickly turned them off because the reflection blinded him. But it was too late. He could not see the water, and as a result, the plane hit sooner and harder than he

---

[52] Walker, Samuel I. 1984. *Up the Slot.*

expected. When they hit, the flight deck flooded immediately. The top turret fell to the flight deck, and the nose crumpled like a giant wad of aluminum foil.

Because they were in a lagoon and the water was calm, the plane stayed afloat for nearly forty-five minutes. The mechanism of the ball turret that had crushed the #6 bulkhead pinned two men, and fellow crewmen quickly released them. Everyone survived except one man, their navigator, Lt. Calvin G. Brown, who could not swim. They tried repeatedly to find him before the plane sank, but they were finally forced to abandon their efforts. They later recovered Lt. Brown's remains, and they buried him at Duncan Municipal Cemetery, Duncan, Oklahoma.

The remaining crew pulled out two rafts from the tip of the plane, grabbed an emergency radio and what rations they could find, and loaded them into the rafts with five men in one raft and four in the other. After sleeping in them that night, they went ashore the next morning. Not knowing what island they were on or whether the Japanese were nearby, they found a cove and concealed the rafts in the brush.

Three search missions from Guadalcanal were launched, unsuccessfully, until finally, on day three, two B-24s reported seeing a parachute held in the air by natives. Then they saw an outrigger canoe that appeared to contain a light-skinned man. Once again, natives had come to the rescue.

The next morning, the stranded crew heard an airplane engine, and when they looked up, they saw a big, beautiful B-24 *Liberator* flying above them. Jubilant, they shot off six flares, and the plane turned toward them. They flashed the letters COBB SOS using the emergency radio light system they had recovered from the plane. Immediately, the plane's radio operator flashed back: "307-Roger." Shortly after that, Lt. Thomas A. Keane of the 370th BS and crew arrived and dropped emergency ration kits to the waiting men. Then about a half dozen natives appeared, fed them, and offered shelter for the night.

The following morning, a PBY showed up and landed easily in the quiet lagoon. Before boarding, the grateful men gave the natives gifts of the raft, flashlight, tarpaulins, and other items, as well as the obligatory but sincere letter stating that the natives were responsible for their rescue and deserving of high praise and thanks.

One of the other planes on that search mission, flown by Lt. Raymond W. Price, did not return. Later, a search and rescue team sent for them discovered the wreckage of a B-24 in a ravine inland from Yenton Point. It appeared as though the plane had been approaching from the sea and probably suffered mechanical problems. They never found any survivors of the eleven-man crew.

They had to split crews up because of illness, death, or injury, and with several planes in repair, men were constantly being reassigned to other pilots for bombing missions. This added to the danger, since they were not accustomed to working as a team. Lyman Clark, an aerial gunner, and his crewmates were lounging around on the morning of July 16th, writing letters home, when they received word that they were to take off late that night to fly to Kahili with Capt. McNeese. The crew went down to the river to take a swim, came back, and wrote more letters, then got some shut-eye for a few hours until flight time.

According to Clark, in his book titled *Missions of Shehasta: A Story of World War II Bomber Aces*, "We pulled eight missions on *Man-O-War* with Capt. Harold McNeese, and we were all pleased to ride with him because he had quite a reputation already when we got to the Canal. He had pulled his crew through some tough missions and was known to come through in a pinch."

As Clark noted, "Kahili was a tough target with plenty of anti-aircraft guns, searchlights, and a master beam that was strong enough to reach up and find our bombers. They also had a steady stream of fighter replacements coming in as quickly as we could shoot them down. At two o'clock in the morning, we were over Kahili Airfield.

"Capt. McNeese went in at fifteen thousand feet, which was low, but at night he felt he could risk it. The first run was dry, not dropping bombs. We were on oxygen," Clark remembered, "and I kept the ball turret moving all the time. On our second run for Kahili, they caught us in the lights, and the Japs started throwing ack-ack up at us as we dropped the bombs. One burst off to my right, making a small puff of smoke. The night fighters did not attack us, but they got a tail gunner in the other squadron. They also shot down a seaplane out on a rescue mission later in the early morning hours."

The squadron returned from bombing Kahili about five o'clock the next morning. Exhausted, they only had a little over twenty-four hours to prepare for a 7:00 a.m. takeoff the following day to bomb shipping in the Shortland Harbor with a fighter screen of seventy-two army and navy planes.

On this second mission, "We were again riding with Capt. McNeese, and on the first run, we could not see the target because of clouds, so we dropped the bombs on an alternative target—a boat in the bay. We got two hits, one on the bow and one on the stern. But those guys were pretty accurate with the ack-ack. They couldn't have gotten any closer without hitting us. Bullets whizzed by the plane," Clark said.

"On the second run, leaving the Russell Islands, Capt. Max J. Sanny, who was leading the 424th BS, developed engine trouble and began losing altitude. The other squadron members followed him down, not knowing he was having problems and going to turn back. By the time Capt. McNeese realized what was happening and had worked into the lead position, the other two squadrons were miles ahead. But McNeese noticed that approximately one-third of the fighters had stayed with them, so he continued and made a single squadron attack. Like a busted football play that sometimes gains good yardage, the two separate attacks worked out remarkably well," Clark said.

"Mac, leading the 424th, along with the 370th Squadron and the B-17s, approached Kahili Airfield from across Lahala Lake and spread their bombs over the runway and to the supply areas on either side, igniting several fires. As we pulled away from the target, we saw sixteen *Zeros* ahead, climbing toward the formation. Fortunately, the P-40s kept most of them away. Only three reached our altitude and made runs on the formation, breaking away early.

"Then came Capt. McNeese, leading the 424th Squadron, again approaching Kahili across Lahala Lake. But by now, towering, cumulus clouds obscured the air base. McNeese led the squadron in a circle north of Kahili, looking for an opening, but couldn't find one through the clouds. Once again, the bombers circled, but the target was still socked in. McNeese then flew across the harbor and bombed Ballale. Partway across the harbor, a target of opportunity appeared—a big, fat, beautiful ship lay directly in our flight path, clearly visible. McNeese decided to pattern-bomb the ship and radioed the message to the other pilots."

The big ship took violent, evasive action and had there been only one bomber, it might have escaped with minor damage. Here, though, the bombs covered too wide an area for them all to miss. Crew members from six of the nine planes reported two direct hits: one on the starboard side amidship, and another on the same side just aft of amidship. Black smoke billowed up. One member of Ward's crew reported that as the ship passed from view, it stopped dead in the water, listing at the stern, and then he saw lifeboats pulling away from the ship.

"Now," continues Clark, "anti-aircraft from the warships was heavy, but McNeese took evasive action as soon as bombs were away, and we avoided being hit. A hole in one plane's left wing was the only damage from ack-ack. The navy PBY squadron and the 5th bomb group each lost a plane and crew to Japanese night fighters. Japs had plenty of fighters available to come up to meet us. They kept a steady stream coming as quickly as our fighters and bombers could shoot them down, and we safely returned to base."[53]

But the month was a particularly deadly one for the 307th BG. The enemy killed sixty-nine members in action.

There was some good news to improve morale for the war-weary men at Henderson, namely, enhancements in recreation on the island. They upgraded the makeshift baseball field with an excellent diamond, including a backstop and dugouts. In addition, they constructed a boxing arena, badminton courts, and several horseshoe pits. The camp looked somewhat organized. They dedicated a new chapel and opened several mess halls and group laundries. And there was always the beach.

• • •

Mrs. Oliver Smith, the mother of Staff Sgt. Robert O. Smith, his radio operator who parachuted out when the plane was about to ditch, wrote Mac the following sad letter. She had not yet received any conclusive word about her son.

July 10, 1943
Dear Lt. McNeese,
Sitting here thinking of nothing but Bob, as always, and thinking hard also of you and the rest of Bob's crew and wondering if you are o.k. and well. I have written you before, but not having received any reply, thought probably that you had never received my letter and also that you are too busy to even find time to write letters outside of your mother and home folks. I know it must be terribly hard to find time to do anything outside of what is assigned to you, but I do want you to

---
[53] Walker, Samuel I. 1984. *Up the Slot.*

know how happy Mr. Smith, Mary Blanche, and I were to receive your letter regarding our Bob and the rest of the crew.

Nothing could have been closer to being Heaven sent than your letter. I have read and reread it hundreds of times and have made copies of it and mailed it to our home folks who, in turn, write us and tell us how wonderful it was to receive a letter so reassuring as that, and from his very own pilot, and we certainly do feel the same way. I know that you are a wonderful pilot, Lt. McNeese, for Bob told us that when we were with him on the 8th of October at Sioux City, which was the happiest day of our lives after not having seen Bob for eleven months.

Then upon Bob's return from Rochester, he wrote to us and said, "Daddy and Mother, After taking this test at Rochester, and with such a wonderful man like pilot McNeese at the helm of our ship, I will fly wherever he or the ship takes us, with no fear in my heart whatsoever." So, you can readily see how we love and feel about you, Pilot McNeese, and like I wrote in my last letter, when this awful affair is over, and you and Bob are safe back with your loved ones, I would love to have you and your dear mother pay us a visit and make our home your home as long as you are to make it so.

I had asked you for a snapshot of yourself, but I now have one that was printed in one of the Chicago papers. And it is very good, I imagine, for it looks like Bob said of you: "He is very smart, alert, poised, and determined." And what else is there to say, and coming from Bob, I know that's true.

We are still praying to God and have put our whole trust in him that someday soon, he and the rest of the crew will be returned safely to us. You and the boys are always in my prayers so many times a day. I will never let you all down. I hope that Bob is safe on some island or that maybe he is a prisoner of war, but just so he is alive is all we ask. We had such a lovely letter from our Chaplain Lertis R. Ellett, and if and when you see him, thank him so much for us, and I will write him in the very near future.

I had a nice letter, too, from Mrs. Lund, Roy's mother, but she said that they had had no further news but were just hoping and praying, too. I suppose you know that John Sargent, the tail gunner, is from Wilmette. Well, I hear from his mother occasionally, but she said in John's last letter, he never mentioned any of his former crew, and she did not know whether or not he knew about what happened or could not write about it.

Well, Lt. McNeese, I will not take up any more of your time, but if you receive this, and I trust you will, please drop us a line. We will be so happy, and I will answer immediately. With all our love and best wishes to you and all the boys we met at Sioux City. I am,

Sincerely yours,
Mrs. Oliver W. Smith

Chapter 30
Capturing Munda Point on New Georgia

In 1942, the Japanese had built Munda Point Airfield on New Georgia Island, the largest island in the Solomons, with plans to erect a large air base there. Construction of the airfield began in mid-November of that year with a great emphasis on keeping this airfield a secret. They cleared the ground for the main runway and put coral down to surface it after they had built most of the supporting structures. To create a canopy so they could work in secret, they wired the tops of the palm trees together. Despite these elaborate efforts to keep it a secret, the ever-vigilant Australian coast watchers discovered and reported it to the Allies, who kept up heavy bombing during construction.

One hundred fifty miles northeast of Guadalcanal's Henderson Field, the Allies considered Munda Point Airfield to be a perfect location for another U.S. air base for the continual advance of the Allied Forces up to Rabaul. This was Japan's main naval and air base in New Guinea, and if it were in the Allies' hands, they could eventually move farther north toward Japan itself. Also, if the Allies controlled Munda, ground troops could advance on Japanese-held Bougainville under the protection of aircraft.

To get close to Munda Point, the U.S. Army and Navy made an amphibious assault on Rendova Island, just south of Munda, on June 30, 1943. U.S. troops quickly overwhelmed the small military garrison the Japanese had on the island and easily captured it. This was important because the U.S. could now use Rendova as a staging area and artillery base to get to the Japanese forces guarding the airfield at Munda Point.

In retaliation, Japanese bombers struck damaging blows on American troops on Rendova during the month, trying to oust them. As the Americans continued to target Munda, the Japanese dive bombers pushed back, protecting the harbor between the two, which they used to supply their airfield. They also continued to focus bombing raids farther south on Guadalcanal and occasionally hit planes and airfields in the Russell Islands near Henderson Airfield.

When Allied ground forces landed at Munda Point, the Japanese blocked the approaches to the airfield. The ground forces made a call for air support. Close air support on New Georgia was tricky to execute and dangerous for the ground troops. At this stage of the war, there was no systematic, target-marking system or good radio communications between line troops on the ground and aircraft above them. Friendly fire could easily hit ground troops.

Despite this, twenty-two B-24 crews, including Mac and his crew, answered their call and managed the delicate assault. The result was the laying of a path a couple hundred yards wide right up to the airfield. The report from the U.S. ground forces was that, "Trees were shattered stumps, pill boxes were caved in, and dead Japanese soldiers were everywhere." There was hardly an area of twenty-five square yards that was free of water-filled bomb craters. But this was just the start.

Over the next two weeks, the ground troops began a very slow progression along the coast up to the Japanese airfield. The jungle was dense and difficult to navigate, and the Japanese were relentless in their defense of their Munda Airfield. As a result, the U.S. troops became separated and disorganized, and their continued advance hit a wall on July 15th. Hungry, tired, and inexperienced, the soldiers began to lose their motivation and forward momentum, and many developed symptoms of combat stress. Historian Samuel Eliot Morison described the chaos that ensued.[54]

"Darkness came to the jungle like the click of a camera shutter. Then the Japanese crept close to the American lines.[55] They attacked with blood-curdling screams, plastered bivouacs with artillery and mortar barrages, crawled silently into American foxholes, and stabbed or strangled the occupants. Often, they cursed loudly in English, rattled their equipment, named the American commanding officers, and dared the Americans to fight, reminding them that they were 'not in the Louisiana maneuvers now.' For sick and hungry soldiers who had fought all day, this unholy shivaree was terrifying. They shot at everything in sight—fox fire on rotting stumps, land crabs clattering over rocks, even comrades."

It was an untenable situation for these young soldiers so recently trained, caught in a war halfway around the world from what they knew. They sent Gen. Oscar Griswold to assess the situation, and he reported back that it was indeed dire. If they were going to take Munda Airfield, they would need at least one other division to break the stalemate. But the movement of reinforcements and supplies from Guadalcanal and the Russell Islands to Munda Point took time, and the Japanese took advantage of the disorder on the American side, launching a counterattack on July 17th. After more than a month-long bloody battle and fierce fighting in the jungle area, on August 5, 1943, the U.S. Army Infantry Forces finally captured Munda Airfield.

---

[54] Miller, John Jr. 1968. *Cartwheel: The Reduction of Rabaul. United States Army in World War II.* 120.
[55] Morison, Samuel Eliot. 1950. *Breaking the Bismarcks Barrier.* 177.

Chapter 31
The Japanese Push Back

As expected, the Japanese struck back from their Munda Point defeat. The Allies received intelligence showing they had a large convoy heading toward the tiny coral atoll in the Gilberts—Tarawa, a Japanese stronghold. They were presumably coming to destroy the American base on tiny Funafuti. They planned a mission to bomb this convoy, and eleven crews from the 307th BG left Espiritu Santo on July 27th for Funafuti, 970 miles to the southeast of the Japanese-occupied Nauru Island.

The year before, the Americans had seized and occupied Funafuti, the largest atoll in the Ellice Islands, ready to turn it into a base to use against the Japanese in the Gilbert Islands. By April 1943, the Americans had built a 6,600-foot airfield on Funafuti, allowing its use by the two Hawaiian-based B-24 Squadrons and the two Guadalcanal Squadrons. Initially, they stationed two Marine bomber groups there, as well as a small seaplane and PT boat base.

Arriving from Espiritu Santo, the B-24 *Liberators* refueled in Funafuti. They searched for the Japanese convoy on its way to Tarawa, but because of the severe weather and poor visibility, they couldn't find it. Instead, they attacked the supply dumps and airdrome on Tarawa. They did some damage, but once again, mechanical problems of the *Liberators* caused the casualties.

Of the eleven planes that took off on this mission, one plane did not reach Tarawa due to engine failure. Two planes ran out of fuel and crashed into the ocean. Maj. Marshall T. Vose's engine stopped as he was making the final approach back to Funafuti, and he smashed into the sea. Fortunately, Vose, Lt. Earl W. Peters, and two enlisted men, Sgts. Stanley F. Grenesko and Harry Tieman, survived. Maj. Vose couldn't swim and struggled until one of the gunners floated by on a bomb bay gas tank and pulled him aboard. The copilot, Lt. James L. Corbett, and the navigator, Lt. Peters, were hanging on a life raft but couldn't get in. Corbett took off his life jacket to mount the raft easier but lost his grip and drowned. Lt. Peters hung on until something nuzzled his foot, and then he launched himself into the raft, propelled like a rocket.

Luckily, a search plane spotted the survivors the next day shortly before they would have had to turn back, low on fuel, about 120 miles from Funafuti. A navy PBY picked up the survivors in the first raft. The second raft was about a mile away, so the plane had to take off again to find it. On the second landing, the seaplane catapulted into the air and pancaked on the water, knocking off one engine, and everyone in the PBY ended up in rafts themselves. This was the only seaplane at Funafuti, so they dispatched a Navy PT boat to rescue all the survivors.

On this mission, only six of the original eleven 307th BG crews, including Mac's, returned to base, and all with an insufficient amount of fuel to taxi in and park. Talk about cutting it close to the wire. The Japanese convoy continued its voyage to Tarawa and soon arrived, and the terrific battle for this critical atoll would ensue a few months later.[56]

---

[56] Britt, Sam S., Jr. 1990. *The Long Rangers: A Diary of the 307th Bombardment Group (H)*.

Chapter 32
Guadalcanal—August 1943

War-weary, the 307th BG flew sixteen missions in August and dropped 119.7 tons of bombs on various Japanese military installations and ships. For the month, the statistics favored the 307th BG. All sixteen missions occurred during daylight hours, and they lost one 372nd BS crew, Lt. Harry L. McDonald's.

On another B-24, Staff Sgt. Albert S. Feller, 370th BS, was killed, and three other men were wounded. However, the U.S. shot down twenty-nine enemy aircraft, damaged five, and had two probable kills. For a gunner to receive credit for downing an enemy fighter, at least one other person must confirm that the plane hit the water, ground, or that the pilot had bailed out. In the heat of battle, it was often difficult to watch what was happening to an enemy fighter when you were being fired upon. Consequently, many kills went unreported or undercounted.

• • •

When compared to the air operation in Europe, the Pacific operation was infinitesimally smaller. The crews in the Pacific did not return home after completing twenty-five missions but had to stay until a replacement crew showed up, which could take many months. They were in a constant state of high stress and acute anxiety, and there wasn't much civilization in the

South Pacific to blow off steam. Crews had nowhere to go between missions or anyone outside to even talk to.

Besides the inherent danger of flying in combat and ducking enemy shelling in between, the B-24 was often unreliable, and they had patched up some planes so many times, they were like old men with a titanium hip, foot problems, a tender back, and a slipped disc. This took a toll on the psyche, and just a small glimpse of civilization could work wonders for morale and mental health.

Finally, toward the end of the month, a full complement of squadrons was on hand in the Solomons, and the group commander instituted a rotation system so that each squadron served a six-week tour on Guadalcanal and six weeks off for training and rest. This could even include some time in Auckland, which must have seemed like heaven to the airmen. The New Zealand food was delicious—steak and eggs, fresh vegetables, ice cream, and other fresh milk products. The airmen would have welcomed almost any food after consuming dehydrated eggs, spuds, and powdered milk for six months, but New Zealand food was good by any standard.

New Zealanders were wonderful and hospitable people who tried to make the airmen's visits enjoyable in every respect, showing them around and inviting the boys home for a drink. The G.I.s learned new customs and got used to driving on 'the wrong side' of the road. Every night was a party, sometimes in restaurants and nightclubs and sometimes in the homes of newly made friends. The men desperately looked forward to leave time and needed it for their mental and emotional well-being.

There was also some good combat news that month. New Georgia Island, where the Japanese had been fighting furiously, was presently in the hands of the Allies, and Munda Field was now being used by American fighters and light bombers. The Allies were making progress up and down 'the slot.'

The rotation of crews began on August 1, so new crews were coming in frequently. That was good, in that there was some relief, but it also meant that many of the crews were green and needed time in the air to work as a team.

They scheduled a daylight bombing mission on August 6th on the supply dump at the Japanese Naval Base at Rekata Bay on Santa Isabel Island. Mac and his downed crew had been perilously close to this base five months earlier, traveling down the other side of the island. Since the U.S. had heavily bombed it in May and June, the enemy had strengthened their base there, which was now a threat to Allied operations in the New Georgia Islands. The hope and goal were that this mission would paralyze the base.

Schedulers coordinated the Rekata Bay mission with B-17 heavy bombers of the 5th group and B-24s of the 307th BG, with two other simultaneous attacks on nearby islands for distraction. Thirty-two fighters were to fly cover for the bombers, and because the B-17s were slower than the B-24s, they were in the lead. The B-24s staggered along behind them, trying not to stall out because they were going so slowly. Few of the B-24 pilots had realized how slow the B-17s actually were, in comparison, until the bomb bay doors opened and it looked like the B-17s had stopped midair. Because of their relatively slow pace, the B-17s slid under and above the B-24s, and with bombs falling from above, below, and in between the planes, miraculously, not one plane was hit by friendly fire—incredible odds. They deemed the mission a success.

As the strike team turned to head back, suddenly, one Japanese pilot brazenly dove through the middle of the B-24 formation with a P-38 fighter close behind in hot pursuit. The men had heard, through the jungle grapevine, that if a *Zero* got up enough speed in a dive, the controls would freeze up, and apparently, that's what happened to this one. A gunner on one of the other planes reported that the *Zero* went down straight into the water without the P-38 firing a single shot.

Next, they scheduled a raid for Ballale Air Base up in the Shortland Harbor area at dusk on August 13th, which turned out to be a horrible affair for the 307th. This time, enemy pilots were hiding in a cloud just above the target, waiting for the B-24s. They began firing into the formation, which broke it up, and in confusion, the *Liberators* began firing at each other. Just two crews could drop their bombs on the target.

On August 25th, another mechanical snafu occurred while a plane was on a sea search out of Espiritu Santo. Lt. Jack C. Stafford's plane ran out of fuel because the engineer had trouble transferring fuel from the bomb bay tank. It forced them to make a water landing, and radio operator Staff Sgt. Jack C. Feller was never seen again.[57]

• • •

A letter home at the end of a busy month:

August 29, 1943
Dear Mother & Curt,
Have been kept pretty busy last few days with my new job as operations officer of our squadron. Am not flying a desk now, by any means, but do have to spend quite a bit of time scheduling our different missions. However, although there are plenty of headaches attached to the job, it does have one big advantage in that the time does go a lot faster.

Our squadron has now moved to APO 706, where we will be located for the next few weeks. It is more of a rear echelon team than 709, so that we are trying to accomplish a good deal of training for our newer crews. Have started transition training for all of our old copilots so that they may all be checked off as first pilots. They have all had a

---

[57] Britt, Sam S., Jr. 1990. *The Long Rangers: A Diary of the 307th Bombardment Group (H)*.

raw deal in that they are not eligible to be promoted to First Lts. until they are qualified first pilots. Inasmuch as most of them have been out of school for more than a year, they are quite understandably "peeved" about the whole situation.

Living conditions here are a big improvement over those of our old base. The quarters are better (screening instead of mosquito netting around the huts). And the food is a little more varied (one fresh egg per man twice a week). We also have our choice of several shows in the evening, so everything considered, it's not so bad. I have my own jeep and no worries about gas rationing. If they could only get some WAACS out here, I think we could make out very well.

Don is living in the same area and is O.F. Don't worry about Carroll, Mother. There is nothing wrong with him mentally as a result of the accident. As a matter of fact, most of the boys say that he was the only smart boy of the crew. At least he's home and we're still "sweating it out." In this tropical paradise. He was sent home on the recommendation of the Auckland Flight Board, who pronounced him "psychologically unfit for combat."

My financial situation sounds great, and I feel like a "bloomin' plutocrat." Don't forget that whatever I've got belongs to you both because I know that the reverse is true.

I sent a form letter to Washington requesting that they use the correct address on allotments sent to you, so I hope that by this time, they have done something about it. Red tape and paperwork are the bane of this man's army and very little I can do out here to straighten things out. I would like to increase my allotment but had better not while I am in this area, as I know from experience that there would be a mix-up.

Am afraid my mail situation is going to be a difficult one to solve. I will be here at APO 706 for the next few weeks and will then return to APO 709 again. If you will write to me at 706 up until about September 20th (date of your mailing) and then to 709 after that, I will be able to get my mail a lot better.

Regarding homecoming, there is nothing definite, but things look very promising for most of us. Some of the boys are not so optimistic, as shown by a few of the campaign slogans making the rounds: "For home we'll strive in '45," and "Golden Gate in '48." However, it's not as bad as that, and I'm still counting on that Christmas dinner.

Love,
Harold

Chapter 33
Guadalcanal—September 1943

In September, the 307th flew eighteen missions from Henderson Field and dropped 269.7 tons of bombs on enemy installations. The group's gunners accounted for ten sure kills, thirteen probables, and two damaged enemy planes. As a group, the 307th BG lost two men and had four wounded.

On the September 3rd strike on the air base on Kahili, Lt. Kenneth Greear had to cut the #4 engine over the target and feather the prop-aligning propeller blades so that the usually curved face is almost straight to eliminate drag. This slowed the plane down and caused him to drop behind the formation. When he was about two miles back, ten to twelve enemy fighters attacked him like a pack of wolves on a wounded rabbit. Five minutes later, two P-40s and two P-39 fighters dropped back and gave him cover until he could catch up to the squadron.

On September 15th, Japanese planes hit Henderson Field, destroying one plane on the ground. The next night, they tried for the runway but missed. On the night of the 21st, a big American reception was waiting for them, and a P-38 pilot shot down two *Bettys*—the Japanese bomber—within minutes of each other. Men got out of their foxholes and cheered as the planes exploded in midair.

Then it was back to bombing Kahili on the 30th, and once more, the enemy pilots were waiting with their attack starting as the bombs dropped, but U.S. fighters kept them away. The bombing lasted about thirty-five minutes before the B-24s headed back to base, all intact and all arriving safely back home.

A fact unknown at the time they were bombing Kahili, but learned from the Japanese after the war, was that during this time, the Japanese stripped their aircraft carriers of all their planes and air crews and based them in the Solomons. They considered the Solomons to be the most important part of the war at the time and tried desperately to stem the tide of the American War Machine, grinding its way northwest 'up the slot' in the Solomons.[58]

• • •

Mac's letter home:

> September 2, 1943
> Dear folks,
> Well, here I am again, sound (?) as ever in mind and body and missing you both very much.
> My new job takes up so much time that I have neglected my letters to you these last few days. I have had no word from anyone at home in 2 weeks, though it is probably due to my change of stations.
> Here at 708, we have been conducting a good deal of training for our different crews, and this means plenty of work for me as the operations officer.
> Last week, I bought $250.00 in war bonds and had them sent out to you. I don't actually come in contact with the bonds, so I can't give you the numbers, but I will hold on to my receipt until you have received them from Washington. They are purchased under our 2 names (co-ownership), and you should receive them by the end of the month. (Sept)
> Love,
> Harold

---

[58] Walker, Samuel I. 1984. *Up the Slot.*

Chapter 34
Guadalcanal—October 1943

The 307th BG kept up the relentless pounding and flew many missions in October. They hit Kahili Air Base nine times, Buka and Kara twice each, Ballale once, and Poroporo, the Japanese evacuation base at Choiseul's northwest tip, once as an alternate target.

But the most notable flight of the month was not a U.S. flight, but a Japanese flight. Flight, as in, they vacated the southern Bougainville area like birds in a bush fleeing buckshot. Before the end of October, the Japanese gave up maintaining air bases at Kahili, Ballale, and Kara and pulled their air units back up to Rabaul in New Guinea. They had been driven out of the Solomons.

Bombing Kahili Air Base into submission during 1943 had been a crucial step toward eventual victory in the Pacific War. It was the first strong air base the Japanese were forced to evacuate, and it was the first crack in the Japanese determination and belief that they had a "so far and no farther" line drawn in the sand, behind which they would not retreat. They retreated from Kahili.

The U.S. continued the air and artillery bombardment of Japanese ships near Munda Airfield since capturing it in August, plus infantry fighting on the ground to keep the Japanese away.

The 424th lost one B-24 crew defending Munda. After takeoff, the plane disappeared and was never seen or heard from again.

By mid-October, Munda had a new, coral-covered runway, and Gen. Nathan F. Twining, Commander of Aircraft, Solomon Islands—one of the first combined air commands in U.S. history, with tactical control of all Army, Navy, Marine, and Allied Air Forces in the South Pacific—moved his army headquarters there on October 20th. Thereafter, because the U.S. bases were perilously close, the Japanese only used the Bougainville Airfields to periodically sneak aircraft in late in the day for small, hit-and-run missions the next morning.

The last six missions flown by the 307th BG *Liberators* in October were with no Japanese fighter opposition at all, and the last four were without even a fighter escort because none was needed. When U.S. ground forces landed in the Treasury Islands near Shortland Harbor in late October, and then set up a beachhead at Cape Torokina on Bougainville November 1st, it had been eight months since the first bombing mission on February 13th. The Allies had accomplished their goal of driving the Japanese out of the Solomons by repeatedly pounding their bases with bombs.

The Allies now knew that contrary to some pre-war, airpower extremists, who said that a few devastating air raids could completely destroy an enemy base, it took constant bombing, day after day, mission after mission, month after month, until they destroyed the enemy's will and ability to rebuild and resist.

Of course, the *Liberators* alone did not accomplish this, but the *Liberators* frustrated the Japanese more than any other aircraft. The ability to operate consistently against them, despite their best efforts, was deeply unsettling. They had no bombers capable of as much self-protection and the ability to absorb as much punishment and still keep flying, as did the B-24s.

Instead of closing ranks in a tight formation, as the U.S. planes did, the Japanese bombers, which were lightly armed and vulnerable to fighter attacks because of their light weight, scattered when under fire as the best means of survival. At first, they expected the U.S. planes to do the same, but the more they hurled fighters against them, the tighter American pilots pulled together in formations. And U.S. gunners threw out protective walls of bullets that the Japanese fighters had to fly through to attack. Commander Masatake Okumiya, a Japanese air staff officer at Kahili in 1943, said after the war, "The B-24 seemed to ignore our fighters and fly into any area of their choice."

· · ·

Here is Mac's letter home after September:

October 1, 1943
Dear Mother & Curt,
Have just returned from another visit to our base at 709. All the boys are fine, though getting mighty anxious to get home. I went there to meet our new C.O. (group commander) who is really a prince. Our old C.O., whom you met in Sioux City, has moved to another job and now wears a star instead of a 'chicken.' Of course, I didn't chase down to meet the 'old boy' on my own hook, but at his request. He has quite a deal cooked up for me and very much to my advantage.

Everything looks very rosy here, and time is passing quickly and growing <u>short</u>.

So glad you liked the roses, Mother. My love to the folks.
Love,
Harold

· · ·

And a letter home the following week:

October 7, 1943

Just a few lines tonight to let you know that everything here is o.k. In fact, it's better than o.k. with the news I've had in the past few days. Time passes very quickly here, and before I can realize it, another five or six weeks will have gone by.

I am in the best of health and still keeping pretty busy with my job. I have moved in with Maj. (Noel S.) Benson, our squadron C.O., and have pretty nice quarters. There are three of us in the shack, including Doc Groth, our flight surgeon.

Received a letter from Bob yesterday, and the old boy seems pretty chipper, though pretty anxious for a reassignment. He tells me he is now section head in his branch, which means he is eligible for a staff sergeancy.

Say hello to the folks for me,
Love,
Harold

• • •

Mac's letter home the following week:

October 11, 1943
Dear Mother & Curt,
Here I am back at 709 with another new job. I am now assistant group operations, which is another rung up the ladder. Actually, however, I would have preferred to stay as squadron operations among the boys I have worked with for the past year. However, that makes no difference, as I wasn't asked, anyway. My new job is very interesting, and I enjoy it. Then, too, I know all of the group staff from our old Ephrata days, so it was very easy to fit in.

Received 2 letters from you when I arrived here, and it was certainly good to hear from you. Hope you and Mrs. DeClercque had a good chat. I saw Don before I came down to 709, and he is fit as a fiddle. Also saw Van here tonight, and he is also well.

Am not permitted to tell you when I am coming home, but the time is not too far away. Take good care of yourselves and write often.
Love,

Harold

By December 1943, the Pacific War had been raging for two full years, and the writing was on the wall. The Japanese would not win, but neither were they about to surrender. The U.S. military had more than recovered from Pearl Harbor; they had trounced the Japanese fleet at Midway and then poked a big, fat hole in the enemy defense perimeter at Guadalcanal and the Solomon Islands.

The Solomon Islands' Campaign had cost the Allies approximately 7,100 men, 29 ships, and 615 aircraft. The Japanese lost 31,000 men, 38 ships, and 683 aircraft. But Guadalcanal was the pivotal, attritional struggle that turned the tide and set up the pattern of multi-domain cooperation that eventually led to Allied victory in World War II in the Pacific.[59] Securing Guadalcanal was critical to paving the way for the Allies to advance north to Japan.

---

[59] Rein, Christopher M. 2018. "A Case Study for Multi-Domain Battle." *Military Review*.

Chapter 35
Mac's Second Tour of Duty—Flying B-29 *Superfortresses*

While the war in Europe was winding down, Japan still needed to be defeated, and the Allies could finally focus on the Pacific Front. Mac was headed home for a brief reprieve after a harrowing and eventful year on Guadalcanal. His last two entries into his flight record for the year on December 12, 1943 were not combat missions but missions toward home. The next to last one shows he left Hickam Air Force Base in Hawaii, only to return within an hour and fifteen minutes after losing his #4 engine. His last entry was a second attempt from Hickam Field to Hamilton AFB in Northern California that same day. That flight was thirteen hours and fifteen minutes. "Arrived home!" he noted.

Mac had flown fifty-three missions from Guadalcanal—double the number usually flown before rotation back to the States, and miraculously, he had survived them all. Few of the original members of the two squadrons were as lucky. He spent a joyous Christmas reunion with family and a couple of months of well-deserved rest.

I can only imagine, though; Mac was champing at the bit, like a restrained racehorse, to get back into the action. He had loved the excitement of combat, swooping in low, avoiding anti-aircraft and flak from enemy planes alike, dropping bombs on ships and artillery compounds, and then darting away like an angry wasp. But instead of heading back to Guadalcanal, the Army Air Forces had new plans for this seasoned, young pilot. They promoted him to major and gave him a new assignment, as his October 1st letter home had alluded.

Another new bombardment group was forming—the 39th with the 20th Air Force—and Mac was to be part of it. They specifically formed the 20th to perform strategic bombardment missions against the Empire of Japan itself. This group was completely autonomous, and its B-29 *Superfortresses*, brand-new bombers, were to be totally independent of all other command structures.[60] The Army Air Forces secretly chose the 20th Air Force to be the operational component of the Manhattan Project that later made the atomic attacks on Japan in August 1945.

Mac received orders for Smoky Hill Army Airfield in Salina, Kansas to join this new bomber group, which they activated on April 12, 1944. They would train him to fly yet another brand-new bomber. But these planes—the *Superfortresses*—were still being built, so they sent Mac to Clovis, New Mexico, where he flew primarily B-25s and B-17Fs in March and April.

The Boeing B-29 *Superfortress* is an American, four-engine, propeller-driven heavy bomber designed by Boeing, flown primarily by the United States during World War II and the Korean War. They named it with a tip of the hat to its predecessor, the B-17 *Flying Fortress*. They designed the *Superfortress* for high-altitude, strategic bombing.

There are two major classifications of bombers: strategic and tactical. They aim tactical bombing at specific targets of immediate military value, such as individual combatants, a military installation, or military equipment. Strategic bombing is done by heavy bombers, such as the B-24 and the B-29, which are primarily designed for long-range bombing missions against

[60] Wikipedia. "20th Air Force."

broad, strategic targets to diminish the enemy's ability to wage war, limiting access to resources by crippling their infrastructure or debilitating industrial plants.[61]

The B-29 could deliver the largest payload of air-to-ground weapons—usually bombs—but was also capable of flight at altitudes up to 31,850 feet at speeds of up to 350 mph. Japanese fighters could barely reach that altitude, and even if they did, few could catch the B-29. The *Superfortress* was the most complicated and expensive weapon of WWII. This big bomber, with its long legs, could travel great distances without having to refuel, and it made it possible to reach Japan itself rather than having troops fighting the war from carriers in the sea. This was the new bomber Mac was now in training to fly. He and the other hand-picked pilots were among the first to fly them.

The *Superfortress* B-29 was one of the largest aircraft of World War II, which also had built-in, state-of-the-art technology. This included, for the first time, a pressurized cabin, dual-wheeled tricycle landing gear, and an analog, computer-controlled, fire-control system that allowed one gunner and a fire-control officer to direct four remote machine gun turrets. The B-29s were also all equipped with microwave radar.[62]

Engineers developed navigational radar to detect German aircraft during the Battle of Britain in 1940, and U.S. and British scientists perfected it to become the most sophisticated detection device to come out of World War II. Microwave radar first appeared in 1943. The development of the cavity magnetron, a high-power vacuum tube, led to higher frequency and, therefore, shorter radio waves into the region of the electromagnetic spectrum called microwave. The shorter wavelengths were easier to focus on in narrow beams. This meant that a distant object would reflect more energy back with greater resolution. Directing anti-aircraft and long-range naval

---

[61] Boot, Max. 2003. "The New American Way of War." *Foreign Affairs* magazine. July/August.
[62] O'Brien, Phillips Payson. 2015. *How the War Was Won*. 47–48. 1st ed. Cambridge University Press. ISBN 978-1-107-01475-6.

guns entirely by radar required microwave frequencies, as did displaying the topography below a plane when they used radar for navigation. It was also useful in airplanes to locate hostile aircraft or ships or to find bombing targets.[63]

So, while early radar was in some of the B-24s, microwave radar became airborne on every B-29 in the 20th Air Force and, for the first time, made possible the night raids on Japanese industrial centers and daylight bombing of targets obscured by cloud cover. It was also an efficient navigational tool that allowed for weather and collision avoidance, delivering fixes in seconds, bouncing off and recovering distance signals from targets en route. What a boon this improved radar system must have been to the bomber pilots and navigators and in providing confidence to the rest of the crew.

However, in early 1944, when the 20th Air Force was being created, the B-29 *Superfortress* was not yet ready for combat. There were an overwhelming number of operational problems, mainly because the engines had an alarming habit of catching on fire. As a result, they held production up. Because of the size of this new aircraft, all work had to be done outdoors, as they were too large for conventional hangars. This, along with the newness of the product and the new mechanics working on them, slowed progress.

To get the B-29s combat-ready as quickly as possible, they sent technicians and specialists from the Boeing Wichita and Seattle factories to the modification centers to work around the clock. They often worked in freezing outdoor weather. But their efforts paid off. By April 15, 1944, on Mac's 26th birthday, they sent 150 B-29s to the 20th Air Force in Smoky Hill Army Airfield in Salina, Kansas, where Mac and the other pilots anxiously anticipated their arrival like expectant fathers waiting during a long labor for the birth of their first child. It was also undoubtedly a wonderful birthday present for Mac.

---

[63] Wikipedia. "Radar in WWII."

Known as the "Fighting 39th," the men who were a part of this elite bombardment group began their B-29 training at the end of April 1944 when they delivered the new planes—now tested, redesigned, and finally blessed for combat.

Mac's flight record shows April 27th "First ride in new baby." However, it was not until well into August and September that most of the ground personnel got to Smoky Hill Army Airfield. When the ground crews finally arrived, they discovered that another bomber group still held the field for training, and that the 39th BG would have to wait their turn until the current group finished and they deployed them overseas. In the meantime, the ground crews of the 39th BG learned as much as they could about this new plane from their predecessors.[64]

On the first of July, Mac joined a large contingent of officers and enlisted men from the 39th BG and attended the Army Air Forces School of Applied Tactics at Orlando, Florida for thirty days of training in B-29 bombardment technique, which differed totally from the B-24 he had been used to. In August, they officially transferred him to the 39th BG and sent Mac to Dalhart, Texas, where he began instrument training school in Galveston and finished a month later, on October 4th. Then it was back to Salina, Kansas to join the rest of the 39th BG.

In Smoky Hill, the 499th Bombardment Group that had preceded the 39th BG finally left for its overseas station in Saipan in October. With their departure, there was now room for final training of the 39th. All facilities could be solely devoted to training for the *Superfortresses*.

Flight training picked up again, and class after class of ground school instruction began for all men of the unit as well. Ground school covered theory, weather, radar, instrumentation, etc. They conducted overnight bivouacs, designed to prepare the men for field conditions in the South Pacific, which, for Mac and some of the other pilots who had previously served in

[64] 39th.org.

Guadalcanal, was unnecessary. Finally, they had fully schooled everyone, and they were almost ready to go into combat operations.

The last phase of flight training began on January 16, 1945, when Mac and all the units of the air echelons went to Batista Field, Cuba for flying and bombing training. Under then President Fulgencio Batista, Cuba had entered the war on the side of the Allies. They designed the practice to simulate a mission in the South Pacific by bombing unoccupied parts of Cuba and surrounding islands. Navigators rehearsed guiding the ship to a practice bombing site and back to base. Bombardiers practiced with the advanced Norden Bombsight, dropping sacks of flour or dummy bombs on selected targets.

Because of the complexity of the B-29, they needed an additional and unique crew position: the flight engineer. His job was to watch the aircraft systems that were usually done on other planes by the pilot and copilot. Gunners also attended ground school to learn the specific characteristics of the machine guns and to hone their skills. In the air, they practiced shooting at drones and canvas sleeves towed behind airplanes. Although female fighter pilots wouldn't exist until 1993, Women Airforce Service Pilots (WASPS) flew some of the tow planes.[65]

With the completion of this training work in Cuba, the group was now considered ready for combat. When the flight crews returned, the rest of the 39th BG was in the last stages of preparation for the ferrying of ground personnel to Marianas Naval Base on Guam.

On January 8, 1945, the ground troops left Salina for the Port of Embarkation at Seattle, Washington, where it would board the S.S. Howell Lykes for the slow trip to the ultimate destination at North Field—Guam. Here, the pilots and crews of the B-29s could and would end World War II.

---

[65] Hmdb.org.

Home for Christmas 1943

Recounting the Guadalcanal experience

Readying for B-29 training

Chapter 36
The 307th in the Solomon Islands—1944

In 1944, while Mac and the 39th BG were training on the new B-29s in the United States, the U.S. Navy, Marines, Army, and Army Air Forces continued their move west toward Japan, taking islands away from the Japanese and setting up and readying air bases that would be close enough to Japan for the B-29 *Superfortresses* that would arrive later to reach.

Mac's former bomb group, the 307th BG, flying *Liberators*, were still kicking what was left of Japanese butts in the Solomons and north of there. The rear echelon of the bomber command headquarters was now moved from Guadalcanal north to New Guinea, an Australian territory that the Japanese swooped in to occupy shortly after they bombed Pearl Harbor. New Guinea was slowly being retaken by the Allies. New crews were sent to the Southwest Pacific Area Center at Nadzab, New Guinea, which processed crews for the 5th and 13th Air Forces. The abandoned Japanese bases on Rabaul and Wewak, New Guinea now served as handy practice targets for the Americans.

Isolated Japanese anti-aircraft gunners were still on Rabaul, however, and they proved they could still damage airplanes, so the pilots were always vigilant. The Allied campaign to totally oust the Japanese from New Guinea resulted in major losses for Japan. They slowly isolated the Japanese troops, and with no food or medical supplies delivered, disease and starvation took its toll and claimed more Japanese lives than enemy action. Up to 97 percent of Japanese troops in New Guinea and surrounding islands never met their enemy, but merely died of starvation or disease.[66]

The 307th continued their relentless assault and flew sixteen more bombing missions to the Truk Islands north of the Solomons and seven to Yap, to the west of Truk. They flew thirty bombing missions that month, plus one search mission. The *Liberators* carried 500-pound demolition bombs to a mission on Dublon Island in the Federated States of Micronesia. This island was then the headquarters of the Japanese Navy, so this was an important target. The bombs hit buildings west of the hospital area and continued across Dublon Town. Lots of fires started, preceded by an enormous explosion, with plumes of black smoke rising several hundred feet into the air. Flames covered an entire city block on the east side.

As Sam Britt detailed in his memoir, *The Long Rangers*, enemy fighters attacked, and six phosphorus bombs burst above and in front of the formation. Then, the enemy dropped about twenty bombs directly on them, and fighter fire damaged ten B-24s. In addition, they hit the 372nd BS's lead plane on the bomb run. Lt. John R. Sawyer, the pilot, was killed instantly by 20mm shells that came through his windshield, entering his head and face, and then exploded. The resulting explosion also mortally wounded Lt. Philip J. Heimlick, the navigator, who was standing between the pilot and copilot. Lt. William E. Way, the copilot, was maimed. The blast cut his right leg, caused his left arm to go limp, and flying glass and shrapnel slashed one side of his face.

When the bullets felled the pilot, it threw him forward on the controls, causing the plane to slip down to one side, almost hitting the wing plane next to them. Lt. Way immediately flipped on the automatic pilot, which caused the nose of the

---

[66] Stevens, David. "The Naval Campaigns for New Guinea." *Journal of the Australian War Memorial*. Paragraph 30. Retrieved 10 March 2016.

plane to come up again, nearly hitting the other wing plane flying on the other side of it. He then leveled the plane using his one good arm and leg. Enemy pilots continued to attack. The nose gunner ran out of ammunition, and the top turret guns went out because the sacks that caught the empty shells were too full. This forced the shells back into the guns, jamming them. One gun in the tail turret went out, and the waist guns were not working properly.

Following instructions from the wounded copilot, the bombardier, Lt. Max O. Tenton, helped fly the plane. When the Japanese fighters finally departed, Sgt. John R. Hall dropped out of the top turret to assist. First, he improvised a tourniquet for Lt. Way, and he and Tenton worked with the other wounded. He then discovered that bullets had shot away the wires controlling the prop governors, and the props were running at too high rpm. At that rate, there would not be enough fuel to reach the base at Los Negros Island, so they jettisoned everything they could out of the plane.

Sgt. Hall then worked to repair the wires to control the props, and the other planes stayed with them for protection. Lt. Way felt it was critical to remain with the formation because without a navigator, they would probably get lost. After finally repairing the wires, Sgt. Hall jumped in the pilot's seat. The copilot now appeared to be semi-conscious, fading in and out.

As they approached the runway for landing, the copilot held the controls with his one good hand. His legs were getting weaker, but when he put his feet on the rudder controls, Sgt. Hall could see what he was trying to do and helped him. Doing most of the flying, Sgt. Hall made a perfect landing—his first. The plane nearly skidded off the runway, but he jammed the left brake and regained control, bringing it to a full stop. The crew helped the injured out of whatever opening they could find.

Heimlick was still alive, and the flight surgeon ran to attend to him. The navigator needed blood, and there was no plasma for a transfusion, so every able crew member rolled up his sleeves and donated blood on the spot. Unfortunately, the surgeon could not save him, and Lt. Heimlick died a few hours later.

Mac also learned that Lt. Harvey R. 'Van' Vanderslice, his copilot on the ill-fated February 13, 1943 flight, was killed on this same mission. A *Zero* pilot made a vertical dive from eleven o'clock, and a 20mm shell entered the right windshield, piercing his right wrist and entering his right leg, then exploding. Subsequently, three 7.7mm bullets entered his chest. He survived all this for about two hours.[67]

• • •

The War Department awarded the 307th BG their first Distinguished Unit Citation for their March 29, 1944 raid on Truk:

GENERAL ORDERS
NO. 63
WAR DEPARTMENT
WASHINGTON 25, DC, 5 August 1944
Section
BATTLE HONORS Citations of units ————————VV
BATTLE HONORS. 2. As authorized by Executive Order No. 9396 (sec. I, Bull. 22,

WD, 1943), superseding Executive Order No. 9075 (sec. III, Bull. 11, WD, 1942), citation of the following unit in General Orders, No. 78, Headquarters Thirteenth Air Force, 27 June 1944, as approved by the Commanding General, United States Army Forces in the South Pacific Area, is confirmed under the provisions of Section IV, Circular No. 333, War Department,

---

[67] Britt, Sam S., Jr. 1990. *The Long Rangers: A Diary of the 307th Bombardment Group (H)*.

1943, in the name of the President of the United States as public evidence of deserved honor and distinction.

The citation reads as follows:

The 307th Bombardment Group (H) is cited for outstanding performance of duty in action against the enemy on 29 March 1944, when it conducted the highly successful bombing of Truk, one of the most strongly fortified and heavily defended enemy bases in the South Pacific, and the key to the Japanese inner defense circle. This mission was in support of and coordinated with a naval task force operating in that proximity and had, as its immediate objective, the neutralization of Truk during our naval action against the enemy. It involved difficulties and hazards greater than in any other single mission previously undertaken by units of the Thirteenth Air Force. To accomplish the assigned task, it was necessary that a flight of approximately 1,700 miles be made entirely over water, without any fighter support, and requiring 13 hours and 30 minutes for its completion. En route to the target, two severe weather fronts were successfully penetrated. From a navigational standpoint, the flight represented a peak in achievement. Two squadrons with 20 airplanes delivered a devastating attack against Eten Airfield, the key airdrome in the Truk Islands, destroying 49 enemy airplanes on the ground and destroying or severely damaging 21 hangars, shop buildings, and warehouses, and scoring 37 direct hits on the concrete runway, making it unserviceable. Immediately following this strike, the formation was attacked by an estimated 75 enemy fighters, and for 43 minutes there ensued one of the bitterest aerial combats ever experienced in the South Pacific area, during which 31 enemy fighters were shot down, 12 probably destroyed, and 10 damaged. The brilliantly successful attack by the 307th Bombardment Group (H) demonstrated the vulnerability of

Truk to our land-based bombers. The success of this mission, which struck such a devastating blow to the enemy, exemplifies the highest type of leadership, teamwork, and flying skill and is in keeping with the highest traditions of the military service of the United States.

BY ORDER OF THE SECRETARY OF WAR:
G. C. MARSHALL,
Chief of Staff
OFFICIAL:
J. A. ULIO,
Major General,
The Adjutant General

Chapter 37
Capturing the Gilbert Islands

During the year 1943, the Allied victories in the Solomon Islands created the platform from which the next advances in 1944 would spring. The goal was to keep moving toward Japan by building air bases on islands close enough for the U.S. *Superfortress* bombers to reach and devastate critical infrastructure. However, the different branches of military brass debated exactly what the best strategy was to advance and where. Japan obviously was heavily and zealously protecting those surrounding islands. MacArthur was firmly lodged in New Guinea and thought the best course of action would be to move next to liberate the Philippines and operate from there, where U.S. bombers could reach Japan. After all, he had a personal interest in helping to free the Philippines, having been driven out by the Japanese after the Pearl Harbor attack.

The navy admirals, however, preferred to bypass the Philippines and capture Formosa, which was much closer to Japan. Powerful men with big egos and differing ideas clashed, and instead of a united strategy, they each went in their own direction. In hindsight, if there had been more cooperation and less competition within the military establishment, the Pacific War might have ended sooner, with fewer lives lost. Eventually, they settled on Guam in the Marianas. It was close enough and probably easiest to reclaim.

The Allies began moving north in a game of island hopscotch, crossing the central Pacific as they moved closer and closer toward Japan. Naval strategy dictated that land-based airfields were preferable to flying off an aircraft carrier, so the U.S. continued building airfields as they moved north. The Allies could then continually weaken the enemy's defenses and protect invading forces as they retook land seized by the Japanese.

At the end of 1943, Adm. Chester W. Nimitz had begun his great drive north. If taken by the Allies, the Marianas would allow the U.S. to reclaim Guam, the largest of the Marianas, putting them a mere 1,500 miles away from Japan—well within the range of the B-29 *Superfortress*. To get to the Marianas, they first needed a base on the Marshall Islands, which was heavily defended by the Japanese. The Marshalls were cut off from any direct communications with the base in Hawaii because the Japanese also had a military base with an airfield on the very tiny island of Betio, on the western side of Tarawa Atoll in the Gilbert Islands. Therefore, to launch an invasion of the Marianas and build a base on Guam, the battle had to start farther to the east at Tarawa, removing the Japanese from Tarawa, then capturing the Marshalls, and then the Marianas. Three giant steps forward.

• • •

The U.S. attack on Betio, Tarawa began when navy ships steamed into the harbor, fronting Betio Island early in the morning of November 20, 1943 with a heavy air raid followed by a sustained, three-hour naval bombardment. This did terrific damage, smashing the Japanese communications net, but the Japanese defenders were sitting in deep bunkers, and many survived to man their guns just as the first Marines hit the north shore.

In Tarawa Atoll, according to some historians, the Japanese weren't even trying to win; they just wanted to kill as many Americans as possible and then die. The navy sent 18,000 U.S. Marines to Tarawa and expected them to secure it easily. However, as other Marines would discover less than a year later in Normandy on the beaches of France, problems with a beach landing can quickly arise. Low tides prevented some ships from clearing the shallow coral reefs that surrounded the tiny island. Japanese guns from the coast blasted away at the ships caught in the harbor, and desperate Marines gave up trying to free boats to paddle in on, and instead, waded toward shore—hundreds of yards away—through chest-deep water amidst enemy fire.

Fire from the Japanese defenders was grim, merciless, and relentless. At day's end, what was left of the American force had barely gotten ashore. Of the 5,000 Marines who attempted to land, the enemy killed or wounded around 1,500 of them. The 3,500 Marines who reached the beach then charged the Japanese troops dug in on Betio. With still heavy resistance from the 4,500 Japanese defenders, the Marines finally took the island after a bloody battle in which both sides suffered heavy casualties.[68] In the end, the Marines ground the Japanese down in four days of tough fighting. Nearly 6,400 Japanese, Koreans, and Americans died in the fighting on this tiny island.[69] But with the American victory, the Gilberts were now firmly in the hands of the U.S., and they could continue next to the Marshalls.

---

[68] History.com.
[69] Editors of History.com.

Chapter 38
Capturing the Marshalls and the Marianas—1944

In the two years since the start of the war, with rapid manufacturing, the United States had amassed a vast array of land, sea, and airpower. At the dawn of 1944, the U.S. Navy boasted seventeen aircraft carriers, twelve battleships, and sixty-six destroyers. In addition, there were another thirty-six types of transport vessels to carry U.S. Marines and Army infantry divisions.

The United States now had over 30,000 men in the Gilberts, ten times as many as the Japanese defenders.[70] The powerful U.S. Navy was next on the move to the Marshall Islands.

Different from the Gilberts, the Marshalls were a much easier landing. No low tides or coral reefs blocked the ships from entering the harbor. The Americans used the lessons learned at Tarawa by outnumbering the enemy defenders nearly six to one with heavier firepower, including use of armor-piercing shells, after the islands took nearly a month of heavy air and naval bombardment.[71] It took seven long months to secure the islands. In the Marshalls, the Americans lost 611 men, suffered 2,341

---

[70] Citino, Robert. Samuel Zemurray Stone, Senior Historian in the Institute for the Study of War and Democracy.

[71] Dickson, Keith. 2001. *World War II for Dummies*. Indianapolis, IN: Wiley Publishing, Inc.

wounded, and 260 missing, while the Japanese lost over 11,000 men and had 358 captured.[72]

After they took the Gilberts and Marshalls, the Allies built naval bases, fortifications, and airfields on the islands to prepare for an assault on the Marianas, the third and final steppingstone in this long path forward toward the Empire of Japan.

This defeat forced Japan to reassess and pull back their defensive perimeter—Absolute National Defense Zone—to now include the Marianas and Palau. They greatly increased their defense on these islands, fortifying them, because they knew that if the Allies captured them, Tokyo would be in range of their heavy bombers.[73]

In June, Adm. Raymond A. Spruance's 500-ship fleet, carrying about 125,000 Marines and sailors, steamed 1,000 miles from the Western Marshall Islands to the South Mariana Islands. This fleet included most of the navy's carriers and battleships, along with many of its transports of the Pacific Fleet.

Guam is in the Mariana Islands, approximately 1,600 miles south of Japan. It became a territory of the United States after the Spanish-American War in 1898, and they ceded the rest of the Marianas to Germany. When the Japanese attacked Pearl Harbor, Guam had been lightly defended, and it was easy for them to swoop in and capture it just three days later. Now, following advances through the Gilbert and Marshall Islands, the Allies set their sights on the return to Guam in the Marianas.

Prior to this, they stationed a few of the new *Superfortress* B-29s at airfields in China and India under Gen. Curtis LeMay. But this turned out to be an almost impossible job to fly from China and India to Japan. Besides the logistical issues of dangerous weather and mountainous terrain, the B-29s could only reach a

---

[72] Rottman, Gordon. 2013. *The Marshall Islands 1944: Operation Flintlock, the Capture of Kwajalein and Eniwetok (Campaign)*. Oxford: Osprey Publishing.
[73] Hylton, Wil. 2013. *Vanished: The Sixty-Year Search for the Missing Men of World War II*. New York, NY: Riverhead Books.

limited part of Japan while flying from Indian and Chinese bases. They needed Guam.

First, the U.S. forces invaded Saipan, the largest of the Mariana Islands, on June 15, 1944. Despite a Japanese naval counterattack, which led to the Battle of the Philippine Sea and heavy fighting on land, this destroyed much of Japan's naval airpower and resulted in the U.S. capturing Saipan and Tinian.

The Battle of Guam lasted from July 21 to August 10, 1944 and was the American recapture of the Japanese-held island. Guam's takeover by American forces also cut the Japanese supply lines with the Caroline Islands territories farther south and pushed their defensive position west to the Philippines while opening the Japanese homelands for aerial assaults. A triple win.

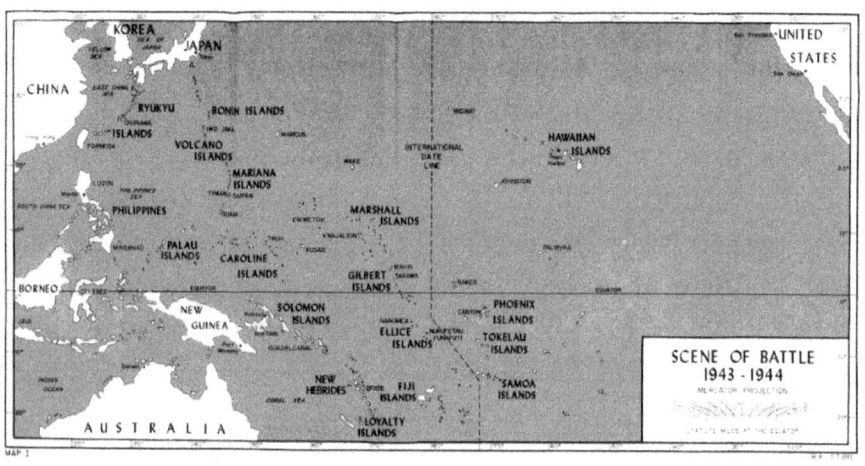

Scene of battles

Chapter 39
The Pacific War—End of 1944 Beginning of 1945

U.S. forces had captured the Gilbert Islands (Tarawa and Makin), the Marshall Islands (Kwajalein and Eniwetok), and the Mariana Islands (Guam, Saipan, and Tinian). With each island they snatched from the Japanese, the United States had moved closer to Japan, hopping like checkers on an enormous game board. Growing superiority at sea and in the air, as well as in the massive number of fighting men, gave the United States increasing advantages. The Japanese were fearsome defenders and fought long and hard wherever U.S. forces met them.[74]

Naval construction battalions—the Seabees—began at once to construct air bases suitable for the B-29 *Superfortresses*, starting even before the end of ground fighting. They built five major airfields: two on the flat island of Tinian, one on Saipan, and two on Guam. Each was large enough to accommodate a bomb wing made up of four bomber groups, housing 180 B-29s per airfield. Ships could also easily supply the bases and, unlike the bases in China, were not vulnerable to attack by Japanese ground forces.

With the airfields now ready, the first B-29s arrived on Saipan on October 23, 1944, and they launched the first combat mission from there on October 28th with fourteen B-29s attacking the Truk Atoll, south of the Marianas in Micronesia. The Truk

---
[74] The National WWII Museum

Atoll was now the Empire of Japan's main naval base in the South Pacific Theater. The next day, the 73rd Bomb Wing launched the first mission against Japan itself from bases in the Marianas, sending 111 B-29s out to attack the Nakajima Aircraft Company—now Subaru—in Tokyo. But the mission was a failure, damaging only 1 percent of the factory.

A gross understatement would be to say that the Marianas were not an ideal location from which to have an air base. Like the Solomons, they were hot and humid and suffered torrential rains and winds. Although meteorologists knew about the jet streams, for the first time, pilots ran into this fast stream of narrow air that moves north to south in both hemispheres, dividing the cold air from the Arctic from the hot air at the equator. Planes encounter it when they fly above 20,000 feet, and the jet stream circles the entire planet. On average, the air moves at about 110 miles per hour, but dramatic temperature difference between the warm and cool air masses can cause jet streams to move at up to 250 miles per hour or more.[75]

Prior to the B-29, planes had never flown that high. The jet stream retreats to the poles in the summer and then back toward the equator in the winter. This was January, and the jet stream was moving westward over Guam, slowing World War II bombers traveling to Japan. The only advantage the Marianas had was that they were islands from which the new B-29s could reach Japan.

Gen. Haywood Hansell was originally in charge of the 21st Bomber Command in the Marianas. He believed that strategic bombing of military installations, not cities and civilians, was the way to win the war. But as shown by the lack of success in trying to bomb Nakajima Aircraft Company, the theory was not working in practice from the Marianas for several reasons. First, the Norden Bombsight could not hit targets from 30,000 feet

---

[75] "When the Jet Stream Was the Wind of War." Archived from the original on 29 January 2016. Retrieved 9 December 2018.

(about the cruising altitude of a commercial jet) with any degree of accuracy. Even at the lower altitudes that Mac flew in Guadalcanal with the B-24s, accuracy was sometimes hit and miss. If planes flew lower, they would encounter the jet stream. Going under the jet stream in daylight would put them in range of the anti-aircraft artillery, which would be suicide. To bomb at night with any accuracy was impossible because the Norden worked only if the bombardier could see the target through the telescope. This strategy of trying to hit military installations clearly wasn't working in the Marianas, and the military brass decided a change in command might create a change in strategy.

They transferred Gen. Curtis LeMay to the 21st Bomber Command in January 1945 to replace Gen. Hansell. After assessing the results of his early raids from China and Hansell's in the Marianas, he decided that the *Superfortresses* would have to come in at night if they were to survive the mission, and they would need to use a new kind of explosive.[76]

---

[76] "Cold War: General Curtis LeMay, Father of the Strategic Air Command." ThoughtCo.

Chapter 40
The National Defense Research Committee

Back on June 27, 1940, a year and a half before the Japanese bombed Pearl Harbor, bringing us into the World War, Vannevar Bush, an electrical engineer and former president of MIT, was concerned that the U.S. was on the brink of war and was behind in the development of weapons of war. After conferring with other scientists, he met with President Franklin Roosevelt, and a new project was born. The president gave a group of scientists, which would later be called the National Defense Research Committee, the assignment to develop new weapons for the American military.

The most famous of these projects became known as the Manhattan Project, which had gotten its start in 1938 when German scientists Otto Hahn and Fritz Strassmann accidentally discovered nuclear fission. The scientists were trying to make uranium atoms with heavier nuclei. To do this, they used a device that shot neutrons at a sample of uranium. They hoped that at least a few uranium nuclei would gain one or more neutrons.

What they discovered was that there were new, lighter elements, such as barium and other elements, that were about half the mass of uranium, showing that atomic fission had occurred. Nuclear fission is the splitting of an atom into two or more atoms of a lower atomic weight. The difference in mass between the original atom and the smaller ones converts to energy. As Einstein taught us with his famous equation $E=mc^2$, a small amount of mass will convert to a large amount of energy. This is because of the huge energy potential that is bound up in an atomic nucleus.[77]

A few months after this discovery, Albert Einstein, a theoretical physicist, sent a letter to President Roosevelt warning him that Germany might try to build an atomic bomb. Einstein was Jewish and had settled in the U.S. after 1933 when Hitler came to power, becoming a U.S. citizen in 1940. It was imperative to Roosevelt that the U.S. beat the Germans to the punch.

In response, FDR formed another group called the Uranium Committee, which included top military and scientific experts to figure out the feasibility of a nuclear chain reaction.[78] They started the Manhattan Project, originally in an office in Manhattan, New York. By 1945, the Allies' Manhattan Project had produced two types of atomic bombs: a plutonium, implosion-type nuclear weapon called 'Fat Man,' and an enriched uranium, gun-type fission weapon called 'Little Boy.'

• • •

In 1942, a separate group of people under the National Defense Research Committee was working on a different way to destroy things—by burning. These men weren't physicists; they were chemists. Brilliant chemists, to be sure: a Nobel prize winner, the president of Standard Oil Development Company, and two professors—one from Harvard and one from MIT.

While experimenting, they learned of a strange occurrence at the DuPont Paint Company that piqued their interest. A compound called divinyl acetylene made paint catch on fire. At

---

[77] Wikipedia. "The Manhattan Project."
[78] Atomic Heritage Foundation.

Harvard, they began cooking up batches of the substance, and when someone put it on the windowsill, the mixture gradually changed from a liquid to a thick, viscous gel. They then discovered, after setting fire to it, that when burned, it did not become liquid but kept its sticky consistency. This suggested to them that if a bomb dropped them, it would scatter burning globs of sticky gel, adhering to whatever surface it landed on, and keep burning, transferring its radiation energy.

This was the birth of napalm.[79]

---

[79] Neer, Robert M. 2013. *Napalm: An American Biography*. Belknap Press.

Chapter 41
The Pacific War—1945

The war in Europe was essentially over, and the U.S. could now devote itself entirely to the Pacific Theater. The Empire of Japan was on the ropes but still fighting, refusing to surrender. Still awaiting the 39th BG, the small number of B-29s stationed in the Marianas continued to pound Japan and the surrounding islands.

Now under the direction of Gen. Curtis LeMay, who apparently was not hampered by the morality of firebombing civilians, the small number of B-29s stationed on the base in Guam began a campaign of incendiary napalm raids that started with the bombardment of Kobe on February 4, 1945. It peaked early with the most destructive bombing raid in human history (even considering the nuclear attacks on Hiroshima and Nagasaki). They conducted Operation Meetinghouse on the night of February 9th and into the 10th, hitting central Tokyo, destroying sixteen square miles, leaving about 100,000 civilians dead and over one million people homeless.[80]

Although capable of precision bombing at high altitudes, the *Superfortress* began dropping incendiary devices designed to start fires or destroy sensitive equipment from a mere 5,000 feet, eschewing the Norden Bombsight completely, firebombing the

---

[80] Long, Tony. 9 March 2011. "March 9, 1945: Burning the Heart Out of the Enemy." *Wired*.

Japanese capital, trying to break the will of the Axis power. They flew under the cover of darkness and had only a tail gunner for protection so that they could carry more napalm.

• • •

Toward the latter part of March, Mac, along with the rest of the 39th BG, began their departure from Smoky Hill, and after processing at Herington, Kansas, set out for the West Coast and the long flight over the Pacific to Hawaii, and then Guam, to join the other bomber groups in the Marianas. Mac's flight record shows that from Herington, he flew to Mather, California. Then, four days later, he flew ten hours to John Rodgers, in Honolulu, Hawaii.

After a brief, two-day rest, he and the crew left Hawaii and made a ten-hour and thirty-five-minute flight to Kwajalein in the Marshall Islands. Three days after that, he flew seven hours and landed in Guam on April 2, 1945. Mac was the lead crew commander and commanding officer of the 62nd Bomb Squadron. They were ready to end the war, once and for all.

On April 26, 1945, flying *Hell's Belle*, Mac flew his first combat mission from Guam against Kokubu Airfield, which the Japanese used for kamikaze attacks on American ships in Okinawa. Two days later, they hit Kushiro, another airfield. On their third strike, they once again returned to Kokubu. It was for this mission that the U.S. awarded Mac's entire crew the Distinguished Flying Cross—Mac's second.

"For extraordinary achievement while participating in aerial flight on 30 April 1945. These individuals were members of the B-29 aircraft that led the entire force of the 39th Bombardment Group in the highly successful strike from a base in the Marianas against Kokubu Airfield on the Japanese Island of Kyushu. Despite shattering barrages of heavy-caliber, anti-aircraft fire at the initial point and during the bombing run, these crew members maintained their plane exactly on the briefed

heading without evasive tactics. At the target, where flak was most highly concentrated, they released their bombs squarely in the center of the airfield. Bombing on the lead airplane, the remainder of the formation laid such an excellent pattern on the airfield and repair hangars that this important base was rendered completely inoperative. During the withdrawal, the formation they led destroyed six, probably destroyed four additional, and damaged nine of an estimated 30 enemy interceptors, which pressed repeated, vicious attacks until after the Japanese coast was left far behind. The gunners from this lead aircraft alone were credited with three damaged enemy ships. The courage and the fortitude displayed by these veterans of repeated assaults against the Japanese homeland, together with their outstanding professional skill in carrying out an important assignment, reflect great credit on themselves and the Army Air Force."

The mining of Japanese ports and shipping routes, carried out by B-29s beginning in April 1945, reduced Japan's ability to support its population by getting food supplies in and moving its troops. Bombing was now fast and furious. Mac and his crews flew thirty combat missions from Guam from April 26 until the end of the war.

• • •

Lowell Thomas, preeminent American radio commentator, explorer, lecturer, author, and journalist, visited Guam and interviewed Mac and others at Depot Field in June 1945. In his radio address, he stated:

"As you have no doubt heard, all the major cities of Japan have been knocked out by the B-29s. That is, the pictures and every raid, photographed in careful detail, show that the industries in those cities have been flattened, the docks knocked out, the rail centers smashed, and the populations have either fled or been wiped out.

"The lads I spent some hours with had just returned from the bombing of Shizuoka, an industrial center eighty-five miles southwest of Tokyo, on the coast between Yokohama and Nagoya, a city with a pre-war population of around a quarter of a million. Until this raid, it may have had as many as 400,000 people.

"The boys are still talking about the May 29th raid on Yokohama. One chap, who came in from this latest night run to Japan, is a Maj. Harold McNeese. 'Mac,' so I was told, could have any job in the air force that he wants, but all he wants to do is bomb Japan. Long ago, he finished a tour of fifty-six missions, in B-24s, in the Southeast Pacific, in the Solomons, New Guinea, and against the Japs at Rabaul. He said he hadn't run into any of the Jap suicide boys. That on the contrary, they seemed to prefer to live, so they play around, do barrel rolls off at a respectful distance. We don't yet know if airpower can win a war, but if the Mikado doesn't decide to call it a day, then these youngsters are prepared to go right on with their bombing until there isn't a city or a town of any size left in the Mikado's empire. Oh yes, our own losses on this latest raid? Out of more than 450 B-29s that flew north into the night, so far, all but two have returned. And now, so long, and all the way back to the NBC in New York."[81]

But still, the Japanese would not surrender.

---

[81] Radio address by Lowell Thomas.

Toasting the new Squadron Commander

Celebrating in Havana, Cuba

Major McNeese – 39th BG

B-29 Superfortress

City of Wilmington readying for mission to Tokyo

Crew of 41 on Hell's Belle – 1st mission from Guam

Major McNeese – 39th BG

B-29 Superfortress

B-29 Superfortress

Bombs over Tokyo

Bombing mission B-29 squadron

B-29 Superfortress

B-29 Superfortress

B-29 Superfortress

Flight Log

AUG 6 - HIROSHIMA; AUG 9 - NAGASAKI!

BREAKDOWN OF TRIP TIME INTO DESIRED CLASSIFICATIONS							REMARKS
TWIN ENG.		4-ENG.		HOODED INST.	NIGHT	LINK	ACTUAL INST.	ENTER IN THIS COLUMN ANY PERTINENT DETAILS OF THE FLIGHT OR OF WEATHER CONDITIONS ENCOUNTERED
1ST. P	CO P	1ST P	CP-GO
		2 15					SLO. TIME # H ENG.
		14 40			10 00		2 40 OGAKI, HONSHU (INCEND.)
		12 35	2 00		10 00		1 35 MITO, HONSHU (INCEND) PATHFINDER
		3 00					SLOW TIME #2 ENGINE — F.O. WILCOX
		15 10			10 00		2 10 MIKAGE, HONSHU (KOBE-OSAKA AREA) INCEND
		8 20					CHECK OUT LT. WESTON
		14 35			3 00		2 35 TOKYO DAY FORMATION (GP LEAD)
							ISESAKI (INCEND) LAST MISSION! WAR OVER
		7 30	7 35				TOKYO DAY FORMATION (SHOW OF STRENGTH)
		25					TEST HOP (LOST ONE ENG.)
			3 10				
		9 05	9 00		6 00		2 00 W/ MAJ LEE DISPLAY FORCE TO KOREA
		1 35	1 35				W/ "STRICLER
		1 15					TEST HOP
		7 50					
		87 35	23 20		39 00		11 00
		1550 45	2592 0	68 30	301 25		104 35
7 20	32 35	1638 20	2824 0	68 30	340 25	23 10	115 35

SEE SEMI-ANNUAL PAGES IN THE BACK OF BOOK AND READ THE INSTRUCTIONS FOR THEIR USE.

Flight Log

Guam is a step up from Guadalcanal

Rest and Recreation between missions

Chapter 42
Ending the War with Japan

With the war in Europe ended, it was time to end the war in the Pacific. With the completion of the atomic bombs, this entirely new weapon required an entirely new unit. They formed this U.S. Army Air Forces unit at Wendover Army Airfield, Utah, in December 1944. This group included flying squadrons that could operate the *Silverplate* versions of the B-29s, which were specifically designed to carry these nuclear weapons. These special bombers used a single, 33-foot bomb bay door in place of the usual four, 12-foot doors. They installed mounting points to allow for different types of bombs, nuclear isotopes, shapes, and firing mechanisms then under study in the Nevada desert. These specially equipped *Superfortresses* began deploying to Tinian in the Northern Marianas in May 1945 and waited patiently.

The Allies then called for the unconditional surrender of the Imperial Japanese Armed Forces in the Potsdam Declaration on July 26, 1945, with the alternative being "prompt and utter destruction." Japan ignored the ultimatum.[82]

President Harry Truman then appointed a Target Committee to decide which two cities would receive the 'Little Boy' and 'Fat Man' atomic bombings. They selected Hiroshima, a manufacturing center of some 350,000 people about 500 miles

---

[82] Wikipedia. "509 Operations Group.".

from Tokyo, as the first target. After arriving at the U.S. base on the Pacific Island of Tinian, they loaded the over 9,000-pound uranium-235 bomb aboard a *Silverplate* B-29 bomber christened *Enola Gay* (after the mother of its pilot, Col. Paul Tibbets). The plane left the base, traveled to its target, and dropped the bomb—known as 'Little Boy'—by parachute at 8:15 in the morning. It exploded 2,000 feet above Hiroshima in a mushroom-cloud blast equal to 12–15,000 tons of TNT, destroying five square miles of the city. Nagasaki was not their second choice originally. Instead, they had identified Kokura as the next target after Hiroshima. In Kokura, 130,000 people lived on the island of Kyushu, where the Japanese operated one of their biggest ordnance factories, manufacturing chemical weapons. The Americans knew all this but had not targeted the city earlier in their conventional bombing campaign. That was one reason the Target Committee thought it would be a good option after Hiroshima.

Nagasaki was an important port city about one hundred miles from Kokura. It was larger, with an approximate population of 263,000 people (about half the population of Wyoming), and had some major military facilities, including two Mitsubishi military factories. Like Kokura and Hiroshima, it also had suffered little from American conventional bombing, but it was the Target Committee's third choice.

After the bombing of Hiroshima on August 6th, ground workers on Tinian Island in the Marianas worked quickly to put the last changes on the 'Fat Man' bomb and prepare it for use. This was a plutonium implosion device of far greater complexity than the 'Little Boy' bomb used at Hiroshima, which used uranium-235 in a fairly conventional explosive mechanism. The scientists and ordnance experts at Los Alamos had agonized for years over how to use plutonium in an atomic weapon, and 'Fat Man' was the result.

The decision to use 'Fat Man' just days after the explosion of 'Little Boy' at Hiroshima was based on two factors: the always-changeable Japanese weather—the appearance of a typhoon or other major weather event could force deployment to be postponed for weeks—and the belief that two bombings following in quick succession would convince the Japanese that the Americans had plenty of atomic devices and were ready to keep using them until Japan finally surrendered. Reports of approaching bad weather convinced the Americans to drop the next bomb on August 9th.

A B-29 *Superfortress* named *Bock's Car* took off from Tinian Air Base at 3:47 that morning carrying 'Fat Man' in its belly, with the atomic bomb already armed. Maj. Charles W. Sweeney flew the plane, accompanied by the regular pilot, Capt. Frederick C. Bock. The *Enola Gay* also took part in the mission, flying weather reconnaissance.

As Kokura, their intended target, came into sight, clouds and smoke from nearby bombing raids obscured visibility. They could see parts of the city, but they could not sight directly on the arsenal that was their target. Air raid signals sounded below, and civilians ran for the shelters. Sweeney flew overhead until Japanese anti-aircraft fire and fighters made things "a little hairy," as a visual sighting of the target would be impossible. He then headed for his secondary target: the city of Nagasaki.

In Kokura, the civilians heard the all-clear, emerged from their shelters, and breathed sighs of relief. None of them knew then, of course, how close they had come to dying. The smoky clouds above had saved their lives and doomed the residents of Nagasaki.

Clouds also obscured Nagasaki, and Maj. Sweeney was running out of fuel, so he turned and was preparing to head toward Okinawa—which the U.S. had captured two months before in one of the bloodiest battles in the Pacific War—to refuel. At the last second, a hole opened in the clouds, however, and Bombardier Capt. Kermit K. Beahan calmly announced, "I can see the target."

So 'Fat Man' began its deadly trip down, detonating over Nagasaki at 11:02 a.m. local time, exploding at an altitude of 1,650 feet over the city with a yield of twenty-one kilotons, about 40 percent more powerful than 'Little Boy' had been. It did so almost directly above the Mitsubishi factories that were the primary targets, rather than over the residential and business districts farther south. Thankfully, Japan had already evacuated tens of thousands of civilians, especially children, from the city. The series of hills bracketing Nagasaki also somewhat confined the initial blast, forming a natural barrier and restricting the damage from spreading too far beyond.

"Still, the impact was devastating, particularly because people had heard the all-clear after an earlier aircraft raid warning and had left their shelters. It annihilated everything within a mile of ground zero. Fourteen thousand homes burst into flames instantly. The blast vaporized people close to it. Those unlucky enough to be just outside that radius received horrific, fatal burns, and farther out, radiation poisoning that would eventually kill them."[83]

In Hiroshima, when the bomb dropped, it killed around 80,000 people at once. In Nagasaki, three days later, the second bomb killed around 40,000 people instantly. Tens of thousands of others died in the aftermath of radiation poisoning and their injuries. They estimated that around 140,000 of Hiroshima's population of 350,000 (about half the population of Vermont) died because of the bombing, and that around 74,000 people were killed in Nagasaki. However, because of the massive destruction of the cities, the recorded death tolls are only estimates.[84]

Yet, even after this second atomic bombing, incredibly, the Japanese still did not surrender.

---

[83] Lengel, Edward G. Former Senior Director of Programs for the National WWII Museum's Institute for the Study of War and Democracy.
[84] Morris, Seren. August 3, 2020. "How Many People Died in Hiroshima and Nagasaki?" *Newsweek*.

Chapter 43
The Final Blow

During all this time, the U.S. insisted on unconditional surrender, with Americans controlling Japan. Faithful to the Bushido Code of Honor, most of Japan's military agreed they would rather die fighting than surrender. The emperor wanted to end the war, but an inside *coup d'état* was plotting to overthrow him and prevent him from surrendering.

Now the U.S. faced an enormous problem, especially since they did not know about the plan to overthrow the emperor. The U.S. did not have a third or fourth atomic bomb at the ready, but the Japanese had no way of knowing that, and many in the Japanese leadership feared we would wipe out the entire nation. Strangely, others in the leadership group welcomed that possibility. So strong was the cultural bias not to surrender that War Minister Korechika Anami actually posed a question to the decision-makers by asking if it would "not be wondrous for this whole nation to be destroyed like a beautiful flower."[85]

At the end of his rope, with the Japanese still dithering, President Truman gave the order: "Give 'em everything you've got." After nearly burning every city in Japan to the ground with the disastrous firebombing with napalm, and then two horrible atomic attacks destroying two cities, President Truman felt they

---

[85] Coffey, Thomas M. 1970. *Imperial Tragedy, Japan in World War II, the First Days and the Last.* New York: World Publishing Co.

had waited long enough for Japan to surrender. They were going to have to force their hand.

• • •

According to LeMay himself in his memoirs: "Our B-29s went to Yawata on August 8th and burned up 21 percent of the town, and on the same day, some other B-29s went to Fukuyama and burned up 73.3 percent. Still, there wasn't any gasp and collapse, even after the second nuclear bomb went down above Nagasaki on August 9th. We kept on flying."

Damage to these areas ranged from 25 percent in Osaka to 43 percent in Nagoya. The *Superfortresses* destroyed half of the aircraft industry in those areas. They burned sixty-four other cities to the ground. The attacks decimated most large Japanese cities and crippled Japan's war industries.

Next, they scheduled a large B-29 raid to destroy the last remaining oil refinery in Akita, Japan. On August 14, 1945, a strike force of 134 B-29 *Superfortress* bombers from the USAAF 315th Bombardment Wing launched a major bombing attack on the coastal part of the city of Akita.[86] The bombers arrived over their target without opposition at 10:30 p.m. and dropped 7,360 100-kg and 4,687 50-kg bombs, with the final bomber leaving the target area at 3:30 on the morning of August 15th. The bombs eradicated the oil refinery belonging to Nippon Oil (the current JX Nippon Oil & Energy Co.) and adjacent port facilities, and the resulting fire spread to the neighboring town.[87]

As the first bomb group left the target, Mac and his crew, along with forty-one other planes, left the runway at 5:40 p.m. With negotiations still going on between the Allies and Japan, the general feeling among the flight crews was that the mission

---

[86] Carter, Kit C., and Robert Mueller. 1991. *U.S. Army Air Forces in World War II: Combat Chronology, 1941–1945*. Center for Air Force History.
[87] *Archived copy.*" Archived from the original on 2013-06-06. Retrieved 2013-10-20. Japanese government site.

might be called off. They planned to recall the bombers en route to their target if the war had ended by Japan's surrender, but no instructions came. Mac and the other pilots continued to target, arriving with no opposition from enemy aircraft, and flak from the ground was minimal and weak. The 39th BG dropped the first bombs at 2:04 a.m. on the town of Isesaki, with no battle damage or injuries to any of the B-29 *Superfortresses* or their crews.

Whereas the two atomic bombs hadn't, these two bombings finally solidified the decision for Japan. Hours later, having survived the coup, Emperor Hirohito finally prevailed. He went on the air and gave a recorded radio address across the Empire on August 15th called the Jewel Voice Broadcast. On it, he announced the surrender of Japan to the Allies. This marked the end—not just to World War II, but to fifteen years of Japan's military rampage across Asia.

President Truman's announcement that the war was finally over came just as Mac and his crew, among the first of the B-29s to return, were touching down on the runway from Isesaki.[88] What exhilarating and welcome news that must have been as they climbed out of *Hell's Belle*, knowing they had made their last combat mission. The war was finally over.

• • •

Mac and the members of the 39th Bombardment Group received the Air Medal (Oak Leaf Cluster):

By direction of the President, under the provisions of Executive Order No. 9158: For meritorious achievement while participating in aerial flights as combat crew member in successful combat missions against the Japanese Empire. All missions were flown under rapidly changing and oftentimes adverse weather conditions. The flights were subjected to enemy anti-aircraft fire and fighter opposition. There were constantly present, difficult navigational problems, prolonged periods

---

[88] 39th Bomber Group-org missions.

of physical and mental strain, and undaunted by the many hazards faced regularly and continuously, each crew member displayed such courage and skill in the performance of his duty as to reflect great credit on himself and the Army Air Force.

View from above

Chapter 44
The Closing Ceremony—Victory over Japan

The official end of the war in the Pacific was quite a different event compared to the one in Europe. Gen. Dwight D. Eisenhower, who wanted an informal, dignified surrender, didn't even attend the signing in a small, dimly lit French schoolhouse in the middle of the night on May 7, 1945.

Gen. Douglas MacArthur, on the other hand, preferred a massive production to conclude the war with Japan. His view was that in the name of honor, the end of this horrible war should be a lesson for the ages. Under the glaring spotlight, with the entire world watching, he wanted the United States to put on an extravagant display of power and domination. This was a historic event, and he desired a flawless performance worthy of this immense accomplishment. Gen. MacArthur decided that the formal surrender should take place on the 45,000-ton battleship USS *Missouri* in the Tokyo Bay, six miles away from the city, on September 2, 1945.

"Swab the decks and get the brass shining like your mother's best cook pot," shouted the chief warrant officer. They threw the entire crew of the *Missouri* into a flurry of unaccustomed activity. Hardened combat leaders, exhausted from nonstop battle, now found themselves acting as theater directors, scrubbing and polishing everything on board the ship. The officers in charge decided where the cast of thousands—Marines and sailors scheduled to be in attendance—would stand and move around, choreographed like performers on a stage. This would also include the position and needs of 225 news reporters and 75 photographers. It was a tremendous undertaking, every bit as complex as a Broadway opening.

The orchestration of this performance also involved hundreds of dignitaries and documents. They commandeered four U.S. destroyers to shuttle the VIPs to the USS *Missouri* and back. Someone commented that next to this elaborate pageant, a royal wedding would have looked like a junior high school play.

Among the military, there were two schools of thought. For most of the Allied top brass, this formality was the culmination of the greatest conflict the world had ever known. It was a day destined to appear in every history book for centuries, and most of them agreed with MacArthur about the need for pomp and ceremony. However, for many of the rank and file, this production, orchestrated by generals and admirals in their stuffy, starched, white shirts and metal-ladened chests, was way over the top. They just wanted to go home.

One thing was for certain—the United States was now, unquestionably, the big dog on the block. To put a sharp point on this, MacArthur barged into Tokyo Bay with an armada of 258 combat ships, showcasing the American forces on full display.

The general, an avid student of military history, wanted to create a powerful scene for the closing act of this war. In centuries past, victors of war forced their defeated enemies to walk under a structure, symbolizing a yoke. With their hands tied, they led prisoners under a wooden arch used to subjugate oxen or, later, an arch formed by Roman spears. This showed the transition from warrior to slave, or winner to defeated. MacArthur planned his own version of this symbolic transition. He would not tie the Japanese's hands, of course, but he would create an arch of weapons over their heads that had turned Japan's cities to ashes—not swords, but American warplanes.

Gen. MacArthur wanted to blacken the sky with squadrons of American warplanes at the exact moment the two countries signed the surrender documents. He imagined it would invoke a powerful image. This would not only serve as a warning to other nations that the U.S. was the world's only nuclear superpower, but they also hoped that it would quell any hope of resistance by the Japanese. The cast of planes would be aircraft from both the U.S. Army Air Forces and Navy, and the B-29 *Superfortresses* would be the stars of the show.

Getting the navy planes to the Tokyo Bay would be simple. They were already there, aboard America's thirty-eight aircraft carriers that were milling about close by. They had been roaming around the eastern coastline of Japan for months, launching sporadic attacks on Japanese cities. After the fighting stopped, they helped locate and deliver supplies to POW camps.

But for the Army Air Forces, getting the B-29s to the location from the Marianas was slightly more difficult. These planes had been pivotal in the devastation of the Japanese cities and had delivered the atomic bombs that ended the war. These were the planes that MacArthur wanted to showcase on the world stage. He was also interested in impressing the Soviet delegation in attendance with hundreds of long-range *Superfortesses* streaming overhead in a seemingly endless procession.

The problem was not only that the five bomb wings operating B-29s from Guam were based over 1,500 miles away, but the *Superfortress* crews knew, better than anyone, that just flying these bombers was often a dangerous undertaking. Incredibly, the average B-29 crewman was much more likely to die in an accident or a mechanical failure than from enemy action. Long, over-water missions in wartime were one thing, many thought, but flying them for show was something else entirely.

They had lived through the war. They had survived months of combat, undertaking white-knuckle takeoffs, avoiding Japanese flak and fighters, and perhaps sweating out an emergency landing or two. It was shaping up to be the most crowded airspace on the planet, and they were not excited about it. This would not be a single formation, but rather, hundreds of planes packed tightly together. What if the plane failed and their number came up?

Some pilots made the trip purely to get another mission credited, since the war technically was not over until the very moment that they signed the surrender documents. The opportunity to fly over Japan once more drew others. They wanted to see, in daylight, the destruction the bombers had created since they had flown most of the missions at night and hadn't dawdled at the time to assess the damage.

For someone like Lt. Col. Thomas R. Vaucher, the 462nd Bombardment Group's operations officer, the mission was not optional. He had led a B-29 raid to Yokohama months before and was now chosen to wrangle the massive group of heavy bombers for their final mass flight. Four of the five wings would take part in the 'display of power' over the *Missouri*. The fifth wing's mission was to drop supplies to POW camps.

For Maj. Harold 'Mac' McNeese, it would never have occurred to him not to make that last flight. As lead crew commander and commanding officer of the 62nd Bomb Squadron, he had led twenty combat missions from Guam over the past four months. As they signed the final peace document, he would now proudly do a flyover, regardless of the risk. This would be his final 'mission,' and for him, it would be a gratifying last curtain call.

The tricky part was that it had been quite some time—if ever—since any of the bombers had flown in a tight parade formation, let alone in front of nearly every VIP in the hemisphere. That hundreds of navy airplanes would also fly through at the same time made the B-29 pilots slightly uneasy.

To arrive at the appointed time, the takeoffs would begin in darkness, at 2:01 a.m. After the long flight from Guam, the roughly 465 B-29s were to join up near Japan's coastline and be prepared to fly in formation by 8:33 a.m. They would raise the curtain of this grand pageant at 9:08 a.m., just as Japan signed the documents.

In order to create the illusion of thousands of planes in the air, they directed the bombers to fly in a huge clockwise rectangle, making it seem to the viewers below that there were twice as many B-29s in the air. Creating this massive illusion, they expected them to cruise in that pattern until 11:30 a.m., or until they were down to less than 600 gallons of fuel, whichever came first.

With all the careful planning and preparation, there were a couple of things even MacArthur could not control. First, the weather was terrible. Surely, clouds would obscure the B-29s at their planned altitudes of 8,000 to 14,000 feet, so the army dropped them down to 3,000 feet. The navy split the difference, tensely planning to thread their 349 *Hellcats, Corsairs, Helldivers,* and *Avengers* through at 1,500 feet, making the whole spectacle that much more dangerous. This compacted the airspace and squeezed the hundreds of planes closer together.

Second, because of the long distance they had to travel, many of the B-29s arrived early and flew over Japan to assess, in daylight, the damage they had done. This made them late to the rendezvous point to get into formation. They were supposed to make the big, dramatic entrance at exactly 9:08 a.m. when they signed the documents, but at the scheduled time, the group hadn't arrived.

At 9:25 a.m., after the Japanese had signed documents and were preparing to leave, MacArthur announced, "These proceedings are now closed." He then grabbed Adm. Halsey's shoulder and whispered, "Bill, where the hell are those airplanes?"[89]

From his autobiography, *Reminiscences*, MacArthur described what happened next: "At that moment, the skies parted, and the sun shone brightly through the layers of clouds. There was a steady drone above, and now it became a deafening roar, and an armada of airplanes paraded into sight, sweeping over the warships. It was over." August 15, 1945 was called VJ Day (Victory over Japan).

Mac and all the war-weary troops had accomplished their mission. And they had survived incredible odds. They could now finally go home.

---

[89] A look inside the WWII surrender ceremony: "My job was to make sure we did not screw up," by Jennie Jarvie. Sept. 2, 2015.

Chapter 45
The Aftermath of the War

World War II lasted almost six years and was the deadliest military conflict in history. Historians and mathematicians dispute the actual death toll, but one estimate finds 70–85 million people perished, or about three percent of the estimated 2.3 billion people on Earth in 1940.[90] Of course, this doesn't consider the tremendous emotional toll and grief felt by families of the dead. For every death, heartbreak and trauma spreads out like ripples in a pond after a skipped stone, affecting countless others. There were millions wounded as well. Their lives and the lives of their loved ones would forever change.

Like Humpty Dumpty, the broken world tried to put itself back together. But unlike Mr. Dumpty, they were successful, but it took time. After Japan formally surrendered, the Allied Forces at once moved in to occupy the country. The occupation lasted for seven years, during which the Allies implemented several reforms. These included the abolition of the Japanese imperial system, introducing democracy, and the prosecution of war criminals. Emperor Hirohito portrayed himself as a powerless constitutional monarch. Many scholars, however, believe he played a highly active role in the war effort. But they marginalized the emperor after Japan surrendered in 1945, and

---

[90] U.S. Census Bureau.

he became just a figurehead with no real political power. The Allies arrested Prime Minister Tojo, who had been responsible for the attack on Pearl Harbor, which started the war between Japan and the United States. They sentenced him to death for Japanese war crimes and hanged him on December 23, 1948.[91]

Japan had initially emerged from the war as a defeated, occupied nation, with its economy and infrastructure in ruins. Yet in the years that followed, the country underwent a remarkable transformation, rebuilding its economy and becoming a major global power. It is today a thriving parliamentary democracy.

• • •

To avert a future world war, the Allied Powers created the United Nations for international cooperation and diplomacy. The members agreed to outlaw future wars of aggression. When they founded the United Nations in 1945, some 750 million people—nearly a third of the world's population—lived in territories that depended on colonial powers. Colonialism, or the aggressive occupation and usurpation of another country's resources, largely drove the Second World War. The wave of decolonization, which changed the face of the planet, began with the U.N. and represents the world body's first outstanding success. The United Kingdom granted independence to India, Indonesia from the Netherlands, and the Philippines from the U.S. Because of decolonization, many territories became independent and joined the U.N. Today, there are only seventeen non-self-governing territories remaining in the world, and fewer than two million people live in them.[92]

Years of war and relentless bombing had also economically devastated the European-based Allies, which also formed an

---

[91] Graff, Cory. *Air and Space* magazine.
[92] Wikipedia. United Nations.

economic alliance, then called the European Coal and Steel Community, that later developed into the European Economic Community and ultimately evolved into the current European Union (E.U.). This provided a common market for important natural resources.

• • •

For the United States, even though the war lasted less than four years, World War II was the costliest war in American history. Adjusted for inflation, the war cost more than $4 trillion in today's money, and defense spending accounted for over 40 percent of GDP in 1945, the war's last year. Almost half of everything produced in the U.S. during that time fed the enormous, hungry war monster.

However, without having to rebuild bombed-out cities, life in the U.S. quickly returned to normal for most people. Approximately 420,000 Americans lost their lives, and countless more returned wounded and disabled. The men who came home were eager to marry, buy homes, and go to work. Women started families. The automobile industry successfully converted back from war planes to producing cars, and new industries, such as aviation and electronics, grew like flowers in springtime.

Stimulated by affordable mortgages, the returning military began buying homes, creating a housing boom that offered employment to all the trades. The jump in post-war births, known as the 'baby boom,' expanded the number of consumers. Increasing numbers of Americans joined the middle class. And at least for the next decade—the 1950s—most families were traditional and intact. Mothers overwhelmingly stayed home to raise children, and dads went to work.

But seeds of change had been planted and sprouted like sunflowers in the summer. The strict roles society had previously assigned to women and men were forever obliterated. War, like a puff of wind scattering dandelion seeds on a fertile lawn, had blown men far away and women into the workplace, most for the first time.

Many women had tasted the freedom of working and earning a paycheck and never again wanted to be assigned to static roles of mother and housewife. Many encouraged their daughters to be independent and to get an education. Choice was the new watchword, and their daughters would lead the Women's Liberation Movement in the 1960s. In addition, the Civil Rights Movement and America's full involvement in the Vietnam War would all have a major impact on that turbulent decade.

• • •

Vietnam, half a world away, was still struggling to free itself from the yoke of French colonization after years of fighting. The tensions would embroil Mac and his family personally. And later, all of America would be involved in Vietnam's war, which would claim over fifty-eight thousand American lives.

Part 2

Chapter 46
The Returning Hero

When Mac returned to his base in California after the war, he visited his good friend Gene Perraud, whom he had known in Chicago and who was now living in Los Angeles. He had met Gene's beautiful cousin, Jerrie, four years earlier when she was a sixteen-year-old high school student. Now at twenty, after finishing a year at UCLA, followed by a year at the University of Mexico, she had blossomed into a vivacious, young woman who modeled part time and was a joy to be around.

Mac was twenty-seven and was as smitten by this smoldering beauty as she was with the handsome, young war hero her cousin had told her so many glowing stories about. They dated, were inseparable, and quickly fell in love. Shortly thereafter, they married, and Jerrie, who had aspired to be a movie star, instead settled down to fulfill her role as wife of an officer and a gentleman. She became pregnant almost immediately, and I entered the world barely nine months later.

With the Army Air Forces now evolving into a new and separate services branch, Mac joined the newly named U.S. Air Force when they formed it on September 18, 1947, and we moved to Davis-Monthan Air Force Base in Tucson, Arizona, where he continued to serve with the 20th Air Force as a flight instructor.

After a year, the Army Air Forces assigned him to the Pentagon, and we moved to suburban Falls Church, Virginia, just outside of Washington, DC. He began taking night classes, and in 1950, he graduated from Georgetown University with a Bachelor of Science degree in Foreign Service. It had been almost a decade and a world war separating his freshman and senior years.

• • •

That same year, 1950, when I was two and a half years old, the Korean War broke out, when North Korea, supported by communist China and the Soviet Union, invaded South Korea, which the Allied Powers backed. When World War II ended, the forces of the Soviet Union occupied the Korean Peninsula in the North and Americans in the South. The country split at the 38th parallel, and the two sides established their own government, both wanting to reunite under their own preferred form.

The U.S. was operating under the Domino Theory—if one country fell to the communists, the surrounding countries would tumble like a cascade of dominos stacked closely together. With Chinese supplies and Soviet support, North Korea looked ready to push the defenders of South Korea into the ocean and take over the entire country. But the United Nations swung into action and passed U.N. Resolution 83, which called for military aid to South Korea to instead push North Korea back up to the 38th parallel. Reinforcements from mainland United States arrived by September, and the Communists found themselves outnumbered.

At the start of the Korean War, the U.S. Air Force promoted Mac to lieutenant colonel and assigned him to be the director of air training for the 20th Air Force. He was in charge of training programs, ensuring that new pilots would learn to fly the latest and most powerful new war machines. These included not only the old B-29 *Superfortress* prop planes, but many new bombers and fighter jets that, for the first time, would be used in a war.

Air forces from the nascent U.S. Air Force and the U.S. Navy wreaked havoc on North Korean infrastructure and transportation capabilities. The war lasted for three years, when finally, an armistice was negotiated.[93]

There were approximately three million war fatalities, and the war destroyed virtually all of Korea's major cities. There were thousands of massacres by both sides, including the mass killing of tens of thousands of suspected communists by the South Korean government, and the torture and starvation of prisoners of war by the North Koreans. North Korea became among the most heavily bombed countries in history. A total of 6.8 million American men and women served during the Korean War period, and there were 54,200 deaths of Americans in service.[94] At the end of the fighting, except for the death and destruction, nothing had changed. Today, North Korea remains staunchly communist and South Korea a democracy.

• • •

I close my eyes and transport myself back to those days in the early 1950s when I was four to seven years old. My earliest memories of Dad are from this time. We were a *Leave It to Beaver*-style 1950s family ensconced in a comfortable, two-story, three-bedroom, red brick home set back on a quiet, unpaved street in Falls Church, Virginia. The homes were on large lots with lush, green lawns. Tall oak trees that surrounded the neighborhood houses seemed to extend their arms to embrace the neighborhood children as we climbed their lofty branches. Here was where my sister Cathe, born one month before my fourth birthday, and I experienced the next few years of our childhood. These were happy, carefree days.

---

[93] Millett, Allan R. "Korean War." *Encyclopedia Britannica*. 30 Nov. 2022. https://www.britannica.com/event/Korean-War. Accessed 10 March 2023.
[94] Fisher, Max. 3 August 2015. "Americans Have Forgotten What We Did to North Korea." Vox. Retrieved 18 October 2021.

Dad drove to the Pentagon each day, in charge of training pilots for another war that was in progress half a world away, and Mother settled into her role as homemaker. Her only escape and link with her desire for fame and recognition was a part-time job as the host of a children's cable show called *Do You Wonder*. On weekends, our household, which always included dogs and cats, would expand when she brought home various exotic animals destined to star in the weekly, black-and-white television show. Our house seemed to suck in neighborhood children like a Hoover vacuum cleaner. Dad loved large-breed dogs and went with each one of ours to obedience school to ensure that they followed his commands and were well mannered. Mother wasn't fussy about training. She embraced all animals as they were, and the stranger the better.

Children in this quiet neighborhood were like nymphs in an enchanted forest where we played hide-and-seek in the trees, tag on the front lawns, and marbles and jacks on the driveways. Our dogs chased happily after us, untethered by leashes, frequently running underfoot, knocking us down onto the freshly mowed lawns. In summers, we ate breakfast on the screened-in porch on the side of the house, and we celebrated birthday parties in the late summer each year surrounded by giggling friends as we played pin the tail on the donkey and musical chairs. The oscillating sprinkler attached to the hose in the front yard beckoned the neighborhood children to don their bathing suits and romp like animated cherubs in a fountain.

Like most young children probably, I had no idea what my dad did during the day. As far as I knew, he disappeared to 'an office' in the morning and magically reappeared for dinner in the evening. At 5'10" and 180 lbs., he was of average height and weight, but he stood ramrod straight and looked imposing and so handsome in the dark, aviator sunglasses and the uniform he wore every day to work.

As I ran to greet him, he picked me up in a giant bear hug and twirled me around him with my legs flying straight out like a carnival swing. He smelled of smoke and shaving lotion. Scrunching my nose, I rubbed the top of his head, brushing the bristly crew cut. As he put me down on the ground, he looked at me with feigned horror and said sternly, "Be careful, Sherry, you'll mess up my hair."

Dad was a prolific reader, and books filled his study and our lives. "If you like to read, you will never be bored, and you can magically transport yourself anywhere, my dear," Dad told me as he opened Rudyard Kipling's *Just So Stories*. "Let's go to India today," he said as I curled up into his reading chair next to him, "and find out why leopards have spots and elephants have long noses, and of course, the burning question of why are cats such jerks?" he said.

With great dramatic flair, Dad read aloud Kipling's poem of *Gunga Din*. In the final three lines, the soldier regrets the abuse and scorn he had so long inflicted on the dying water boy. In the last line he intones, "You're a better man than I am, Gunga Din," (meaning character is not determined by status in life but by deed). Dad and I often repeated that line to each other over the years when either of us did something noteworthy, pointing at the other in appreciation. We read Kipling's story of "Rikki-Tikki-Tavi," the brave mongoose who defends his friends and home against their enemy, the cobras.

By example and teaching through books and stories, Dad taught me about traits and habits worth nurturing and developing, like courage, character, and honesty. There were always morals to the story, lessons to be learned, and glorious adventures to be enjoyed. He was the consummate teacher, and I was his curious, eager student.

Dad had a great sense of humor and introduced me to the poetry of Robert W. Service. Sitting on the couch with ankles crossed, I listened intently to him read aloud. I would howl with laughter at "Bessie's Boil," voiced by him in a cockney accent. There was also great adventure in many of Service's poems, and it was a thrill to experience the dangers and ironic happenstances the characters found themselves in while in the Yukon wilderness. "The Ballad of the Ice-Worm Cocktail," "The Shooting of Dan McGrew," and "The Cremation of Sam McGee" were among our favorites. These stories inspired my imagination and beckoned me to read more, like a mythical siren calling to a lonely sailor.

• • •

Fall began the holiday season with birthdays, Halloween, and Thanksgiving. By mid-December, Dad would take us to the Christmas tree lot to pick out an enormous tree that reached the ceiling. Then Mom would supervise the decorating with lights and ornaments and tinsel. Anticipation of the magical arrival of Santa, who would slide down the chimney with bags full of toys, began. On Christmas Eve, we'd leave out cookies and milk for the big guy and carrots for the reindeer, then hurry to bed.

"It's Christmas," I shouted at the sleepy adults as I burst into their bedroom. "Get up. Let's go see what Santa brought us." Dad had been up late assembling the bikes and dollhouses and would have liked a few more 'winks,' as he called it, but dutifully, if not entirely cheerfully, got up at my urging. He pulled a dark-blue, terry-cloth robe over his pajamas and fastened it with a belt around his waist. Then he slid his toes into his brown bedroom slippers, looked at me, and pointed at the bathroom, where Mother was getting ready.

"Hurry, Mother," I yelled to her as she brushed her teeth and threw cold water on her face. She pulled back her hair and twisted it into a ponytail. "Come on," I said as she swirled a silk robe around her nightgown. I pulled on their hands, leading them to the top of the stairs, urging them forward. Mom held Cathe, and together, we started cautiously down the stairs.

"I don't think Santa was here last night," Dad said. "I didn't hear anything. Maybe Mrs. Santa was angry and didn't let him leave the North Pole. Maybe Rudolph was sick." Knowing my father's penchant for teasing, I was not the least bit fooled or worried.

I ran down the stairs, and as I peered around the corner, my eyes opened wide with wonder. In the corner of the living room stood the giant fir tree, sparkling with tinsel and lights. It looked like an enormous, dazzling cornucopia, spilling gifts out into the middle of the room. There was a jumble of boxes covered in tinfoil, and brightly covered wrapping paper with ribbons splayed out in a sea of color and texture.

I jumped on the painted, wooden rocking horse and marveled at the large dollhouse. There was a bright-blue bike, complete with training wheels, and a special doll for each of us. Santa had brought the unwrapped gifts, and the beautifully decorated boxes were from Mother and Dad. We took turns opening each gift and giving hugs and kisses as Cathe and I jumped in the wrapping paper after we tore it to shreds and wadded it up into balls of color.

Mac and Jerrie marry

Happy in Los Angeles

Sherry joins the family

Tucson, AZ

Chapter 47
Falls Church, Virginia, 1951–1955

"Dinner's almost ready," Mom called from the kitchen one evening. "Come help me set the table, Sherry." Dad closed the book we were reading, and I slid down from his lap and ran to assist her. Dad picked up the newspaper, lit another cigarette, and sipped his martini. Cathe, now a toddler, was playing with her dolls on the floor while our Dalmatian, Yankee, napped under Dad's feet.

I carefully placed the knives and spoons on the right and forks on the left, with folded, cloth napkins planted underneath each fork. I put a glass in front of each plate and brought out the salt, pepper, butter, rolls, and water pitcher.

As we took our seats around the dining room table, with Cathe in her highchair next to us, I put my napkin in my lap. "Sit up straight, Sherry. Lean over your plate and bring your fork up to your mouth vertically and then horizontally, like this," Dad instructed me, demonstrating the delicate, right-angle maneuver. "That's why they call it a square meal. And," he added, "for heaven's sake, pull your elbows in, Sherry. You eat like a snare drummer."

Looking down at a plate of stew Mother set before him—a jumble of meat, potatoes, and vegetables—Dad wrinkled his nose, bent close to me with his hand covering his mouth in a gentle aside, and asked in a conspiratorial whisper, "Do I, or did

I?" meaning, do I eat this, or did I already eat this and threw it up? This always evoked the intended giggles from me.

There were never any arguments, but Dad encouraged debate, and we discussed news of the day.

"Now, Sherry," he said, opening his eyes wide and cocking his head at me, "how was school today?"

"Good," I said, slinking down a bit in my seat. "Miss Ross moved me to the Bluebirds reading group," I said a little too loudly. I thought this would impress him immensely, since everyone knew the Bluebirds were the highest reading group in the first grade.

"Miss Ross reprimanded her at school today," my mother said, "and sent her to the principal's office for talking too much during class, and then talking back to her."

Dad looked at me sternly, his lips pinched in a clear sign of disapproval. I knew what was coming. Dad solemnly meted out all punishment for transgressions after dinner.

"May I be excused from the table?" I tried hopefully, not wanting to delve further into the subject that I felt would only serve to increase my punishment.

"No, you may not," Dad replied. "Not until you've eaten your vegetables and Mother and I have finished our meal." After what I thought to be an inordinate amount of time, he wiped his mouth, rubbed his stomach, and said rather nonsensically, "I feel more like I do now than I did then. Thanks, Jerrie." He looked at me, and I puzzled over this odd phrase, repeating it, trying to make sense of it. Then, bringing me out of my deep thoughts, he pushed back his chair and held out his hand. "Now you may be excused," he said, and led me down the hall to my bedroom like a prisoner on her way to solitary, my eyes downcast.

It was always the same scene and the same script. Dad sat next to me on the bed and looked incredibly sad and disappointed. He rehashed my crimes and elicited from me an apology and a promise to do better in the future. Then, he motioned for me to 'assume the position.' I lay over his lap, white undies lowered to expose my pink and soon-to-be red rear end.

As I silently repeated the words that I knew by heart right along with him, he began, "Sherry, you know I would cut off my right arm for you. This is going to hurt me more than it is going to hurt you." Then he delivered five or six hard whacks with the palm of his hand. I was dubious that the words were completely true, but I understood his meaning. I had let Dad down. He did not deliver the spanking in anger. I had committed a rule infraction, and this was the consequence. Bad choices sometimes have painful consequences.

Those times were thankfully few. Most often, Dad's green eyes sparkled with humor. He loved to tell jokes and had the Irish gift of storytelling. "Shaggy Dog" stories were a favorite.

"Wow, is your dog actually playing chess?" the man asked the farmer. *"He must be the smartest dog in the world!"*

"Oh, he ain't so smart," the farmer drawled. *"I beat him two out of three games."*

• • •

"Time for your bath, girls," Mother called out around seven o'clock each evening. It was always annoying to stop playing with my Betsy Wetsy dolls or dressing paper dolls and shift gears into the bedtime ritual, but I didn't hesitate long.

"Coming!" I called back, grabbing Cathe's hand and leading her upstairs. Mother ran a bath, and Cathe and I soaked and washed, our hair rinsed under the faucet until it was squeaky clean. After toweling off, we brushed our teeth, put on our pj's, and hopped into our beds, ready for Dad to regale us with a bedtime story. Usually, it was an episode of *Tarzan of the Apes* that he made up on the spot and always ended it with a cliffhanger. We eagerly looked forward to the next 'chapter' the following night, like a modern-day Netflix series.

"Sweet dreams, sleep tight, and don't let the bedbugs bite," Dad said, then kissed us lightly on our foreheads before leaving the room.

When it was Mother's turn, she sat on one of our beds and sang lullabies and other songs, or recited nursery rhymes or read stories to us. The night ended by saying our prayers. "Dear God, hear and bless the beasts and singing birds. And guard with tenderness small things that have no words. God bless my mother, my father, my sister …" Then we were allowed just a sip of water to 'wet our whistles' and ended with a kiss good night. Mother switched off the lights, and we drifted into a blissful slumber.

Falls Church, VA

Falls Church, VA

Falls Church, VA

Mimi visits

Dad with Stormy and Jezabel

Chapter 48
Mac Appointed Air Attaché—French Indochina

It is hard for me to picture my dad without a book, newspaper, or magazine in his hands. He was either learning about something or reading for pleasure. But, if he was sitting, he was reading. A cigarette smoldered in the ashtray on the coffee table beside him, and his martini glass with two olives sat next to the ashtray. I would frequently read with him, and he would welcome my questions or observations without irritation for the interruption from a perpetually curious youngster.

Sometimes, he was studying. He received a master's degree in government from George Washington University and was inducted into the Pi Gamma Mu Honor Society in 1955. This is the oldest and preeminent honor society for the social sciences, extending membership to business administration, education, cultural and area studies, public administration, and organizational behavior.[95]

That same year brought another promotion. The U.S. Air Force selected him to be the air attaché for Saigon, Laos, and Cambodia to replace the current attaché, who would be leaving in 1956.

The United States had long had a vital interest in these three countries, which were formerly called French Indochina from

---

[95] Wikipedia.org/pigammamu.

the time France declared them a colony in the mid-1800s. U.S. involvement with Vietnam began as far back as 1942, when Japan occupied the country during WWII. In September 1945, shortly after the war ended, U.S. Army Air Forces' P-38s flew over as Ho Chi Minh, the new president, declared Vietnamese independence. USAAF planes had flown aid to Ho Chi Minh and his group of Vietcong guerrillas and carried some French authorities, who were still hoping to reestablish France's colonial claim on Indochina.[96]

Ho Chi Minh, an avowed communist, had become president of the Democratic Republic of Vietnam (North Vietnam) in 1945 after WWII, and while free of Japanese occupation, he wanted the whole country to be independent and free of French rule, which they kept in the south. Ho Chi Minh was a formidable leader and had been the head of the Vietnamese nationalist movement for nearly three decades.

Although full-scale fighting broke out between the French and the communist-affiliated Viet Minh at the end of 1946, the United States didn't begin its more substantial engagement in the region until 1950, after China had fallen to the communists under the leadership of Mao Tse-tung.[96]

In an effort to prevent the further spread of communism, the USAF delivered the first military aid to the French in South Vietnam in 1950, and over the next four years, the United States loaned France its entire fleet of aircraft. USAF officers and enlisted airmen served in Saigon through the U.S. Military Assistance Advisory Group (MAAG) from the time they established it in 1950, as did the men who were assigned as air attachés to the U.S. Embassy in Saigon.

The U.S. began extensively helping the French in their fight to keep Indochina their colony, as then-President Harry Truman was fearful of worldwide communist militancy. He approved a National Security Council memorandum that proclaimed that

---

[96] https://media.defense.gov/2019/feb/22. Wikipedia. "The History of the Vietnam War."

former French Indochina was a key region, and the United States would provide support against any communist aggression. To back it up, Truman authorized fifteen million dollars in military aid to the French.

By 1953, the USAF stationed mechanics in Vietnam to service the planes they had donated, in numbers that grew to nearly 500 airmen by the time Dien Bien Phu fell and North Vietnam defeated the French, in May 1954. By this time, Americans were providing 80 percent of all war supplies used by France.

The French had tried for years to beat back Ho Chi Minh's encroaching army following WWII. Having lost the political will of the French people, they conceded defeat. French Indochina, for all intents and purposes, no longer existed. Vietnam, Laos, and Cambodia became three separate countries, each struggling to set up their own system of government, and the United States was interested and concerned about the type of governments they intended to set up. President Truman and the U.S. government still believed firmly in the domino theory. U.S. leaders were determined to prevent the spread of communism, so when France lost the battle at Dien Bien Phu and left the fight, the Americans redirected the war supplies to the South Vietnamese Army. Between 1954 and 1956, there were essentially two separate Vietnams battling against each other.

• • •

The Geneva Convention, which followed France's withdrawal, partitioned Vietnam at the demilitarized zone along the 17th parallel. Called the "Democratic Republic of Vietnam," communist Ho Chi Minh controlled the north, and the south became the Independent State of Vietnam, first under Emperor Bao Dai and then under President Ngô Đình Diệm. This left the south fighting to restrain the ever-encroaching Viet Minh (now called Vietcong) Army from the north with the heavy munition and tank support of the United States.[97]

As the French slowly withdrew, American military personnel gradually began replacing them as strategic advisers to the South Vietnamese, accompanying the growing stream of U.S. tanks, planes, artillery, and other supplies that were being sent to South Vietnam. Mac, as the next air attaché, would plan, organize, and collect overt intelligence in Indochina, or what used to be called Indochina. He would be the principal air force adviser to the ambassadors of the three nations—Vietnam, Laos, and Cambodia—from April 1956 to January 1958.

---

[97] Wikipedia. 1954. "Geneva Convention."

Chapter 49
Readying to Move to Saigon, Vietnam

Running full speed into the house, I pushed open the screen door to the kitchen. It was the spring of 1955, and I was in the second grade. "Daddy" I said, "you're home!" I raced past Mother, who was standing at the sink, preparing dinner. The smell of roast chicken wafted through my nostrils as I zipped by her, heading for the living room. I had spotted his turquoise Plymouth parked in the driveway from down the street, where I was playing tag with my friends.

"Don't let the door slam behind you," my mother called as the screen door banged against the wooden frame. Yankee was right on my heels, jumping and wagging his tail as if Dad had been missing for months.

"Yes indeed, I'm home, my little gnome," he said, purposely mispronouncing it 'ganomie.' He took off his glasses and put down the newspaper he'd been reading, then pulled me onto his lap. "I have some exciting news to tell you. We are going on a grand, new adventure. It's an odyssey, really."

"What's an odyssey?" I asked.

"It's a good word for you to know, Sherry. Let's look it up in the dictionary." He opened *Webster's Unabridged*, which he kept on the reading table. *Any extended wandering or journey*, we read. "We're going to live in another country called Vietnam for two years. How about that for an odyssey?" he asked. "They don't speak English in Vietnam, so we will need to learn to speak French, which the Vietnamese people speak as well as their native Vietnamese. That's how we will talk to people. *Parlez-vous francais?*" he asked, smiling. "You will soon enough."

"Vee et nom," I pronounced carefully, the V whistling through the gap in my mouth from a missing tooth. "How do we get to Vietnam, Daddy, and when do we go?" I couldn't wait for this new adventure to begin.

"We'll start out this fall. This odyssey will begin with a plane ride to Chicago to visit relatives on my side of the family. You'll meet my brother—your uncle Bob—Aunt Mary, and your cousins, Mike and Sue. You'll also get to meet my uncle Free and Aunt Jeanne, with whom Bob and I lived after our father died. Then we'll fly on to Los Angeles for a long visit with all four of your grandparents. You and Mother will stay with Mimi and Grandad for a couple of weeks while I fly back to Virginia to prepare for my new job in Vietnam. While you're in Los Angeles, you'll continue in third grade, then"—he paused dramatically, as I sat raptly forward, elbows on my knees, hands on my chin, eyes opened wide—"when we are ready to go, I'll join you, and we'll fly to San Francisco. Then we'll take a long trip on a gigantic ship," he said, holding his hands wide apart.

"How big is the ship?" I asked excitedly.

"It's as big as a city, with swimming pools and playrooms and restaurants," he replied. "And the best part of all," he said, "is that we will live in a country that is vastly different from America, and very far away. Here, I'll show you on the map." He pointed at a spot on the globe that he kept on the desk in the front room. "Vietnam looks a bit like the crook of an arm nestling the countries of Laos and Cambodia, doesn't it? And look how close it is to India," he said. "We will live in the southern part of Vietnam, in the city of Saigon. It's right on the ocean in the South China Sea." Pointing, he said, "Here's where we live now, and here is where we will be going." He traced his finger around the globe. "As you can see, Sherry, it's exactly halfway around the earth. It's as far away as you can travel from here before you come back around."

"Wow," I said. "Do they have wild animals in Vietnam like India?"

"Oh yes," he said, "they have lots of animals—elephants, tigers, and monkeys. There are jungles in Vietnam, just like we read about in India." Prudently, he didn't mention the snakes, poisonous lizards, or mosquitoes … just exciting jungle animals. But I wouldn't have cared. I was already on board.

• • •

With Dad, we were either reading about adventures or taking them. We had just spent three weeks the past summer driving from our home in Virginia to Los Angeles to visit our grandparents, touring many of the national parks along the way. "Look at this mobile playroom," Dad said, proudly pointing at the back seat of the car. "You and Cathe can color, read, and nap during the drive across the country." He had laid a custom-cut piece of plywood over the back seats that extended to the back of the front seats. Then he covered the board with a mattress and sheets and propped two pillows up on the sides.

"It's great," I said, jumping onto it. "I can take books and see everything as we pass by. Cathe can nap and play with Susie." Cathe named all her dolls Susie, and she had a growing collection.

Dad drove us through the country on the southerly route, partly on the famous Route 66 through towns and villages, staying at the ubiquitous roadside motels that dotted the country. In New Mexico, we drove south to the spectacular Carlsbad Caverns National Park. Imagine, a stunning 250 million years ago, the limestone area around the caverns had been home to an inland sea. It was an eerie underworld kingdom with stalactites hanging from the tops of the caves, fashioned by drips of minerals, lava, and sand over millions of years. Droplets that hit the floor of the cave, year after year, produce stalagmites, Dad told us, gradually rising upward in a conical shape. The effect was breathtaking. It was like looking at horns of ancient unicorns or into the mouth of an unholy monster.

I stood in the safety of the huge, ballroom-like areas of Carlsbad Caverns and imagined exploring beyond or taking the relatively open paths carved into the cavern like an archaeologist discovering the secrets of the ancient past. Dad taught me a new word: *spelunking—exploration of caves, especially as a hobby.*

We motored on to Arizona. The mantra, "Are we there yet?" now resounding in all of our ears prompted Dad to say irritably, "We'll be there when we get there," which puzzled but oddly satisfied me. And finally, we were there.

Standing at the north rim of the Grand Canyon, its magnificence awed us, stretching for miles and miles and as colorful as an artist's palette. No matter how many times I have seen it since, it never fails to evoke feelings of wonderment and awe.

Next, we drove north through the magnificent Colorado Rockies along winding mountain roads overlooking beautiful towns like Ouray, nestled in the valley. We passed ski resorts and mines, then headed up through Wyoming to see Old Faithful erupt at Yellowstone National Park, and then on to Redwood National Park to see the trees big enough to drive a car through.

It was an eye-opening experience to appreciate the wonders of nature in our great country, and Dad, ever the teacher, delighted in sharing these treasures with his daughters. Perhaps this was exactly his intent—to show us the beauty and grandeur of our own country before we headed out to experience and live in another country on another continent, halfway around the world.

. . .

Secure in our family and excited to be going on this great, new adventure to Vietnam, I wasn't sure what to expect, but I knew it was going to be a romp into the unknown—an odyssey, as Dad called it. If I had heard of the country of Vietnam before this, which I hadn't, I was certainly oblivious to the political environment we were about to enter.

For me, my father's new assignment meant only that we were about to embark on 'the great adventure of my lifetime.' How could I have known then, at age eight, that I was about to be exposed to an exotic, new world, visiting a host of cities and countries in the Far East while experiencing other cultures, foods, and lifestyles that I could never have possibly imagined in our Falls Church, Virginia suburban cocoon.

Gearing up for our big move from Virginia to Vietnam, there was a flurry of family activity—what to take, what to leave behind? We were moving to a partially furnished home for two years, but what belongings were we going to take with us? Of course, Yankee, our Dalmatian, made the short list. A locked gate and security fence surrounded the yard and house we were moving to, but Jezebel, our cat, might have been vulnerable with the huge, open windows and a cat's penchant for roaming. I believe we decided, for her own safety, to leave her behind, as I have no memories of her in Vietnam.

Over the next few months, we visited the base infirmary to get the obligatory and painful weekly immunizations for a large array of dreaded diseases, like the plague, polio, tetanus, typhoid, and malaria, and later continued booster shots in Saigon at the American Embassy. And as my storybook heroine

Pippi Longstocking might have prepared, we took French lessons.

In January 1956, as promised, the four of us, along with Yankee, boarded a plane. After a brief stop in Chicago to visit our relatives, we landed in Los Angeles. Mom, Cathe, and I stayed with Mimi and Grandad Perraud, whom we adored. Their apartment had a flat, tar roof that I could climb up to using the fire escape and have a bird's-eye view of the neighborhood. I couldn't see the ocean from that vantage point, but I could inhale it. The air aroma was a mixture of smog, tar, and ocean breezes, which I savored as I breathed deeply through my nose. The roof was my getaway spot to be alone with my thoughts and dream about the adventure awaiting us. I fantasized about the next chapter of my life, but the reality was more than I could have ever imagined.

Shortly after we arrived in Los Angeles, Dad took us to visit his mother, Margaret, and stepfather, Curt, who also lived in the city, so we could say goodbye before we left for our two-year sojourn to Asia. Nana, as they instructed us to call his mother, was not particularly interested in grandchildren—especially the female variety—and that was fine with Cathe and me. The rare visits were always strained and formal, and this one was no exception. Curt did his best to entertain us with a rubber alligator that he hid under the carpet, and I chuckled appreciatively, while Nana puttered around the kitchen, making lunch and worrying about our move to Vietnam. In my child's eye, she was a nervous person, fretting about all kinds of inconsequential things, it seemed to me. She was a stark contrast to Grandmother Mimi, who was funny and outgoing, even with her proper English demeanor.

A few days later, Dad flew back to the Pentagon for seven weeks to prepare for his new assignment as air attaché, and

Mother enrolled me in the third grade in a Los Angeles elementary school while we anxiously awaited his return. We were about to embark on an ocean journey that would take us to a land of enchantment and experience—a world completely different from anything we had ever known.

Disneyland before we sail

Chapter 50
The SS *President Cleveland* and the Voyage to Vietnam

In February 1956, after a day's adventure in the newly opened Disneyland, we said goodbye to all four of our grandparents, and with Yankee in tow, we flew from Los Angeles to San Francisco. They transported our crates, luggage, and Yankee directly to the ship and loaded them on board.

We spent the rest of the day visiting Fisherman's Wharf, riding a trolley car, gazing at the Golden Gate Bridge, and eating Chinese food. Then we strolled up the long gangplank to board the SS *President Cleveland*. Our eyes widened like tea saucers. I was eight years old, and my sister Cathe was four. After checking out our cabin, we came up on the top deck. We stood at the railing, wearing jackets and gloves, and waved to the crowds of people gathered below as they released balloons.

As the big ship pulled away from the dock, streamers attached from the boat to the dock broke free and floated in the air like undulating rainbow flags. A band on board the ship played loudly, and passengers danced as the tugboat guided us out of the harbor and into the vast Pacific Ocean. It seemed as magical and surreal as any ride at Disneyland. It was definitely an 'E' ticket.

Glenn Ford, the American movie actor, and his entourage were also on board the ship. They were on their way to make the movie *The Teahouse of the August Moon*, a satire comedy about the occupation and attempted Americanization of Okinawa right after WWII. The movie also starred Marlon Brando, but he was not on board this ship. During the multi-week sea adventure, we became great friends with Mr. Ford's bodyguard, whom we called 'Funny Bunny Brother Bill.' He was our one-man entertainment host, playing games and exercising Yankee as we ran around the oak-stained, wooden deck of the ship and dove into the swimming pools.

The SS *President Cleveland* was relatively small compared to ocean liners today. It carried only 579 passengers (379 first class, 200 economy class) plus a crew of 352. But this was a first-class luxury liner. She was all leather and polished brass. No tacky chrome or plastic for that classy lady. The grand staircase in the middle, leading to the upper decks, was elegant, featuring a swirling, polished, mahogany banister. We had two swimming pools to choose from—one fresh and the other saltwater. There were games, activities, and children's events highlighted by a talent show in which all the children took part, complete with costumes and a choreographer. Glenn Ford graciously served as a judge of our children's talent show. The trip was the most fantastic floating excursion imaginable.

Our first stop was Honolulu, Hawaii, where we spent a day or two visiting with friends of Dad's who lived on the base in Mokulē'ia, where he had trained before going to Guadalcanal. Then we toured Pearl Harbor and checked out the white-sand beaches of Waikiki before boarding the ship again and continuing our journey west to the China Sea. What memories the trip must have evoked from Dad as he floated in the Pacific Ocean, headed to Asia instead of flying over it.

• • •

The only time I ever remember seeing my dad angry was when we docked in Yokohama, Japan. I was alone in the children's playroom one afternoon when a man walked in, smiling and waving his arms up and down, like a duck preparing to fly. He was about thirty, brown-skinned, slender, and casually dressed. The man hurried toward me, not speaking at all, and suddenly grabbed me, kissing me on the mouth. I remember feeling momentarily frozen. "Stop," I said. I didn't want to be rude, but this didn't seem right, even if he was an adult, and he was smiling.

I broke away from him and ran to find my father, who, upon hearing what happened, was furious. Never had I ever seen him so outraged. He took me immediately to the ship's doctor and waited outside the exam room, pacing and seething. The ship went into a lockdown, but they never caught the man, and the Yokohama trauma concluded with a clean bill of health for me. Dad must have felt so responsible for not being able to protect me at that moment.

After six weeks of Hotel SS *President Cleveland*, we finally arrived in Saigon. As tugboats slowly towed her into the harbor, we watched dozens of small, wooden boats propelled by men who pushed them forward with long oars dragging in the water. When they came closer, the men stood up, smiling and waving. As they beckoned and called, passengers threw money to them, and we watched, mesmerized, while they dove for the coins beneath the clear-blue water. When the ship docked in the harbor in the South China Sea, we waited with great anticipation, wonder, and excitement about what lie ahead. Our lives and lifestyles were about to change forever. What new experiences and adventures awaited us? I could only imagine, and I didn't have the experience of imagining anything close to reality.

Together, the four of us slowly walked down the gangplank, holding hands and drinking in the sights and sounds of our new, unfamiliar country. Everything looked different from anything I had known—the buildings, the noise, the smells, and the people.

It was March, and yet, the weather was hot and sticky. The people all had brown skin and luxurious, thick, black hair that women wore long to the middle of their backs. Everyone sported thin, loose-fitting garments that covered most of their skin, and many wore conical-shaped straw or bamboo hats, tied to their heads with a silk scarf, protection from the sun's fiery rays. Men pulled or pedaled passengers in two-seater conveyances that we had seen nothing like before. It was as different as if we had walked with Alice *Through the Looking Glass*.

At the end of the long ramp, a military car and driver waited to take us to our new home. Something would bring our belongings later. The driver solemnly saluted Dad. "Col. McNeese," he said, "I'm Pvt. Ron Riley, your driver. Welcome to Saigon."

"Thank you, Pvt. Riley," Dad replied formally, returning the salute. "We look forward to our stay here."

Riley opened the doors for us to get in as crates with our belongings were being hoisted on shore. They whisked us away like celebrities going to the Academy Awards. Within minutes, we rolled up to an iron gate that was swung open by a smiling, young man. He was tan and thin and wore an untucked, white shirt with sleeves rolled above his elbows, loose, black pants, and sandals. *"Bienvenue à la maison,"* he said with a broad smile. We slowly and excitedly stepped out of the car and entered our new house, half a world away from our home in Virginia.

When our family arrived in Saigon in March 1956, the last of the French military were leaving. There were, however, still a lot of French civilians living there. The European influence was pervasive.

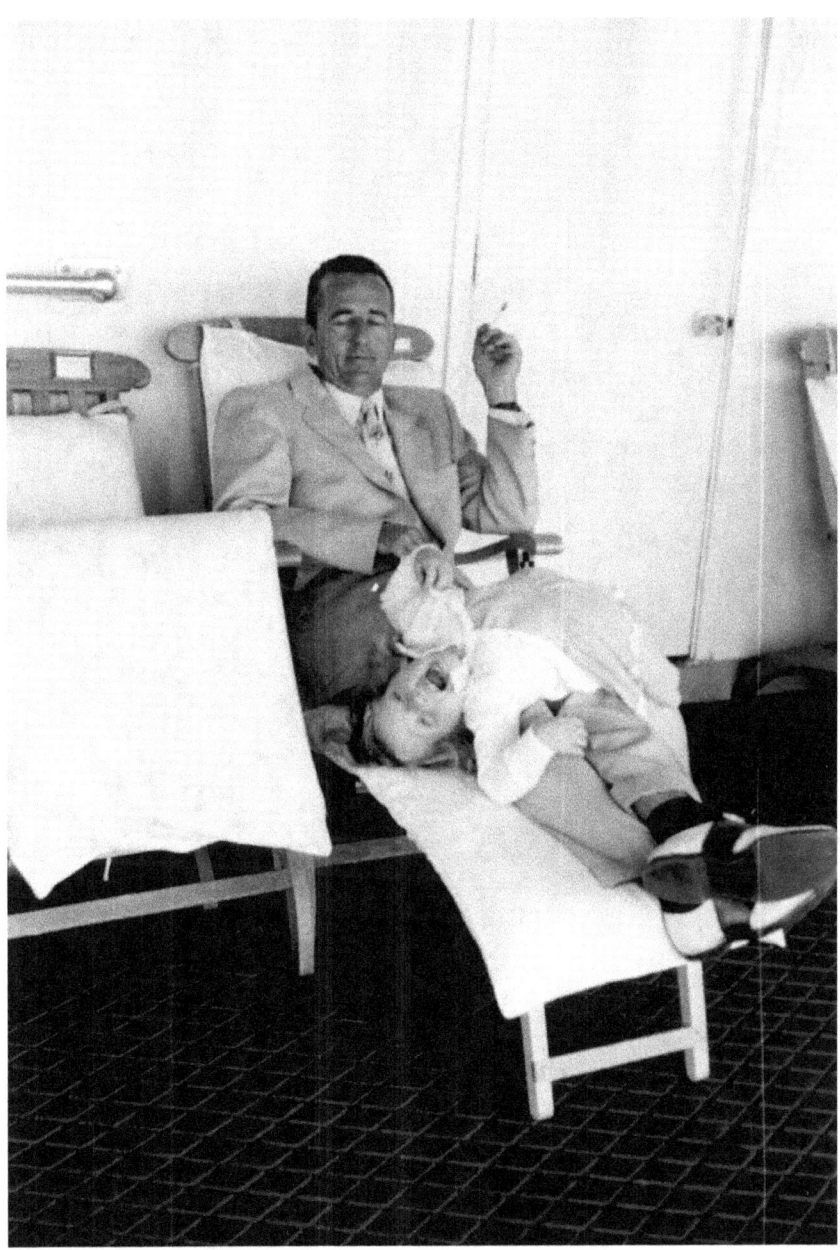

Relaxing aboard the SS President Cleveland

Showtime with Glen Ford

Chapter 51
Our Home in Saigon, Vietnam—1956–1959

I ran to explore the house that we would live in for the next two years. It was a large, white, two-story, French colonial mansion on a street called Truang Minh Giang, catty-corner from Ambassador Elbridge Durbrow's even larger residence, and a half mile from the opulent, white palace where the president of South Vietnam, Ngô Đình Diệm, lived.

Fenced and gated, our home included servants' quarters, an oblong, two-story edifice in the back where our cook and his wife both lived upstairs above the laundry room. There were seven 'servants,' as they were called, who became friends and companions to Cathe and me over the next two years. Kim, who had first greeted us when we arrived, was number one houseboy, and Thanh was our nanny. Yankee had the run of the fenced and gated yard, and we quickly added Hercules the monkey to our family as well.

My bedroom was enormous and occupied the front part of the second story with a view of the gate and street beyond. Mother and Dad's bedroom was in the back, next to Cathe's. Facing the house, on the left side, was the driveway that ended under the second-story porch, which did double duty as a carport. The porch was white stucco with a high roof matching the high ceilings inside the house. We frequently ate lunches or dinners out there when it wasn't raining. An outdoor ceiling fan whirred above the porch, and ceiling fans were in every room of the house, circulating the hot, humid air.

My father's military driver entered and exited the gated property each day to chauffeur him to and from work, pulling the car up under the carport. On the front corner, extending down the right side of the house on the first floor, was another porch just off the living room, where a large, oval, bamboo cage swung gently from a black, metal hook. This housed a variety of pets. Two ducks—a gift from a staff member—greeted us initially, but during our stay, the bamboo cage also housed a mynah bird, occasionally Hercules, and briefly served as a jail cell for a guest monkey. More about that later.

Papaya, mango, pamplemousse, and banana trees grew abundantly in our yard, and the fruit was deliciously sweet. Pamplemousse, much like grapefruit but larger and sweeter, was my favorite. I loved being able to pluck fresh fruit for a snack whenever I wanted. There was also a big, red-stained tree stump that loomed ominously in the center of the side yard. It was here that Diem beheaded the occasional chicken he had brought from the market. With one chop of his hatchet, he decapitated the bird and prepared it for dinner. Then he used a makeshift, outdoor grill nearby to cook the fresh meat barbeque style. The smells were wonderful; fragrant spices, previously unknown to us, permeated the air.

Only nuoc mam—the horrible-smelling (to our noses) fish oil dipping sauce—was never integrated into our diet. Like poi in Hawaii and vegemite in Australia, nuoc mam is an acquired taste that we never quite developed. Meals consisted mostly of chicken and fresh fish from the local market and locally grown produce, with only supplemental condiments coming from the commissary on the nearby base. Mother told us that our family's good health during our tour overseas was because of the fresh, local cuisine we ate, instead of relying on packaged commissary foodstuff. We always boiled and refrigerated water for drinking water, however. Orange soda, with its thick, sugary taste, was popular everywhere and an occasional treat. Or we could buy Shasta 'It Hasta Be Shasta' at the commissary. But that was rare as well.

As the morning sun streamed through the large, shuttered window beside my bed one morning, I slowly opened my eyes, blinking at the light. I could smell the citrusy fragrance of the papaya and the pamplemousse trees drifting in from the courtyard below. The air smelled like a tropical fruit salad surrounded by plumeria leis.

I remembered it was Monday and a school day. I was finishing the third grade in my third school, but I didn't mind. For me, changing schools and homes was like the change of seasons on the East Coast of America—anticipated for the break in monotony that promised new things to come. Cathe and I adapted, as did most of the other children of American diplomats and military personnel.

Lying in bed for just a few minutes, I listened quietly to the chirping of house geckos bustling about on the walls and ceilings, telling me good morning, or so I imagined. These bug-eyed creatures fascinated me. They seemed in constant motion, ever vigilant, their jerky body movements stopping, starting. Their heads swiveled as if they were constantly on the alert for prey and predator, like tropical prairie dogs, comical and crafty. The thick, heavily woven mosquito net draped over my large, four-poster bed like a tent prevented me from seeing them clearly at first, but I knew they were there, noiselessly scurrying around, going about their business of locating and catching insects, diligently finishing up the night shift and getting ready to clock out gecko style.

I loved the sense of security my netted encampment provided, but with light streaming in and the day before me, I carefully unzipped the flap of the netting and exited my enclosure. Thanh's smiling face greeted me. She had carefully laid out my clothes for the day on a large, wicker chair: a light-colored, short-sleeved dress with flowers on it, white underwear, and brown sandals.

Thanh had already opened the shutters of the windows, which were kept tightly closed at night to keep out unwanted critters, winged and footed. Once in a great while, a poisonous lizard found its way into one of our bedrooms. It was identifiable by its colorful, striped hide and large size, and Dad would dispatch it with a baseball bat that he kept at the ready for just such occasions. There were no screens on the windows, so at night, mosquito nets protected us from being bitten by the little, blood-sucking insects and contracting malaria and other mosquito-borne diseases.

The ceiling fan pushed the hot, moist air down as it whirred softly above my bed, gently cooling the room with the breeze. The warmth of the tropics was sheer happiness to me. I loved the sun on my face and the smell of fruit trees in the air.

Dressing quickly, I bounded down the stairs to the kitchen for breakfast. Diem, the cook, had laid out morning fare of cereal, eggs, fruit, and les croissants. *"Bonjour, mademoiselle,"* he said formally.

"Bonjour, Diem," I replied. Diem was a somber fellow—formal, polite, and proper. His wife, who lived with him in the back, was shy and reclusive, like a little mouse briefly emerging from her habitat, then scurrying back inside. She did the laundry, which was on the lower floor of their quarters, and we rarely saw her. Kim and Thanh were all smiles, laughter, and fun.

I kissed Mother and Dad good morning, and the four of us sat at the kitchen table at the back of the house, chatting happily about the coming day's plans and yesterday's events. Thanh dressed Cathe in shorts and a halter top for preschool, Dad was in his uniform, and Mother, who sported a sundress and sandals, had expertly applied her makeup, including a penciled-on beauty mark, and pulled her dark hair, now blonde, up in a ponytail. Yankee half-napped nearby, taking it all in, his head on his paws, waiting for the sound of the gates opening.

With the run of the open house and large yard, Yankee had sentry duty and began barking when he heard the gate creak open. Pvt. Riley pulled slowly into the driveway and under the carport, waiting for Dad to emerge from the house so he could chauffeur him to work. His driver seemed so serious, an enlisted man charged with driving the colonel to work. I waved to Pvt. Riley and, kissing Mother and Dad on their cheeks, ran out the front door to meet Kim, who was standing next to his bike, propped up against the house, waiting for me. Kim grinned. After Dad's car backed out of the driveway, he gave me a hand up on the back of the two-seater bike, and together we rode down the tree-lined streets, passing houses and businesses as we made our way to my school through the cacophonous streets of Saigon.

•   •   •

I learned, years later, that on June 8, 1956, two months after we arrived, Staff Sgt. Edward C. Clarke, USAF, shot and killed Tech. Sgt. Richard B. Fitzgibbon Jr., USAF, in Saigon. The two men served together as flight crewmen assigned to the Military Assistance Advisory Group (MAAG). Reportedly, Fitzgibbon had reprimanded Clarke for an incident on a flight that day. Clarke fled the shooting scene and exchanged fire with Vietnamese policemen, who were chasing him. During the pursuit, Clarke jumped or fell to his death from a second-story balcony. In 1998, the Defense Department recognized Fitzgibbon as the first U.S. service member killed "in the line of duty" in Vietnam and added his name to the Vietnam Veterans Memorial in Washington. His son, L/Cpl. Richard B. Fitzgibbon III, USMC, died in action in Vietnam in 1965. Clarke's name does not appear on the Vietnam Veterans Memorial wall.

Our home

Kim with Cathe and me

Chapter 52
Day-to-Day Life in Saigon, Vietnam—1956–1958

Experiences are gifts so much more valuable than "things." While physical objects deteriorate and become obsolete, experiences last forever in our memories. And what memories I have from those two years.

Saigon was called 'Little Paris' then, and indeed it was a beautiful, European-style city. Bustling, open-air markets and sidewalk cafés filled the city center. Relatively few cars were evident, but those that were, shared the road with pedestrians, bikes, *les pousse-pousse* (pedicabs), rickshaws, and even caribou-drawn lorries. Everyone was going somewhere, it seemed. Slender women donned blousy, peasant pants with billowing, white tops, or the more elegant, long, ao dai garments slit at the waist, enveloping black, silk pants. Some wore scarves that covered their heads, and both men and women sported conical hats to keep the sun off their faces.

In the middle of the intersections, policemen stood on round pedestals, directing traffic and blowing whistles. They wore white shorts, crisp, white shirts, white knee socks, and white helmets and gloves—a very French uniform. The smells from the coffee shops and eateries were everywhere, filling my senses with the sweet aromas. Signs on building fronts in both French and Vietnamese advertised their businesses. It was a bustling blur of activity, lights, and sound.

We filled each day with adventure and excitement, beginning with the bike ride to my Quonset hut school campus. The American school in Saigon had a small main administration building, but the classrooms consisted of two military Quonset huts that resembled oblong, metal igloos. They insulated them, and they were quite comfortable for most of the day, even in the tropical climate. Because there were so few American children, they combined the grades with about fifteen children in each classroom. The teachers, who were volunteer American wives, individualized our studies with workbooks from military-supplied programs called the Calvert System. They dismissed classes early, as the afternoon sun often heated the metal buildings by the afternoon.

Cathe, four that first year, attended Croix Rouge-Jardin D'Enfant. The French had founded Croix Rouge (Red Cross) in South Vietnam four years earlier to attend to the needs of Vietnamese civilians caught in the middle of the First Indochina War, and the Jardin D'Enfant (Children's Garden) was their preschool. The school was filled with mostly Vietnamese children, making Cathe the odd child out, at least in terms of looks, dress, and language. But she played happily with the other children and learned to sing songs in several languages.

After school, our parents assured that we were immersed in the many cultures that formed the diplomatic community in Saigon. I recall particularly enjoying birthday parties at the homes of Asian children. The games and activities differed from American parties, more sedate and orchestrated, it seemed. The food and rituals were unlike our Virginia birthday parties where we played pin the tail on the donkey, musical chairs, and ate birthday cake. I especially cherished the delicate party favors we received. When it was our turn to host birthday parties, I am sure the other children found ours as strange and delightful as we found theirs.

During the summers, I took horseback riding lessons at the Saigon Equestrian Center with Cirque Hippique Saigonnaise, a French riding academy. This was not my idea, but my parents thought a proper, young lady should know dressage. I looked smart in my jodhpurs and black riding boots and carried my crop as a prop.

Walking up to them, I was slightly fearful of the large Arabian and Australian horses that they saddled me with (pardon the pun). And, at less than one hundred pounds, I desperately clung for dear life to the practically nonexistent horn of the English saddle as the horses ran their own route over an obstacle course of barrels, brushes, and fences. Above the fenced-in paddock was a viewing area with seats where spectators sipped cool drinks and watched the entertainment below, and I am sure I contributed much to their amusement.

During weekly shows for which we practiced, there was a prescribed route and order of jumps, and we, meaning the horse and I, usually followed them correctly. However, the horse I was riding occasionally decided—either out of boredom or, more likely, out of a lack of direction from me—to take a different series of jumps. Clearly, I was not in control of these animals, and they knew it. My horse frequently went on strike and declared, with an equine stubbornness, that he just wasn't in the mood to take the jump at all and abruptly stopped in front of it, sending me flying over alone, landing in an awkward face plant, covered with dirt. I racked up an impressive number of faults and penalty points, if that counts for anything. Dad and Mom smiled and clapped proudly, as if that were part of the act.

Throughout Dad's assignment, Mother's 'job' in Saigon as a diplomat's wife was primarily to entertain. Years later, I found a resume she put together in which she declared that she herself had been a diplomat in Saigon, reporting directly to Ambassador

Durbrow. But like her claim that she had graduated from UCLA, and later, that her children were practically world renowned in their respective fields, Mother's penchant for creating her own reality by inflating her and her children's accomplishments was an endearing peculiarity we always found alternately embarrassing and/or humorous.

Jerrie was born for her role as diplomatic spouse, however. Beautiful, charming, and raised with the etiquette and know-how of proper entertaining, she was the ideal hostess—gracious and vivacious. Together, she and Dad hosted frequent parties, some costumed. I would sit on the stairs and watch the guests laughing, dancing, and drinking adult beverages. They were also frequent guests at the many formal dinners required as members of the diplomatic community.

On one occasion, a hugely elegant affair, tapeworm was served (beautifully presented, I am sure, and it probably tasted just like chicken). Mother, who had a most adventurous and expansive palate, apparently decided that this delicacy, along with a proffered fish eyeball, was one step too far in the culinary exploration she usually embraced. Not wanting to offend her hosts, she discreetly covered her mouth with a napkin and ever-so-delicately dropped the tapeworms from the end of her chopsticks down the front of her low-cut gown. Apparently, no one was the wiser. She was quite proud of her diplomatic subterfuge and told that story often in the years to come.

We usually spent our weekends either at the large, local, community swimming pool called Cirque Sportif, where we swam and sunbathed, or at the beach called Cap Saint Jacques in the China Sea. There were endless family staff parties, normally centered around some body of water to escape the tropical heat.

Dad took us to the Michelin Rubber Plantation on several occasions. It was about forty-five miles northwest of us, between the Cambodian border and Saigon. My parents had friends or colleagues, or perhaps Dad had military business there, but I have happy memories of swimming in the Olympic-size pool and riding around the plantation in a jeep with our host's pet python resting quietly on the floorboards in the front. I recall that later, a group of us posed for a picture, holding this twelve- or fifteen-foot reptile. Wanting to be as far away from the head as possible, I stood somewhere closer to the tail, when suddenly, a small scale slid open, and I learned firsthand how a snake does his business. I can appreciate reptiles for the unique creatures they are, but I prefer to admire them from a distance or, even better, in a glass cage. However, if it were necessary, I would still prefer holding the business end of the scaly creature to holding the head, as long as someone else is gripping the head firmly.

• • •

In mid-1956, contractors completed a U.S.-aid-built, 7,200-foot runway at Tan Son Nhut Airport in Saigon and began work on a 10,000-foot concrete one. Tan Son Nhut and Bien Hoa, seventeen miles to the northeast, became the main airfields for the Vietnamese Air Force. Mac flew weekly out of Tan Son Nhut, mostly to Cambodia, Laos, and to Clark Air Base in Manila. The VNAF based its 1st Fighter Squadron and its air depot at Bien Hoa. The United States also funded a highway between Bien Hoa and Saigon, built strong enough to withstand heavy military traffic.

Sherry on big *cheval*

Chapter 53
Nixon in Saigon, Vietnam—1956

On Friday, July 6, 1956, at 3:30 p.m., as recorded in our invitation from Mr. Tran Van-Lam, president of the Vietnamese Constituent Assembly: "Parents are urged to send their children to this important event," Raymond Pagan, chairman of the American School Board, extolled on the invitation.

Cathe and I, along with the other children and teachers at the American School, attended a special session of the assembly in honor of Vice President Richard Nixon, who was visiting Saigon. Let the record show that Cathe and I were in attendance and certainly listened attentively to each pearl of wisdom Mr. Nixon imparted as they sailed swiftly over our heads. I have absolutely no recollection of the event and, consequently, must have been unimpressed with Mr. Nixon. (History shows that I was an excellent judge of character.) Cathe, who was not quite five, was completely politically unsavvy and wouldn't have recognized Nixon in a lineup of gorillas. But there we were, seated in bleachers as instructed.

During Nixon's visit, Dad spent considerable time in the company of the vice president, and Mother went with Mrs. (Pat) Nixon on a tour of the local hospital and orphanage where she regularly volunteered, and on a longer trip to Cambodia. At the orphanage in Saigon, Mother showed Mrs. Nixon the colorful cartoon characters she had painted on the walls to brighten the grim surroundings, and the boxes of soap and other cleaning supplies donated by American companies that she had helped to secure for the orphanage. These were also great photo ops for all concerned.

Curious to know more about the events that brought the vice president to Saigon on that date in history, I later googled it. I discovered that on July 6, 1956, the day of our assembly, Vice President Nixon had just arrived in Saigon. He was there to present President Ngô Đình Diệm with a letter from President Eisenhower stating, "The U.S. looks forward to many years of partnership with South Vietnam." Why he wanted to speak to American elementary school students is a puzzle, but again, I am sure the cameras were recording it and it made for good politics.

July 20, 1956, the date set by the Geneva accords for unification elections in Vietnam passed without an election being held. The North Vietnamese had continued to press for consultations to prepare for elections, but with only lukewarm support for their position by the Soviets and the Chinese, they had little leverage. Ho Chi Minh remained firmly in control of the north, and President Diệm, with America's backing, held the reins in South Vietnam. In a speech to the Vietnamese Constituent Assembly, Nixon announced: "The march of communism has been halted."

History shows that he was incredibly wrong about that, and in the north, Ho Chi Minh angrily shot back: "The U.S. imperialists and the pro-American authorities in South Vietnam have been plotting to partition our country permanently and prevent the holding of free general election as provided for by the Geneva Agreements."

This was partially true. America did not want an election to take place, as the U.S. was afraid it would cause a victory for Ho Chi Minh, who would engulf the south in communism—another domino falling. America did not want to partition the country, either, but wanted the entire country to be democratic, just as Ho

Chi Minh wanted it to become communist. They were at an impasse.

The following year, in January 1957, the Soviet Union and China proposed a permanent division of Vietnam into north and south, with both nations to be admitted separately to the United Nations. But the U.S. rejected that proposal, unwilling to recognize communist North Vietnam at all, and Ho Chi Minh used that as an excuse to increase efforts to unite the country. North Vietnam continued to send messages to Diệm through 1960 that called for the consultations to be held, but the words fell on deaf ears. President Diệm, backed by the U.S., had refused to take part, and they did not hold any elections.

Mac smoking rice liquor

Diplomatic dinner

Jerrie at orphanage

Jerrie meets Chris

Mac talks with Mrs. Earl Warren

Mother behind President Diem

Saigon 1956

Chapter 54
Dad Takes Us on Unexpected Flight to Clark Air Base, Philippines

"Mom, Mom, come quick! The monkey's choking!" Cathe and I shouted, jumping up and down. We had been waiting at the front gate for Dad's car to pull up. He had flown to Clark Air Base in the Philippines on military business and had been gone for several days.

A few minutes before, an elderly Vietnamese man walked up to the gate and stood, grinning, on the other side of the fence. His mouth pulled back in a broad smile, revealing teeth blackened by the betel juice he chewed. He had an array of wares strung around him, including pots, pans, and a small monkey on a rope that appeared to be tightening around the monkey's neck.

Hearing our cries, Mother ran out of the house and reached out her hand, trying to loosen the rope on the animal's neck. The monkey, undoubtedly frightened with all the screaming and yelling going on, jumped on my shoulder and onto Mother, biting her on the hand. "Ow," she yelled, looking surprised, blood streaming down her finger. "He bit me."

Just as this commotion was taking place at the gate, my father's car arrived. The maelstrom of people swirling about parted, and the gate slowly opened. As the car pulled under the carport, Dad hurriedly joined the growing group of people shrieking and pointing.

"Daddy, the monkey jumped on me and bit Mommy on the hand," I cried. "She's bleeding!" Dad quickly paid the old man for the monkey and told Kim, who had also joined the crowd, to get the bamboo cage off the porch and bring it outside. The brown simian jumped agilely into the cage, looking happy to be off the leash.

"*Ecoute-moi! Nous allons à l'hôpital en Manille,*" Dad told Kim. "We're leaving for the hospital in Manila. We'll be there for a few days. While we're gone, give the monkey food and water, but don't let anyone touch him," he said in French. "And I want him under strict observation for the next few days until I give you further instructions," he said. "*Comprenez vous?*"

"*Oui, monsieur le colonel. Je comprends.*" I understand, Colonel, he said solemnly.

Dad took charge, barking more orders. "Private," he said, turning to his driver, "wait here. We're going back to Tan Son Nhut. Call the airfield and have them refuel the plane and prepare it for another takeoff." Addressing Mother, he said, "We must get to the hospital as quickly as possible. Jerrie, go up and get yourself and the girls packed enough for a few days. We need to leave here in half an hour."

We ran upstairs, and with Thanh's help, we quickly rounded up suitcases and several changes of clothes. Everyone looked anxious and hurried around. Kim put the packed bags in the back of the staff car, and the three of us climbed in the back. Dad sat up front next to the driver.

The monkey in the bamboo cage hooted and howled like a prisoner, taunting his jailers as we backed out of the driveway. "What were you thinking, Jerrie?" Dad admonished her. "I know you were trying to save the poor creature, but you know the risk of rabies in wild animals here in Southeast Asia."

"Rabies?" I repeated dumbly. I had read *Old Yeller*. "Are you going to die, Mother?" I asked frantically.

"No, I'll be fine, Sherry. Dad is flying us to the hospital for the medicine. Don't worry," Mother said with conviction.

But I was worried. Everyone seemed worried and distressed. Mom appeared to be fine. The monkey had bitten her, but she wasn't bleeding anymore. *Why are we racing to the airport?* I wondered.

What I learned, years later, was that if the monkey was, in fact, rabid, the serum had to be administered before symptoms start, and that can be as short as three days. Once the symptoms begin, death is inevitable. There is no cure for rabies. The first sign of rabies can look like the flu with fever and headaches. Then it rapidly progresses through the body, causing inflammation of the brain, paralysis, confusion, and paranoia, leading to delirium and eventually to a coma. The treatment consisted of twenty-five injections in the stomach or arm over thirty days. Even today, once symptoms develop, there is no known cure. Treatment must begin before symptoms appear, and time was running out.

The hospital was on Clark Air Base in the Philippine Islands, where Dad had just returned from, at least a three-hour flight away. Hospital pharmacies could not easily stock the vaccine. It had to be 'fresh' to be effective. If they didn't have any on hand, it would have to be flown in from the U.S., eating up more precious time.

We had three days to start treatment. Fortunately, we didn't have to deal with airlines or reservations or tickets or security. We were being whisked by car to the Tan Son Nhut Air Base in Saigon, where my father's plane was waiting for us. We were Dad's only passengers, and he was as tense and anxious as I had ever seen him. A car was there to meet us when we landed, taking us swiftly to the American hospital. We used almost a day getting there. Would the vaccine be available?

How many hours or days we waited there in Manila, I don't know. I remember we stayed on the base and enjoyed the facilities for some period of time, and once they had the vaccine, doctors immediately started giving the first of the series of painful rabies shots to Mother. Then seven doctors—apparently without input from either of my parents—deliberated my fate. I was young, and the monkey had only touched me, so it was a medical judgment call. If the monkey turned out to be rabid, it was possible for me to have contracted the deadly disease through a cut or scrape on my body. The monkey would have to be quarantined for ten days. Of course, if the monkey turned out to be rabid, it would be too late to give me treatment. The anti-rabies serum in those days was powerful enough itself to cause paralysis or even death, and because of my age and size, they risked the delay and waited for the monkey to develop symptoms during the quarantine period before giving me the first injection. They did not share the urgency and reasons for it with me. It would be several years before I understood the gravity of the situation.

Mother, who was always as irrepressible as a newly opened bottle of champagne, felt well enough to go dancing at the officers' club that evening, and so they did. Suddenly, though, she felt a strange sensation in her right arm and numbness, and Dad took her back to the hospital. This, according to the doctors, showed that continuation of the treatment might mean permanent paralysis. We waited for the monkey to die or show signs of rabies.

'Monsieur le singe' (Mr. Monkey) died the following day. They spared me the cause and manner of his death, but Kim told us that there was foam on his mouth, which sent everyone into a panic. Evidently, rabies affects the nervous system, and the animal can't swallow its saliva, which causes foaming at the mouth.

They shipped the carcass to the hospital for examination, and two days later, the results showed that, luckily for us, he did not have rabies, and we were winging our way back to Saigon. My parents speculated about the foam. Had they given him poison or soap? No one was ever sure, but we had averted the immediate crisis. Without further injections, the numbness in Mother's arm proved temporary, and she was understandably relieved that she didn't have to undergo the complete series of shots and risk permanent disability. They spared me from having to endure any part of the treatment.

The monkey incident was over, and life returned to our day-to-day normal. Thanh took charge of our activities once again, and Kim transported us whenever we needed to go by bike. Lesson learned, though. From then on, we avoided street vendors hawking wild animals like the plague that they could be carrying.

The monkey cage

Chapter 55
Exploring Asia

During our stay in Vietnam, Dad traveled to various other countries. He was the air force's representative to the ambassadors of Laos, Cambodia, and South Vietnam and was on business frequently in all three countries. In addition, he spent some time at Clark Air Base in Manila, but always returned home within a few days.

We accompanied him periodically and took frequent vacations. We saw beautiful and exotic Bangkok, Thailand. Dad always made sure that he exposed us to stimulating experiences or were on an adventure, learning and growing.

On one such occasion, we stayed with English friends in beautiful Hong Kong for a few days. Their home, high on a mountain, overlooked Kowloon Bay, where we gazed at a stunning panorama of city buildings tucked into a cove of the ocean like dollhouses. I recall the magnificent view of the harbor below as we stood behind the short, white retaining wall in the backyard. We immersed ourselves in the bustling city of Hong Kong before returning home to Saigon.

Twice we visited the Philippine Islands. Once, with the rabid monkey scare, and once, we stayed at a resort in Baguio, high in the Philippine mountains, during the summer months. Family vacations were exotic, fantastic, and memorable. It seems incredible that we could travel and vacation as often as we did.

Perhaps some of it was because Dad had business nearby. I do not know. I wish I had asked him about it when I grew up.

One unforgettable fantasy vacation was a trip to Kashmir, India where Dad rented a houseboat for the four of us. Kashmir is in the northernmost part of India in the Himalayan Mountains and was, until 1947, a 'Princely State' under the British Indian Empire. Then it became a disputed territory between Pakistan and India, and fighting for control continues even today. But in the summer of 1956, it was paradise.

The wooden houseboat had three bedrooms, a dining area, and kitchen. Intricately carved wood paneling blanketed the interior, and flowing drapes and soft, colorful pillows gave it the look of an exotic room you might expect to find in Casablanca, Morocco. We aquaplaned—standing on a board that was pulled by a speedboat—up and down the Himalayan River most days.

"We're going on an adventure ride," my dad announced one morning, "in a boat called a shikara." As we all settled in, two men using paddles and poles guided the boat up the river on a meandering trip until we turned into a pool of water hidden from view. I opened my eyes wide, not believing what lie in front of us. There, at the back of the pool, was a rocky hill with a waterfall cascading down from the top over rows and rows of planted flowers embedded in the hill. It was incredible and so unexpected. As I think about it today, I envision it as a gigantic Monet painting set in motion—an ethereal experience, to be sure, and one that is seared into my memory.

Another day, Mother dressed us in traditional Indian garb, and we played happily on the bank, pretending we were Indian princesses. Out of nowhere, a group of people suddenly appeared, carrying elegant silver platters, utensils, and tablecloths, which they spread on the ground. Next came plates of food, and we had an evening picnic feast fit for kings.

Like a colorful, whimsical tattoo, Central India is indelibly etched in my memory. We spent another week visiting several cities, including New Delhi and Old Delhi, which is a walled part of New Delhi, founded in 1639.

Most of urban India was a blur of the senses. What I recall most vividly in 1957 was the incredible poverty and streets crowded with people, vehicles, and animals, colliding and swerving like bumper cars at a carnival. There seemed to be beggars and cows everywhere. Since Hindus consider cows sacred, they meandered through the streets and markets as the mood struck them, as carefree as their fellow bovines that roamed ranches in the American West. It seemed the cows in India knew they were special and flaunted their status, acting like rulers of the city, going about their business protected and unafraid, swatting flies with their tails and pushing their noses up and into whatever they wanted. Humans just had to tolerate the large, gas-passing animals and watch where they stepped. The pungent smell of the food vendors cooking kebabs and curries wafted throughout the open-air markets and competed in the nostrils with the scents of the cows, chickens, and dogs like a colorful, odoriferous field of flowers and stinkweeds.

There were myriad street entertainers with dancing bears and snake charmers and fights to the death between hooded cobras and mongooses. These little carnivores of the meerkat family are fascinating creatures—smart and communicative in a group. They are largely immune to the poison of cobras and are lightning fast with powerful jaws and sharp teeth. This was gruesome 'entertainment,' but like watching a train wreck, hard to avert your eyes.

Hooded cobras swayed to the music of men who sat cross-legged in front of a large, woven basket playing flute-like instruments. There were snakes in some canals running along the dirt streets in the rural areas, and I was mindful of not losing my footing. With the sounds of cars honking, vendors hawking, and bikes whirring about, the animals and people blended in a cacophonous festival of sound and activity.

We flew to the city of Agra, 140 miles outside of New Delhi, to see the Taj Mahal, the stunning, white mausoleum studded with semi-precious stones built in 1632. It was breathtaking to behold. We rode elephants and felt a part of this incredible carnival.

During the last summer, Dad took us on a getaway week in the French resort town of Dalat—located high in the mountains in the middle of Vietnam—to escape the heat. We hiked, explored, and enjoyed the cool mountain air. I recall a staircase banister at the lodge where we stayed that Cathe and I delighted in sliding down to the scolding of our caretaker. *"Pas comme il faut! Pas comme il faut!"* (Not proper!) she shouted in her 'Frenchnamese' to mostly unhearing, giggling children.

There was also a jukebox in the lodge with American songs from the '40s and '50s that we played over and over, memorizing the lyrics.

Two weeks in the mountains and then back to the tropics; what an amazing time and place to spend one's formative years. I knew even then that I was privileged and lucky to be having this Dorothy in Oz-like experience. I hoped I didn't wake up one morning to discover that, like Dorothy, I had only been dreaming after receiving a sharp blow to my head.

Aquaplaning in Kasmir

Cobra and mongoose – India

Dancing bear – India

Chapter 56
War Comes to Saigon

On February 22, 1957, a would-be assassin, who was a member of the communist Vietnam Workers' Party, shot at but missed President Ngô Đình Diệm after he spoke at an agricultural fair in Ban Me Thuot in the Central Highlands. Communists in the south had planned the attack, supposedly without Hanoi's approval. But the political tension was building.

In mid-1957, the USAF transferred to the Vietnamese many of the more antiquated aircraft that had been on loan to the French. Although this period was technically one of peace between the wars in Indochina, shifts across Southeast Asia portended more conflict. In North Vietnam, radicals who favored revolution to reunite the country gradually gained more influence in the politburo. In the south, with tacit support from Hanoi, communist cadres and eventually militias began forming to oppose the Ngô Đình Diệm government. Diệm responded harshly, driving more of the groups that disagreed with him into the communist camp.

In September 1957, when I turned ten years old, I started hearing whispers of war from my parents' hushed conversations—a bombing here, an assassination there. As I have since learned, an anti-government crowd had broken the relative peace in South Vietnam during our last year and a half when they killed seventeen people in a bar. The killings were apparently the beginning of a low-level campaign targeting government officials, schoolteachers, and village chiefs' families. In October, someone threw a bomb into a Saigon restaurant, injuring a dozen people. A bomb killed an American army officer near Nha Trang. Then, on October 22nd, in three successive attacks aimed at U.S. installations in Saigon, bombs injured thirteen American soldiers.

A Saigon newspaper highlighted the growing violence in the countryside of South Vietnam: "Today the menace is greater than ever, with the terrorists no longer limiting themselves to the notables in charge of security. Everything suits them—village chiefs, chairmen of liaison committees, simple guards, even former notables. In certain areas, the village chiefs spend their nights in the security posts, while the inhabitants organize watches." Fortunately for me, there were no televisions and therefore no nightly news to disturb my childhood paradise. Mother and Dad rarely discussed these current events around me.

• • •

The first week of November 1957, Dad left for an Air Attaché–MAAG Conference at PACAF Headquarters in Hawaii, where he delivered a speech. As revealed later, the *Vietnam, Cambodia, and Laos Final Report from the Conference* stated: "Lt. Col. Harold G. McNeese, the air attaché in Saigon, said that the MAAG believed that North Vietnam could overrun South Vietnam 'within thirty days' if the south received no reinforcements. McNeese conceded, however, that intelligence gathering about North Vietnam was 'very slight,' with few good sources of information. From what little the Americans in Saigon could learn, they thought that economic conditions in the north were 'bad.' McNeese described Diệm as a 'strong man' and the key to both the strengths and the weaknesses of South Vietnam. He also said that relations between South Vietnam and Cambodia were 'bad and have worsened in the past six to eight months.' The embassy saw Cambodia as '100 percent neutral' because it had accepted aid from both the 'Soviet orbit' and the 'Free World.' As for Laos, it was 'divided into two entities—the Kingdom of Laos and the northern area controlled by the Communist-led Pathet Lao.' According to Ambassador Durbrow, the military attachés attached to the embassy had much better intelligence sources than the MAAG did."[98]

• • •

By the end of December 1957, the Diệm government fought back strongly and decimated the communists who had infiltrated South Vietnam. According to reports, the government killed two thousand suspected communist party members and sympathizers and arrested sixty-five thousand. But communists had also killed over four hundred South Vietnamese officials. The war had moved swiftly from the rural areas to the city of Saigon and had entered our beautiful city.

Mac's two-year tour of duty was ending, and it was time for us to go home. The air force was sending Mac back to the Pentagon. A new air attaché would arrive to take his place. In February 1958, as the fighting increasingly encroached, we said a tearful goodbye to our friends—especially Kim, Thanh, and Diem—and all the many people we knew and loved. The staff stood along the driveway and waved as the military car pulled out and we left our beautiful home and life in Vietnam. Over the years, I have often wondered how our kind companions fared during the coming escalated war that would last until 1975.

• • •

Mother, Cathe, Yankee, and I boarded the SS *President Hoover* for the return voyage to the States. During the weeks-long trip, we traveled without our SS *President Cleveland* companion, Funny Bunny Brother Bill, who had long since returned home, but

---

[98] McNeese, Lt. Col. Harold G. "Vietnam, Cambodia, and Laos." Final Report, Air Attaché–MAAG Conference. November 4–8, 1957. AFHRA, reel K7241, frame 1436.

Chief Officer Bill Kahili filled his role and was a delightful companion and good friend to our family for many years to come. Bill Kahili entertained and taught us about the many joys of sea travel, and we could play with Yankee, who was, by now, a seasoned sailor and world traveler.

The ocean trip back home was as much fun as the trip two years earlier, with two exceptions. First, we were told that the air force urgently needed Dad at the Pentagon and he had to fly back ahead of us, so he couldn't accompany us. This was probably true, but the main reason wouldn't be disclosed to Cathe and me until we had returned from Vietnam and were back in California.

The second reason the return trip was marred was that somewhere in the vastness of the Pacific Ocean, we ran into a terrible storm, and the ship rolled violently from port to starboard and back for hours. Everyone was terrified. Our lifesaving drills became real as we huddled together topside wearing life jackets, drenched in the pouring rain. The seas were so rough that even the grand piano became unbolted and slid across the dining room, along with most of the other furniture. As the giant ship dipped deeper with each wave, we mentally prepared for the worst. Thankfully, the large ship eventually weathered the storm. A band started up, the entertainment resumed, and we continued our extraordinary trip back home to America.

Chapter 57
Home on Both Coasts—1958

We docked in Tokyo for a few days, and Mother introduced us to Chris, a charming Frenchman who she said was a friend of hers from Vietnam. We explored the vibrant city, buying countless souvenirs with the five dollars' worth of yen he gave to both Cathe and me. Then, we reboarded the ship and spent five more weeks steaming across the ocean.

After docking in San Francisco, we traveled south to once again stay with Mimi and Grandad, this time in their new home in Anaheim. We were eager to see Dad, but he was across the country at the Pentagon, terribly busy, we were told.

The day after we arrived, we sat in my grandparents' kitchen, and Mother pulled me onto her lap and hugged me tightly. "Sherry," she began slowly, "there's something I need to tell you. Your father and I are going to get a divorce." She paused for several moments, allowing me to absorb her words.

"Divorce?" I repeated, stunned. I knew what the word meant, but I had no frame of reference in my happy life. My parents never argued or said a cross word to each other, at least that I ever heard. "Don't you and Dad love each other?" I asked.

"I've fallen in love with someone else," she said simply. My mouth dropped open. "Do you remember that nice man you met when the ship stopped in Japan last month … Chris?" She went on, "He's going to be your new stepfather."

ZAP. My storybook life ended just like that at age ten and a half. It was as if a large cartoon lightning bolt had descended from the sky and slashed through the middle of *My Book of Childhood*. The first half was a fairy tale filled with adventure, sunshine, and rainbows, and the second half was now gray and cloudy. I did not know how black the pages would later become. *What would life be like without Dad?* I couldn't imagine. I didn't want to imagine.

Mother's words made no sense to me. I couldn't process what she was saying. "Divorce? Why?" was all I could manage. *We were a happy family. What was happening? How could life, as I knew it, have changed so drastically overnight? One minute I was a happy child in a wonderful, loving family, and suddenly, I wasn't.* I desperately needed to talk to my father back in Virginia.

"Daddy," I cried into the phone, reverting to baby talk, "why are you and Mommy getting a divorce? I love you so much!"

"This is your mother's decision, Sherry, not mine," Dad said. "But just you remember, I will always be your and Cathe's father. You are my girls. Nothing will ever change that. I will always be here to love and support you," he said solemnly. "Write to me once a week and tell me what you're up to, and I will faithfully write back. And we'll continue to talk by phone frequently. Maybe while your mother is getting settled, you could come and stay with me for a while? You'd be a big help to me in my old bachelor pad," he said, trying to put a positive spin on the situation. "I'll talk to your mother about it. Would you like that?" he asked.

"Yes," I said as I blinked back tears. "I'd like that, Daddy."

I cried a lot each night after that and took to wetting the bed. As a toddler, I had rubbed the silky rim of my blanket and sucked my index finger for comfort, and now I reverted to this security measure at night as well. I even walked in my sleep once, making it out the front door and down the driveway before my mother put her hand on my shoulder and gently guided me back into the house. I was grieving and perhaps in a bit of shock over this new, life-altering revelation.

Dad needed me, I decided, more than Mother did, so a month later, in April 1958, Mother arranged for me to fly to Washington to live with him at Langley Air Force Base. I knew Mother's affair and their pending divorce had blindsided and crushed him. At almost eleven, I felt like I could help him with meals, the house, and the healing. But gone were the halcyon days of my childhood.

While I lived with Dad at Langley, Mother and Cathe moved to Boulder City, Nevada so that she could get a quick divorce, as the state required only a six-week residency. Chris remained in North Africa where he was manager of an air corporation. I finished the last two months of fifth grade in Virginia, where I felt every bit an outcast. We lived on a military base, and I was separated from my mother and sister. I was profoundly lonely, and Dad knew it. He did his best to be a mother and a father, but he worked long hours. He also understood that Cathe and I needed to be together and with our mother.

"Do you miss your sister, Sherry?" he asked me one day.

"Yes," I replied, "and Mom."

"Then I'll bring them back," he said simply.

A few days later, Dad flew to Boulder City, rented a car, drove to Cathe's school, and picked her up. Then, together, they flew back to our apartment in Virginia. He called Mother before they left to tell her, and she was furious.

"You're kidnapping her," she screamed into the phone.

"No," he calmly replied, "the courts have awarded me full custody. If you want to be with the girls, you'll need to move to Virginia."

When the state of Nevada finalized Mother's divorce, she came to the East Coast and rented an apartment in Washington, DC where the three of us, and Yankee, lived. In October, Chris flew to New York from North Africa, where Mother met him after a month of correspondence filled with lust and sexual innuendo, both eager to be together at last. They were married quietly on Halloween in New Jersey, with her relatives in attendance. We didn't know then how appropriate their wedding date was—a day of frightening monsters and screaming banshees.

Chris then flew back to North Africa to wait for his new family to join him there. When Mother finally told him that Dad would not allow us to leave the country, he gave his notice to the air corporation and prepared to move to Washington, DC, intent on making a new life in America. Cathe, Mother, and I had been there almost a year now.

Sadly, Dad was now only a weekend father, and we couldn't wait to be with him after school on Fridays. Like horses suddenly discovering the barn door was open, we raced to his waiting convertible. He took us bowling, miniature golfing, and to the movies. It was two days of fun and games. But it certainly wasn't like having him come home to us every evening.

· · ·

After Dad returned from his assignment as air attaché in Saigon, he spent the next four years at the Pentagon as chief directorate of plans, "responsible for all actions involving resolution of differences among the military services." The air force promoted Mac to full colonel in May 1960 when he was forty-two years old.

Knotts Berry Farm – Buena Park, CA

Chapter 58
A Stepfather and Chaos Enter Our Lives

When Chris arrived in the United States, he spoke very little English and had no immediate job prospects. Although he held college degrees, he couldn't even be employed as a French teacher because he lacked citizenship. He was angry about having to uproot his life and start over in a foreign country. He never appeared to resent Cathe and me for this major life change, but he blamed Mother, and his anger never abated.

They rented a house in Silver Spring, Maryland with a large kitchen overlooking a backyard pool. The second half of *My Book of Childhood*, no longer cloudy, was about to be darkened in. The Author of Life and his illustrator would need very few bright crayons ... just lots of black ink. Butterflies and rainbows filled the first half of *MBOC*. The second half would be littered with skulls and crossbones, lightning rods, and mushroom clouds. We were born in the magical land of *Narnia* until Mother suddenly shoved Cathe and me through the wardrobe into Hades, never to return.

A mere two months after Chris joined us to live in America, Mother and Chris had their first wedding anniversary. This was a family celebration, we were told. We were planning to go to the Ice Capades after a typical American-style dinner of beans and franks, which Mother thought he would appreciate. As she set the plates down in front of us, Chris swept his meal onto the floor and shouted, slamming his fist on the table. We were all stunned, staring at each other.

"*Putain!*" he spat at her, using the most vulgar of French epithets. "*Putain!* You give me bean and hot dog on our *anniversaire? Ta foulle! Imbécile!*" Suddenly, Chris grabbed my mother by her blonde ponytail and held her head under the kitchen faucet, the tap full blast. She sputtered and screamed and kicked her legs at him, trying to extricate herself from his grasp. Water was everywhere.

All I could think of was that he was going to drown her. Jumping up from my chair, I ran to the sink and pushed him as hard as I could. "Stop it! Get away from her!" I yelled. He fell back, releasing her. Mother dropped to her knees, coughing. Cathe stood next to her, rubbing her back, crying hysterically.

Chris's face was bright red as he yelled in French and English, flapping his arms up and down like he was about to take off into a strong headwind. "*Nom de Dieu,* stupid girl," he said to her.

Wearing her new, red-flowered dress that she had bought for the occasion, Mother now lay on the floor next to the iron pot. Her arms and legs splayed out amongst the brown beans and franks, sprinkled on the green, linoleum floor like a Salvador Dali oil painting. We never made it to the Ice Capades. Instead, we spent the evening consoling our mother and wishing she had never brought this horrible, angry man into our lives.

Through the years, the anger and the yelling never stopped; it only intensified. Like a tiny pimple, he'd pick and pick at some misunderstanding or perceived slight until he had swollen it into an enormous pustule, and all the hate and anger he was holding inside would burst out. No matter what started the tirade, it always devolved into fits of jealousy and hurling accusations of infidelity at each other.

"*Merde!* I am lee ving zees house and you; you dare tay peek chairs," he spat out, his lips curling up in disgust. Calling her 'dirty pictures' became one of his top insults, which I never quite understood.

We escaped each weekend to be with Dad, but never spoke to him about Mother and Chris's relationship, and he never asked. After a year, we moved across the country to California with Dad's reluctant permission. Chris had developed business contacts with a French company, and we moved to Anaheim, where our grandparents lived. I hated being so far away from Dad. Having him close made me feel safer, even if he didn't know we needed protection. I wrote letters diligently and talked on the phone frequently, but Mother and Chris had turned our life upside down, as if they had thrown us down the rabbit hole after Alice. Everything was topsy-turvy.

• • •

Cathe and I flew back East to visit Dad during the summers and holidays. Life was still a learning experience whenever we were with him. During that first summer, he took us to New York City. Entranced, we rode to the top of the Empire State Building, explored the museums, marveled at the synchronicity of the Rockettes at Radio City Music Hall, and had lunch at an automat—a strange, new, technological device that dispensed food items on plates. This amazed and delighted us.

The summer of 1959, we cruised to Havana, Cuba months before Fidel Castro rose to power and had a wonderful week exploring the island. Dad recounted his time there in 1944, training on the B-29 *Superfortresses* before being stationed in Guam. Time with Dad was a respite from our life with Mother and Chris, but we never betrayed Mother by disclosing to him the cyclonic storm we felt trapped in, living with them.

As I look back, life with the new stepfather seems like a Jerry Springer episode on steroids. Where once we lived in peace with quiet discussions and the occasional disagreement, now we endured daily screaming matches. Into this chaos, brother Derreck was born in July 1960, and Valerie made her debut three years later. Chris tried one new job after another, hampered, in part, by his heavy accent, his lack of U.S. citizenship, and possibly his temper, although he turned on the charm around other people.

We moved around Southern California every year, from Anaheim to Buena Park, to Tustin, and back to Anaheim as he changed jobs and Cathe and I changed schools. This at least taught me to make new friends quickly and became a deft skill I developed. People were transitory, but their brief appearance was like a piece of a puzzle pressed into my human experience. I have few lifelong friends, but I have countless friends in my life.

Unhappy new family

Chapter 59
Mac Remarries—Moves to Paris, France

A few years after Mother and Dad's divorce, a charming, precocious, twelve-year-old girl named Cynthia knocked on Dad's apartment door in Alexandria, Virginia selling light bulbs for the Job's Daughters. Cynthia remembers being very scared to knock on strange doors, but this nice man—who turned out to be Mac—opened the first door she timidly rapped on.

"Is that pretty lady who sits on the balcony on the third floor your mother? She has beautiful legs."

"Yes," she said, a bit surprised.

"If you introduce me to her, I'll buy all of your light bulbs," he said with a broad grin. Cynthia agreed enthusiastically and introduced the colonel to her mother, Bara. Cynthia had no idea what he did with the dozens of light bulbs he purchased, but a romance was certainly brightly lit.

Helen Bara Burns, a divorcee whom Mac called Bara B, worked at the Pentagon as a secretary and was indeed beautiful, bright, and well read. She didn't need to draw attention to herself but was adept at bolstering Dad's ego, and he delighted in her doting attentiveness. They soon married and moved to a larger, bottom-floor apartment in the same complex. It thrilled me, knowing Dad deserved happiness and the love of someone who truly appreciated his many good qualities.

Cynthia quickly became devoted to him, calling him Daddy almost immediately, hungry for a father figure and someone to look up to. I was also secretly a bit jealous of Cynthia, who had my father full time. Cathe and I spent summers with them, enjoying the pool, and we three girls attended a two-week summer camp in the mountains of Virginia.

Living in California, as far away from Washington, DC as one could be in the continental U.S., I missed Dad, separated by all of the flyover states. We talked on the phone and wrote letters, but I longed for his daily presence. Dad and Bara, happily married, now lived with Cynthia and her brother, Eric, who was away at college much of the time, in a beautiful apartment in the Chevy Chase, Maryland area.

Mac graduated from the NATO Defense College and was chief of the Command and Control Branch and Directorate of Plans, Headquarters, USAF, which meant that he was responsible for the development of U.S. Air Force positions on matters related to the Worldwide Military Command and Control System.

Mac's cousin, William Bradford, with whom he was very close, had joined the Foreign Service in 1950, and now, coincidentally, worked in the U.S. Embassy in Saigon, where he was employed from 1962 to 1964—three years after Mac and our family left. Small world indeed.

• • •

In the early sixties, the fighting between North and South Vietnam ramped up and moved down the country, and things began to change. Although communists had infiltrated the south during the two years we lived in Vietnam, most of the fighting took place in the north, near Hanoi, nine hundred miles away, and I was oblivious to it. Tempers appeared to cool for a while, and Ho Chi Minh continued to press for elections. But the Vietcong were becoming a growing threat to the south.

Assassinations of local officials continued, and efforts to control villages and rural areas were becoming more difficult.

The U.S. realized the training it had provided to the South Vietnamese Army during the previous five years had not applied to combating an insurgency. They changed their policy to allow the Military Assistance Advisory Group (MAAG) to provide anti-guerrilla training to the South Vietnamese Army. U.S. generals, backed by CIA intelligence, did not believe the communists could mount a political revolt that would threaten the survival of South Vietnam. But they were wrong. They underestimated the strength of the Vietcong guerrilla army.

South Vietnam's government slid into religious chaos. The Roman Catholic president, Diệm, who was hanging on to power by a thread, had refused to make concessions to the Buddhists, and the government threatened to implode under the pressure. The CIA was in contact with Vietnamese generals who were planning to "remove" Diệm, and they were told that the United States would not oppose such a move or punish the generals by cutting off aid. Subsequently, his generals overthrew and executed President Diệm, along with his brother, on November 2, 1963.

The press reported that President Kennedy was stunned. Following the coup, chaos ensued. Hanoi took advantage of the situation and increased its support for their guerrilla fighters. South Vietnam entered a period of extreme political instability, as one military government after another toppled in quick succession.

Incredibly, just twenty days after Diệm's assassination, on November 22, 1963, I was sitting in English class when the intercom crackled on. A shaky voice intoned: "May I have your attention, please? The President of the United States, John F. Kennedy, has just been shot in Dallas." Everyone froze like a tableau. It was as if the world had stopped revolving. Mr. Taylor, our teacher, slowly tilted his head back, put his fingers to the bridge of his nose, took a deep breath, and walked out of the classroom. I don't remember when, if ever, we saw him again.

His picture did not appear in the school's yearbook that year. The principal dismissed school immediately, and we went home to watch television and listen to the stunning events that played out over the next four days.

They declared President Kennedy dead a half hour after he was shot in the head and neck. Technically, Vice President Johnson became president at that moment. A little over ninety minutes later, flanked by still-bloodstained First Lady Jacqueline Kennedy and his wife, Lady Bird Johnson, Vice President Lyndon B. was officially sworn in by Texas federal judge Sarah T. Hughes aboard Air Force One. The nation was in collective shock.

Two days later, as the world waited to learn the motive and details from the assassin, Lee Harvey Oswald, a man later revealed to be Jack Ruby shot and killed Oswald on live TV. Millions of viewers watched this jaw-dropping, singular occurrence that defied belief. These events were seared into the nation's—and, in fact, the entire world's—psyche. That someone would kill the beloved, young president was beyond comprehension.

Once again, I needed to talk to my dad and called him. We spoke for an hour. He was as saddened and as moved as I was. A lifelong Republican, he admired the Democrat Kennedy for his integrity and drive. He had met President Kennedy at a Rose Garden reception four months earlier, where the president congratulated him on his graduation from the NATO Defense College. His assassination was just unthinkable.

· · ·

Shortly thereafter, Mac called to tell Cathe and me that he had been assigned as the special assistant to the Deputy Chief of Staff, Plans and Operations, SHAPE–(NATO), and he and his family would be moving to Paris, France.

A dozen European and North American countries had founded the North Atlantic Treaty Organization, signed in

Washington in 1949 in the aftermath of the Second World War. Its purpose was to secure peace in Europe, to promote cooperation among its members, and to guard their freedom — all of this to counter the threat posed at the time by the Soviet Union. NATO committed the signing Allies to democracy, individual liberty, and the rule of law, as well as to peaceful resolution of disputes. Importantly, the treaty sets out the idea of collective defense, meaning that they consider an attack against *one* Ally as an attack against *all* Allies. The security of its European member countries is inseparably linked to that of its North American member countries. The organization also provides a unique forum for dialogue and cooperation across the Atlantic. Supreme Headquarters Allied Powers Europe (SHAPE) was then headquartered in Porte Dauphine, near downtown Paris.

In his new role, the air force tasked Mac with the development and implementation of policy directly supporting global operations, force management, weather, training, and readiness across air and space. He and his new family, including his twice-widowed mother, moved to an apartment in St. Cloud, France, a wealthy suburb of Paris, while they waited for housing at SHAPE Village, an international housing complex, to open up, and Mac began work at NATO Headquarters.

The air force quickly promoted Mac to principal assistant to the Deputy Chief of Staff, Plans and Operations, SHAPE. Almost fifty years later, Cynthia fondly remembered the day when her mother, Bara, was ill, and Mac invited her to accompany him to a luncheon with some German generals at a posh restaurant in Paris.

"I was the colonel's daughter, who sat between the colonel and the general, and had no idea what to do or say," she told me. "I was barely eighteen. Mac was so gracious and courteous, never reprimanding me when I tried to speak German in my clumsy accent to the general, who called me a 'silly girl.' Dad never treated me like a silly girl," she said.

• • •

In another of life's coincidences, Mother informed me, toward the end of my junior year in high school, that she, Chris, and their two young children were moving to Paris. "Chris needs to find work with French aviation companies. There's no room in the small apartment for all of us, so you and Cathe are going to live with your dad. I will stay part of the time with the kids in Moncontour, helping his parents."

Excellent, I thought. *A year in Paris, and we will live with Dad. A twofer.* We had been to central France the summer before and stayed in the small, rural town of Moncontour du Poitou, where Chris had grown up and Cathe and I had spent the previous summer. I had kept up my French from Saigon, continuing it each year in high school, along with a year of German. Although I would miss my friends, houses and acquaintances had always been temporary. I always expected a move. We left that summer and flew to Paris. Another adventurous chapter in my life was about to begin with Mac.

• • •

On August 2, 1964, an international incident occurred off the coast of North Vietnam just as we were flying to Paris. The USS *Maddox* destroyer, which was stationed in the Gulf of Tonkin, reportedly fired three warning shots, and the North Vietnamese attacked with torpedoes and machine gunfire. The news reported two days later that the North Vietnamese again ambushed the USS *Maddox*. There was great public skepticism. But it wasn't until the early 2000s, after decades of government secrecy, that the National Security Agency (NSA) revealed the truth when they declassified and released nearly two hundred documents. The documents showed that there was, in fact, no attack on August 4th. U.S. officials had lied about the Gulf of Tonkin incident for their own gains—and perhaps for Johnson's own political prospects. As many Americans suspected, the "incident" that propelled America into fighting in the Vietnam War never happened. The U.S. promulgated it to justify sending ground troops to Vietnam.

• • •

Arriving in France, Cathe and I somehow wedged ourselves into the small apartment that Dad and Bara had rented with his mother and Cynthia in St. Cloud. They had not expected Cathe and me at the time they first moved there, almost a year before, so when a space in SHAPE Village became available, we moved to a much larger accommodation—a four-bedroom apartment in Saint-Germain-en-Laye, also in the suburbs of Paris.

Grandmother Nana kept to herself, mostly staying busy in the kitchen, helping Bara with household duties, and then scurrying back to her bedroom lair like a scared, little mouse. She never appeared interested in any of us girls, except she seemed sure that I, the more exuberant teen in the family, would somehow disgrace her beloved son. Her disapproval surrounded me like a cold blanket. She never forgave our mother for divorcing Dad, and it felt like she had transferred all that resentment to me. Mostly, I ignored her.

Dad chuckled at his mother's constant cloud of doom that seemed to surround her as she tsk-tsked her way through life. She was not happy about living in France and complained that "the stupid French people couldn't even speak English." Reminding her we were in their country and that she should be the one at least attempting to learn their language made no apparent dent in her firmly held conviction—the French were stupid, and she was trapped. She spent most of her time in her bedroom, where she no doubt sulked.

By fall, Cynthia was away most of the time for her freshman year at the American College in Paris. Cathe attended eighth grade, and I began my senior year at Paris-American High School. A regularly scheduled army bus connected SHAPE Village to Camp des Loges, the U.S. military base, Paris-American H.S., and downtown Paris, making a regular route. At seventeen, I took full advantage of the easy access to Paris several times during the school year, sliding down in the seat as we passed the school to 'ditch' for the day. Most weekends, I visited the city with friends, taking off my high heels Bara insisted I wear in Paris and replacing them with sneakers so I could walk miles through the streets, enjoying the shops, cafes, museums, and exploring the city.

• • •

In response to the Gulf of Tonkin "incident," in December 1964, the air force's Tactical Air Command (TAC) deployed a squadron of C-123 *Provider* assault transports from the 464th Troop Carrier Wing at Pope AFB, North Carolina to Clark Air Base, Philippines, then on to Tan Son Nhut Air Base, South Vietnam to set up a tactical air cargo transportation system.[14] These were two airports Mac knew intimately well. TAC headquarters was at Langley Air Force Base, Virginia and provided a balance between strategic, air defense, and tactical forces of the post–World War II U.S. Army Air Forces—then in 1947, when it became the U.S. Air Force. As the command responsible for training aircrews for overseas duty, TAC maintained Readiness Training Units in the United States to train pilots and other aircrew members for fighters, reconnaissance, and troop carrier squadrons in the Pacific.

The air force's TAC sent pilots and support personnel to Da Nang Air Base, as well as Phan Rang Air Base in South Vietnam, and Takhli Royal Thai Air Force Base and Korat Royal Thai Air

Force Base in Thailand. Initially, TAC began deploying squadrons of F-100 *Super Sabre*, RF-101 *Voodoo*, and F-105 *Thunderchief* aircraft to these overseas installations.

I thought back to my life in Saigon. It seemed like a dream now. When we left that beautiful country a mere seven years before, I could never have imagined that they would send young American men, now my age, to fight in the jungles. Nor could I have imagined what a devastating effect it would have on a generation.

Summer in VA

Dad marries Bara

Reading in the park

Meeting JFK in the Rose Garden

Chapter 60
Life with Dad in Paris, France

Dad was strict about following rules, and his expectations were high. Young men who wanted to ask me out on a date needed to come to our apartment beforehand to meet the colonel and request his permission. This was an intimidating experience for any young man. His stock question— "Well, son, do you think you'll ever amount to a hill of beans?"—was always a conversation starter.

This caused me to sneak out through a window several times to go on a date with a young, American soldier named Butch because Dad did not approve of me dating an enlisted man. But he was a charming, handsome, young soldier stationed far away from home, and we had great times exploring Paris and dancing at the Enlisted Men's Club. This would have horrified all three adults in the household and would have surely given Nana the vapors.

Dad encouraged me to be adventurous, and I was. There were two incidents that come to mind that happened in Paris. One was when a girlfriend and I snuck onto a movie set.

"They're coming to Paris next week to film a movie called *The Great Race*," my friend Anne screamed. "Let's go down there and watch. Tony Curtis, Jack Lemmon, and Natalie Wood will be there. Maybe we can see them and get their autographs." Anne shared my sense of adventure and was always up for doing something offbeat.

"Let's go," I said. We took the military bus into Paris and then the metro to the Eiffel Tower. They had roped the entire area off, and trailers surrounded the perimeter like Conestogas circling a campfire, ready to fend off an Indian attack. In the middle, costumed extras were milling about. Cameras, booms, and lighting poles were everywhere. It was *très* exciting.

"Look," I said to Anne, "I think we can get under this rope and sneak into that trailer. Let's pretend we're extras." She and I peeked into several trailers before we found one that was devoid of people and awash with nineteenth-century costumes.

After donning long dresses and bonnets, we stepped out of the trailer into the sun and onto the movie set. The dresses were slightly ill-fitting, but we figured they would work well enough to get by.

After a few minutes of walking around, trying to blend in, I spotted Tony Curtis. Excited, I ran over to him and blurted out, "Mr. Curtis, I am such a huge fan. Could I please have your autograph?" But in my exuberance, I did the unthinkable. I stepped on his gleaming, white shoes, leaving a dark smudge across the top of one of them.

"Get her out of here!" he roared, and someone swiftly escorted my friend and me back to the trailer, told us to get dressed in our own clothes, and unceremoniously marched us off the set. I was never a big Tony Curtis fan after that. The story I later told delighted Dad and Bara. Bara called us plucky. Nana just sighed and retreated to her lair. I returned to that scene of the crime many times. The most memorable was for the senior prom, which was held in the restaurant on the second level of the Eiffel Tower.

The second incident took place inside a Paris police station. My friends and I were shopping at the *Galeries Lafayette* department store, and one of them was taking a five-finger discount on pretty much everything she could stuff in her bag. Carrie and I were unaware until the last moment, when it was too late. Security swiftly escorted us out of the store, down to the basement, and perp-walked us to the local station. It was humiliating and frightening.

A police captain smiled down from a remarkably high desk and asked for our ID cards. *"Alors,"* he said, smirking. Continuing in French, he said, "All daughters of colonels. Two Americans and one Canadian. Not a pleasant picture." He clucked his tongue on the roof of his mouth several times for emphasis. "Lucky for you, we will not charge you, but since you are not yet eighteen, we will release you only into the custody of your parents. What are their phone numbers?" Frantically, we swiveled our heads back and forth, staring alternately at each other, looking like young, female versions of *The Three Stooges*.

I thought about the phone call my father would receive. *"Allô, ici, le Commissariat de Police. Votre fille a été arrêté pour vol!"*

"VOL?" I repeated to myself, *"Your daughter has been arrested for stealing!"*

"Non! Not in a million years. I would rather rot in this jail than give you my father's phone number!" I said rather theatrically, but convincingly, I thought.

"Tant pis (too bad)," he said, turning away to shuffle some papers.

I held out like the prisoner of war that I felt I was for at least an hour. We sat on benches and took several pictures of ourselves behind bars from an open cell. Then, as it got dark, I knew Dad would be worried about me, and I was getting hungry. I finally gave in and gave up the phone number, as did the other two girls. I snatched the phone from the sergeant making the call, though, and screamed into the mouthpiece, "Don't worry, Dad, it's all a huge misunderstanding. So sorry to trouble you. I'll explain everything. I love you, and I'll see you soon," then handed the phone back to the stunned policeman.

When Mac arrived, along with Bara and Nana, who fortunately waited in the car, they took each of us girls into a separate room with our respective parent or parents. Mac, who spoke fluent, but slow and deliberate French, listened, cupping his ear and squinting to understand the words that the policeman was spitting out at breakneck speed. Mac was obviously uncomfortable and took several deep breaths. The sergeant was detailing 'the heist' in rapid French. Three girls, shoplifting all afternoon, blah-blah-blah. But because of our ages, we were being released into the custody of our parents with no charges filed.

"What was that last part?" Dad asked me.

"Dad," I said, "he wants you to know that I was an unfortunate bystander in this whole sordid situation, and he apologizes for the inconvenience. I am free to go."

"Merci beaucoup," Dad said, standing up quickly and offering his hand. His face was a study in granite. As we pulled away in the staff car, I could see my Canadian friend—the perp—leaving in her parents' station wagon, banished to the third row of seats facing backward. Her sad face looked forlornly out the rear window, like a convict being transported to prison by surly guards driving her away. It was a comical picture, and I suppressed a giggle.

Dad was firm, and I endured a brief lecture as he cautioned me about being careful of 'the company you keep' and about appearances of wrongdoing, etc. My grandmother wouldn't speak to me for weeks, sure that I had finally ruined my father's career. They put my Canadian friend into therapy for kleptomania, and the experience was definitely a teaching moment for me. I would be forever scrupulously honest, making sure I returned even the smallest items like paper clips, rubber bands, and pens to the office when I entered the adult world. *Effrayé tout droit*—a French version of *Scared Straight*.

Dad was serious about proper behavior, but he certainly did not keep so tight a rein as to restrict my growth or impede my learning about life. Quite the opposite. He gave me enough rope to hang myself, as he said, and encouraged my adventurous spirit.

At seventeen, after my senior year, it did not surprise me that he agreed to allow me to travel alone with my friend Dawnelle McCluskey on a train adventure to Italy. After all, when he was my age, he had joined the Merchant Marine and sailed around the world visiting exotic ports of call. Not content to go on the school trip to the island of Majorca in Spain and lie on a beach with our classmates, I wanted an escapade. I was my father's daughter, obviously. Dad's only requirement was that he book the hotels in advance.

There were no high-speed trains in those days, so there were many stops, but we enjoyed the slow ride past the charming houses, farms, and vineyards of France and Italy. Our first destination was all the way to the tip of Italy. From Naples, we took a ferry boat to the island of Capri and then a seventeen-mile bus trip to the ancient city of Pompeii, preserved just as it was in AD 79 by the lava from the volcano Vesuvius. The bodies and artifacts transfixed us. Years later, the Italians moved many to a museum in Rome.

Traveling back up north, we saw the ruins and beauty of Rome and the Vatican, and I was stunned at the incredible painting by Michelangelo on the ceiling of the Sistine Chapel. Continuing north, we sunned on the beaches of Portofino in Genoa on the Italian Riviera like two celebrities enjoying a holiday on the Cote d'Azur.

Traveling and seeing the world was always on the agenda. At Christmas, Dad took the family on a vacation to Germany and Austria. We visited Berchtesgaden, Germany and saw the infamous Eagle's Nest, which was a symbol of Hitler's power. It still stands for the evil of the Nazi regime, where they planned for war and mass murder. Garmisch-Partenkirchen, Germany, a world-class resort area in the Bavarian Alps with stunning views of majestic mountains and crystal-clear lakes, charmed us. We swam and hiked and watched the skiers glide down the mountain trails. Then we spent a few days in Munich, where Mac had business, and visited picturesque, storybook towns in Austria. Later in the year, on spring break, a girlfriend and I stayed for a week in London. The memories are sweet.

Ball at Versailles

Mac and Bara

In Rome with Dawnelle

A day in Paris

Chapter 61
Leaving Paris—Summer of 1965

What a glorious year and a half for a young woman not quite eighteen. It was not only magical to experience the splendors and history of Europe, but to have my father in my life full time once again was a joy and a respite from the chaotic life with Mother and Chris, which was like living with Richard Burton and Elizabeth Taylor in a never-ending scene from *Who's Afraid of Virginia Woolf?*

On March 8, 1965, while I was happily finishing my senior year in Paris, France, President Lyndon Johnson ordered U.S. Marine battalions to defend the American airbase at Da Nang, Vietnam, which is approximately equal distance between Saigon and Hanoi. Thirty-five hundred U.S. Marines landed near that city, and the landing marked the first time the U.S. inserted combat troops into the war. American boots were now solidly on the ground in Vietnam.

Three months later, I graduated from high school. The commencement was held at the Maison Internationale de La Cité Universitaire in a huge auditorium in Paris. I had been accepted at the University of Illinois, Champaign-Urbana campus, and it excited me to start this new phase of my life, for the first time a free bird on my own ... or so I thought.

It was the summer of 1965. America had officially entered the Vietnam War, and Mac was to be the director of war plans, headquarters Tactical Air Command (TAC). He and Bara were moving back, this time to Langley AFB. Mother and Chris had recently moved to Indianapolis, Indiana, where Cathe would start high school, and I would await the start of university in the fall.

"Sir," I said with feigned seriousness as I gave Mac a sharp salute, "request permission to remain in Paris and attend the Sorbonne or the American College like Cynthia did her first year."

"Permission denied, soldier," he replied with equal seriousness as he returned the salute. "We are going back to Washington, DC, and I am not leaving you alone here in Paris, even if you are almost eighteen."

What could possibly go wrong?, I thought.

• • •

American troops were now being sent to Vietnam in record numbers. The escalation that began in March continued throughout 1965, and by the end of the year, two hundred thousand American troops were in Vietnam. In 1966, the troop level doubled to four hundred thousand.

Almost all of my fellow Paris-American H.S. classmates had been accepted at colleges around the U.S., many of the young men at West Point or the Air Force Academy. But that wasn't the case with some of my previous classmates from my California high schools, and indeed from high schools all around the U.S. The army immediately drafted many high school graduates, who were not college bound, into the army and sent them to Vietnam to fight. It was an enormous incentive to go to college and keep their grades high. All men who reached the age of eighteen were required to report to their local draft board for classification. The selective service's November 1965 draft call was the largest since the Korean War.

The selective service boards in each state could issue deferments for a variety of reasons, including college attendance, dependent children, or they could classify a registrant as "available for service" and require that he undergo pre-induction testing. They could order men who passed the tests to be inducted and report for duty, depending on the needs of the military and the allocation of national manpower requirements to the local draft boards.

Some young men, imbued with the patriotism of their WWII-generation parents, enlisted. Others, resisting the idea of Americans fighting in a foreign civil war, fled to Canada. TV, virtually in every household now, brought war into the American living room for the first time. The nightly news became a horrific, tragic reality show as the reported enemy "body count" kept mounting steadily. This tally was how the U.S. military showed the American people that the U.S. was winning the war. The count included not only enemy soldiers, but unarmed civilians.

• • •

Mac led the Tactical Air Command as director of war plans during these first two years of American involvement in Vietnam, as TAC was consumed by operations in the former Indochina—Vietnam, Cambodia, and Laos—the three countries for which he had served as air attaché. Daily, flight crews trained by TAC would hurl themselves and their planes at targets across the area of operations, including over the skies of North Vietnam.

Chapter 62
We Move to Indianapolis as the Vietnam War Escalates—1965

Flying from Paris, Cathe and I landed in Indianapolis, Indiana, where our mother and stepfather had just moved into a rented home on the north side of the city. Chris had secured a management position with Lake Central Airlines (which later merged with Allegheny Airlines, which became USAir, which became U.S. Airways) to buy and maintain French airplanes—the *Nord 262*. He frequently and blessedly traveled to France, giving the household some occasional peace and normalcy.

Strongly encouraged by my mother to stay in Indianapolis instead of going to the University of Illinois, and with a desire to referee the fight nights when Chris was at home, I instead started Butler University in downtown Indianapolis, and Cathe began her first year of high school. Derreck was now five, and Valerie was only two.

Jerrie was always a kind and loving mother to the four of us, but she never understood the damage their constant screaming matches were having, particularly on her two youngest children. As a young teen, I would cuddle and try to reassure them. As I got older, I would sit on the stairs in full view of the combatants, listening and watching, silently ready to call the police if he struck her, which he had done on occasion.

The near drowning on their first anniversary was never far from my mind. I was not personally afraid of Chris, just what he might do to Mother. My presence, however, both reassured and emboldened her. With me in the room, she felt safe to hurl insults and accusations back at Chris, extending the confrontation hours longer than it might have otherwise lasted. *Just stop talking, Mother,* I thought as Derreck and Valerie huddled upstairs, crying. There was such fear in their eyes, their small bodies shook as if shivering from the cold. The loud battle going on between two people who were supposed to make them feel safe and secure terrorized them.

As the months and years and endless battles wore on, Chris not only revealed himself to be a volatile, bitter person, he was, in fact, a cheat and a philanderer with no moral compass to guide him. The contrast in character and temperament between Mac and Chris was stark. They were as opposite as sunset and dawn.

From the start of their marriage, Chris had several affairs. Now Simone, his Moroccan secretary who spoke three languages fluently, and whom he praised constantly for her business acumen and intellect, became increasingly integrated into our lives. They spent a great deal of time together, and he talked about her constantly.

Simone was plain looking with short, dark hair, and she dressed in dowdy, unflattering clothes. She smoked Benson & Hedges 100's, one after another, often lighting a second one with the lit cigarette she currently held. She was soft-spoken with a quiet, intellectual demeanor, a striking contrast to our outgoing, glamorous, and emotional mother.

Mother, of course, graciously welcomed Simone into our family circle, frequently including her for dinners and holidays. Whenever Chris and Mother argued, he screamed at the top of his lungs, "Jer REE, you am-bay-seal." Then came the inevitable comparison to Simone, the smart, calm businesswoman he now called 'Simi.' I suspected there was more to their relationship than business.

"You bitch!" I heard my mother scream one afternoon. "Get out of my house!" I was upstairs in my attic loft, studying, when I heard the familiar thundering sound of voices blaring from below. But something was different; these were both female voices. As I came down the ladder, I saw that Chris had come into the house with Simone, and she and Mother were standing several feet apart, yelling at each other.

"Oh, I'll leave all right," Simone spat, "but I'm leaving with your husband. We're in love, and he's leaving you to marry me."

"Over my dead body," Mother yelled back.

I took my customary seat on the stairs, assumed the listening position, and briefly tuned in. 'Simone' was apparently madly in love with Chris, and they were going to run off together. I was ecstatic.

Take him, I thought. *Take him and good riddance!* Most of the ensuing confrontation took place between the two women. At twenty-nine, Simone was about ten years younger than Mother, but Mother was not to be replaced so easily. As the two women hurled vicious and vile insults at each other, Chris mostly held back, enjoying the cat fight over him. He was smiling and so uncharacteristically calm. The yelling went on for almost an hour. My mind drifted as it always did during these pointless, repetitive confrontations. The words were a blur of blah-blah-blah, like a cacophonous symphony on a never-ending track.

I was now a sophomore in college. For about seven years, I'd been listening to variations of this scene. I tuned it all out and thought of my dad, so calm and reasoned. So different from the hysterical people, screaming insults at each other. Then, I thought about the one thing Dad had gotten wrong and Mother had been correct about. *I was not in college to find a husband to take care of me, as Mac had envisioned. I was going so that I would be prepared to take care of myself. I would be a success and prove to be better at my job than any man. Marriage would never trap me as it had my mother. If later I married, it would be for love, not money or security.* I had not yet found this man, who I knew would be much more like Mac than my stepfather, but I was only weeks away from meeting him.

I left my own thoughts and drifted back into the present. My habit was to stay neutral and quiet, but I continued to silently root for Simone. The match wound down. Clearly, Simone did not have the stamina needed to endure these long battles. Chris and Jerrie could easily scream for hours at a time. Simone obviously wasn't in fighting shape.

At the end of the evening, the tables had turned dramatically, and Simone did not leave with her 'prize.' Chris had magnanimously decided to stay with Jerrie. It was as if he had been refereeing a prize fight and, after twelve rounds, declared Jerrie the winner based on points. I almost expected him to raise her arm in victory. She was beaming at her hollow triumph. As for me, I felt as disappointed as though I had placed a million-dollar bet on the outcome and lost it all. Of course, the real winner was the unscrupulous Chris, who would keep both women—one as wife and one as mistress—for the rest of their lives.

• • •

As the Vietnam War raged on, most Americans turned their focus away from the domestic Civil Rights Movement and on to the Vietnam War. The army, now at its peak, had around 4,368,000 young Americans deployed, the marines, 794,000, the navy, 1,842,000, and the air force, 1,740,000. That's almost nine million young men whose lives were forever, unalterably, changed. Many would never return home. Many who did, came back broken physically, mentally, and emotionally.

On college campuses, students—baby boomers—were growing increasingly angry over the war that many considered interference in another country's civil war. Protests erupted across the country on college campuses. "Hey, hey, LBJ, how many kids did you kill today?" people chanted.

Everyone seemed to know someone who had either been killed or returned wounded and traumatized. A new term developed—Post Traumatic Stress Disorder. The war, previously called a "conflict" because war was never officially declared, was now referred to as the Vietnam War, and it divided this country by generations. Most of the WWII generation considered dissenters and protesters cowards and un-American. Many of their children viewed this war as unjust, driven by power, ambition, and politics. No one had attacked America, and there wasn't a Nazi madman killing millions of people and attacking our Allies.

To most in the baby boom generation, it was a needless waste of young, American lives. The rock music of the sixties and seventies telegraphed their voices with songs like "We Gotta Get Out of This Place," by the Animals, and "Fortunate Son," by Creedence Clearwater Revival and written by John Fogerty, highlighting the disparity of the wealthy who could often avoid the draft. "What's Going On?" by Marvin Gaye, and then the clearly anti-war song "War (What Is It Good For?)" recorded by Edwin Starr in a dramatic, angry vocal, reached number one on the charts and stayed there for three weeks. But Midwestern campuses where I was ensconced were largely insulated from the turmoil, protests, and demonstrations happening on campuses on both coasts. Only when a few college friends returned from Vietnam, or I watched the nightly news, was I reminded of the war.

A cease-fire was called for Tet, the Vietnamese New Year. On January 30, 1968, the first day of Tet, the North Vietnamese Army and Vietcong mounted an immense surprise attack on more than one hundred cities and towns in South Vietnam, notably Saigon. Although they were repelled and pushed back, the Tet Offensive seemed to shake the confidence of the U.S. which, by the end of 1968, had peaked at nearly 450,000 troops. The Tet Offensive hastened the withdrawal and was a turning point in the war.

It was probably inevitable that horror stories of civilians being gunned down began to be reported in the U.S. press, including the tragic Mỹ Lai Massacre in March 1968. This was an ugly war that squandered countless lives. The Vietcong were fighting for control of their country, and American soldiers, mostly, were reluctant combatants.

In 1969, Richard Nixon, whom Dad had met and spent time with eleven years before in Saigon, succeeded Lyndon Johnson as president. He had run on the promise to reduce the U.S. troop levels in Vietnam, calling his plan "Vietnamization." He said that the U.S. would gradually withdraw from the war, allowing the South Vietnamese to shoulder the bulk of the fighting, but that didn't exactly happen. American ground troop levels in Vietnam not only remained high, but the Nixon administration even expanded the war into the neighboring countries of Laos and Cambodia. American soldiers had now been fighting and dying in Vietnam for three years.

The Vietnam War, or the Second Indochina War, was decades old. It was extremely difficult for the French, Americans, and South Vietnamese—all conventionally trained—to win against the Vietcong, who were guerrilla warriors who used ambushes, sabotage, and raids against their enemies. Fighting took place in the jungles and the rural village towns of Vietnam. The Vietcong didn't always wear uniforms, and to fool the U.S. soldiers, they could exchange weapons so that U.S. troops could not distinguish North and South Vietnamese by the guns' country of origin (mostly Russia and the U.S.).

The North and South Vietnamese soldiers looked alike, and seemingly friendly villagers—even women and children—could be armed and extremely dangerous. Villagers often built booby traps or helped house and feed the Vietcong. For U.S. forces, simply finding their enemy was difficult. Since Vietcong hid in the dense brush, U.S. forces dropped Agent Orange or napalm bombs, which cleared an area by causing the leaves to drop off or to burn away from the trees. Unfortunately, this poison later proved to be physically detrimental to our troops as well.

When the young men returned home after a tour of duty, the American public not only didn't welcome them with open arms, regarding them as heroes as it had done with soldiers in WWII or Korea, they vilified them. They were called baby killers and routinely spat on. It's no wonder that so many Vietnam veterans were emotionally, spiritually, as well as physically scarred. Their country had turned their collective back on them, shunning them like lepers.

The army had not equipped the young men to do much with their lives when they returned as civilians, having been primarily trained to kill. Many returned traumatized, lost, shamed, and sometimes ashamed. Some turned to drugs and alcohol. Some became homeless. But as the war went on, the public was becoming inured to the term "body count." There were so many dead bodies on both sides of this terrible war. And both countries would continue putting young men through the military meat grinder for ten years.

Chapter 63
Mac Serves in the U.S. Arms Control and Disarmament Agency Before Mandatory Retirement—1970

Having finished his assignment with TAC at Langley AFB, the air force assigned Mac to Weapons Evaluation and Control Bureau, for the U.S. Arms Control and Disarmament Agency as military staff assistant. The emphasis of this agency was to gain an understanding of the strategic weapons capabilities of the Soviet Union and People's Republic of China. It expanded the electronic reconnaissance capability of the United States through federal agency research and private contract research, using radio frequency and optical technologies. The theory of this mission was that a clearer understanding of other nations' strategic capabilities was an important initial step in the prevention of nuclear war.

Mac's responsibilities included the development of basic U.S. positions on arms control, particularly in connection with the Strategic Arms Limitation Talks (SALT) with the USSR. America continued to be in a Cold War with the Soviet Union. I recall that all during junior high and high school, we had duck-and-cover exercises in school where we had to hide under our small desks, which were supposed to protect us from the radiation of a nuclear blast. Many people built bomb shelters in enclosed basements under their houses. I felt more reassured talking to my dad on our weekly calls than huddled under a wooden umbrella.

• • •

Letter from Dad:

> *September 8, 1969*
> *Dearest Sher and Cath,*
> *Will kill two little birds with one stone and make a copy of this letter for each of you. I have enjoyed good, newsy letters from each of you both recently and realize that I've been delinquent in keeping you up to date on our own news.*
>
> *Our move to the "boonies" is now almost complete, and what a job it was! I took a week's leave and moved all but the heavy items of furniture in the car. Down the elevator, into the garage, load up, drive 12 miles to Virginia, and up three flights of stairs with books, clothing, dishes, etc. It was good for me, however, as I managed to lose a few pounds of "muscle" around the waist. Bara and Nana did their share, and more, and Bruce Bradford helped out on one occasion. At any rate, we're all a little pooped and glad that the worst is over. By next week, we should be back to normal.*
>
> *I know that you are both looking forward to school, but perhaps for slightly different reasons. You, Sherry, because it means the windup of a long, long pull; and you, Cath, because you are just starting on a grand adventure. Be sure to adopt good study habits right from the start. This takes self-discipline, but will pay wonderful dividends in the future. If you get off on the wrong track to start with, it is so difficult to get back on course. Discuss this with Sherry, as she can be very helpful to you.*
>
> *Speaking of schools, I will be enrolling again at George Washington for another 6 semester hours in the fall. Managed to pass my French examination this past summer and am now some 9 hours advanced*

toward my PhD goal. Should be at the halfway mark by the end of the spring semester. Hope I can hold out!

My work here at the Arms Control and Disarmament Agency continues to be interesting, though I am not too optimistic about the prospects of an arms control agreement with the Soviets. Two of the papers, which I have written recently, will form a small part of the U.S. position on arms control when and if we do sit down with the Russians to negotiate.

I hope you both had wonderful birthdays. Please write to me soon.
All my love,
Dad

For his work at the ACDA, Dad received the Joint Service Commendation Medal.

"Colonel McNeese made vital contributions to the development of positions adopted by the United States for the Strategic Arms Limitation Talks with the Soviet Union. His outstanding military expertise was recognized throughout the Agency, as evidenced by his widely sought advice on airpower matters and his highly skilled presentations pertaining to Department of Defense plans, programs, and organizational studies. By his exemplary performance of duty, Colonel McNeese has reflected great credit upon himself, the United States Air Force, and the United States Arms Controls and Disarmament Agency."

• • •

I stood at the back of the church, at the start of the long aisle separating the pews at the White Harvest Methodist Church in Indianapolis as my father stepped to my side. He was breathing deeply and standing tall. A tight, proud smile made his lips curl up slightly. Friends and family were on either side of the aisle. I wore a beautiful, off-white, satin dress that Mother had borrowed from a friend's daughter. We had it altered, and it fit me perfectly. Dad gave my elbow a tight squeeze. It was as if he were saying, "Okay, Sherry, prepare for takeoff."

We strolled down the carpeted path to the waiting group of friends. Cathe was my maid of honor. I closed my eyes and blinked away tears. It felt as if I were taxiing down a beautiful, white runway. At the end of the carpet stood Mike, my tall, handsome copilot, beaming. As we reached the podium, Dad gently let go of my arm, and Mike reached for my hand. Mac leaned down and whispered, "Hold on to the throttle, Sherry. It's your time to soar."

• • •

Mac had served his country for thirty years, and because of mandatory retirement, he hung up his wings in 1970, the same year that I married Mike. Dad was only fifty-two years old. He was a full colonel with an eventful and distinguished military career under his belt. Too young and full of life to actually stop working, he began consulting for the Federal Emergency Management Agency as a planning officer. George Washington University awarded him a graduate teaching fellowship, having completed the requirements for a PhD in International Relations, and he consulted to the National Security Affairs as an independent contractor.

My brother, Derreck, recalled one afternoon when Mac and Bara invited Jerrie, Valerie, and him to lunch at their apartment in McLean a few years after Mac retired. Once again, in a strange twist of fate, Mother and Chris had moved from Indianapolis to Falls Church in 1970 when he started a business selling airplane parts, and they lived very near Mac and Bara. Derreck, then in his early teens, remembered fondly how Dad took him aside and told him, "You're Jerrie's son, and that makes you my son as well. Don't be a stranger." Derreck, who struggled with the outrageous behavior of his father, Chris, said that the fact that a man of Mac's caliber and character would consider him a son made him swell with pride, and does to this day. He told me he, too, regretted that he wasn't able to spend more time with Mac.

Mac and Bara enjoyed a peaceful, happy life, dining at the Officers' Club and taking advantage of the many benefits of what was then Fort Myer in Arlington, Virginia. There were also occasional sailing outings with daughter, Cynthia, her husband, Tony, and their young family.

"I have only wonderful memories of Mac," Cynthia told me recently. "He was a genuine hero who always treated me as a daughter when I was only a stand-in, and he would have much preferred you to be there."

• • •

In January 1973, representatives of the United States, North and South Vietnam, and the Vietcong signed a peace agreement in Paris, ending the direct U.S. military involvement in the Vietnam War. The terms included a cease-fire, release of POWs, and the promise of new elections to be held. As events played out, the cease-fire agreement was a sham and not worth the ink it took to sign the papers. The Vietcong began firing on the South Vietnamese even before the last American troops departed on March 29th. By early 1974, full-scale war had resumed, and the South Vietnamese authorities reported Vietcong had killed 80,000 of their soldiers and civilians during the year, making it the most costly year of the Vietnam War. Ho Chi Minh wanted his entire country back, after decades of fighting the French and another decade of fighting Americans.

I called Dad on his fifty-seventh birthday and again eight days later on April 23, 1975 when, after failing in a last-ditch effort to get Congress to approve additional funding for the South Vietnamese government, President Gerald Ford declared the Vietnam War had ended "as far as America is concerned." Saigon was about to fall. I wanted to get his thoughts and concerns.

Six days after President Ford's announcement, on April 29th, the communists in North Vietnam rushed in to Saigon and shelled Tan San Nhut Air Base, preventing planes from landing. As a prearranged signal from U.S. Ambassador Graham Martin, the embassy played the song "White Christmas" over and over, and the evacuation of Saigon began. Because planes couldn't land and the Vietcong had blocked the sea lanes, the only option was a helicopter evacuation.

I learned from Dad that his younger cousin, Bill "Brad" Bradford, who had served at the embassy a decade earlier, was being sent back to Saigon to assist in the last of the U.S. Military's evacuation. When the Vietcong attacked the defense attaché compound, the U.S. Embassy became the only departure point for helicopters.

Originally, the U.S. had planned to evacuate only Americans, but Ambassador Martin insisted on evacuating South Vietnamese government officials and the embassy's local staff as well. There were also about 10,000 South Vietnamese people awaiting certain death from the communists, who pressed against the gates of the embassy, hoping to leave Saigon in helicopters. For two days, from April 29th to April 30th, helicopters landed at the embassy every ten minutes, including landing on the roof. Some pilots flew for nineteen hours straight. Incredibly, marines evacuated over 7,000 people, including 5,500 Vietnamese, in less than twenty-four hours.

As they airlifted the last people out of Saigon, the communists rushed in to capture the city and united the entire country under Ho Chi Minh's communist regime. The new government changed Saigon's name to Ho Chi Minh City to honor the man who had fought for thirty-plus years to throw off the yoke of foreign invaders. But even today, most residents still refer to it as Saigon.[99]

American troops had been fighting this extremely unpopular war in Vietnam for eight years, and the U.S. had been involved for two decades, spanning five presidential administrations from 1953 to 1975. The Vietnam War was over, but the human cost on all sides was high. Fifty-eight thousand American soldiers, about one million North Vietnamese, and between two hundred thousand and two hundred fifty thousand South Vietnamese soldiers were killed in action. Sadly, there were also two million Vietnamese civilians who lost their lives in this war. And this doesn't account for the wounded and traumatized, whose lives it would forever change. Once again, this war, like others, was a costly, lengthy exercise in futility.

• • •

On a different continent, within days of the end of the Vietnam War, another war was taking place, and this war would also embroil our family. In the middle of Africa sits the country of Chad. It is a landlocked country, sometimes referred to as the "Dead Heart of Africa." Many anthropologists believe it is one of the areas where the human species originated. Chad had been a French colony from 1920 until 1960, when it became a sovereign state under its first president, Francois Tombalbaye. But it was a tumultuous governance, and after fifteen years of war and unrest, the military ousted Tombalbaye in a coup d'état. It was under this dangerous and unstable new government that President Gerald Ford appointed Bill Bradford as ambassador to Chad.

Mike and I flew to Washington for the family celebration at the Officers' Club at Langley AFB, and I danced with Brad, congratulating him on his appointment. He seemed both pleased

---

[99] Wikipedia. "Operation Frequent Wind."

and excited about the new undertaking. Dad had mixed feelings about the appointment, and we spoke about his concerns frequently over the next two years. He was certainly proud of his younger cousin but concerned that Brad's entire family, including his elderly, wheelchair-bound mother—Mac's dear aunt Jeanne—was going with him to this very unstable war zone. The U.S. Senate confirmed Bill Bradford as ambassador to Chad on October 15, 1976, and he served there until 1979.

• • •

I regret not being around Dad as frequently as I would have liked during my adult years. There was so much more that I wanted to learn from him. We lived on two different coasts, and the visits were too few. He was busy with obviously important business, but he was always thrilled when I called, chatting as if he had all the time in the world. We corresponded over the years through letters, and while phone calls and in-person conversations were always more satisfying in the moment, I am delighted to have saved all of these written documents of life with my father. Memories fade, but the written word, carefully preserved, lasts a lifetime or more.

Dad rarely brought up his own work, but he was intensely interested in me, my family, and my life. He was such an incredible role model and caring father. I could always count on his well-thought-out, studied opinions.

During my adult years, when I visited Dad, we talked at length, at dinner and in the evenings, about current events, philosophy, politics, and history. As he relaxed in his comfortable armchair with his pitcher of martinis, taking puffs on his cigarettes, I would prompt him to tell me stories about his early flying days, and he would lean back and recall. The tales always had a humorous bent and were self-effacing. Like most men of that era, it seems he wasn't one to brag or talk much about himself or his exploits.

· · ·

Letter written September 1, 1991:

Dearest Sherry, Mike, and Brett,

First (and most important!) happy birthday to you, my dear girl. I note that the big event will be on Friday next, so you will have a long weekend to celebrate with the family. Have a ball!

Am so delighted to note the progress that Tokos's stock has made on the exchange. I am sure that your labors are largely responsible, Mike. Congratulations.

I am also pleased to hear that you, Sherry, are negotiating with your employers for a new, less stressful working relationship. I hope things work out well, dear. As for Brett, we were delighted to hear how well he is doing with Tokos and what a mature, young man he is becoming. We share your pride in his progress.

Bara and I are both well, but poor Jeanne is quite ill with the "shingles." She is improving under strong medication but feels "poorly." Bill and Jody are in Europe and will be gone for another week, so we have been doing what we can to assist—visits, shopping, overnight stays, etc. Bruce, Laurie, and Kate have been carrying the major load, but since they work during the day, Bara and I have tried to be helpful.

You asked my opinion on the breakup of the Soviet Union and dissolution of the CP. I concur with you that it is an almost incredible event, perhaps the most significant since WWII. I know of no one who predicted such a self-destruct scenario nor would have thought it possible in such an authoritarian society. On balance, I would say that it is very good news for the free world and Soviet citizens, but the transition from a totalitarian society to a free-enterprise, market economy will be long and difficult and, I fear, fraught with dangers for all. I think our president is acting wisely and prudently, i.e. moving slowly until we can sort out needs and mechanisms. I favor humanitarian aid for the difficult winter that lies ahead and technological assistance to help in the transition to a more democratic society. Later, a multi-lateral, Marshall Plan type of assistance may be in order. Let's stay tuned!

Have a wonderful special day, Sherry dear. I'll be thinking of you and will call. Use the enclosed check to help with the celebration!

Love,

Dad

Dad visited us several times as Mike and I moved about the country with job promotions, and our regular holiday trips back East kept us connected. Mac had been involved in war—or trying to prevent it—his entire career. He served his country through WWII, the Korean War, and the Vietnam War. Mac had seen the rise and fall of many dictators and believed strongly in the value of democracy. He understood that the nature of politics was compromise, and that compromise was necessary for good governance. That is how democracy works.

"Always keep an open mind," he counseled. "Debate and argument are vital to finding common ground in a world of differing opinions and problem solutions. Listen to another point of view and learn from each other as both sides move closer to common ground."

Mac was a student of history and would often quote George Santayana, who William Shirer popularized in *The Rise and Fall of the Third Reich* in 1959, who said, *"Those who cannot remember the past are condemned to repeat it."* He also believed that because, as Lord John Edward Acton observed, "Power corrupts and absolute power corrupts absolutely," the integrity of those in power had to be of utmost consideration. Too much power in the hands of a few is a recipe for disaster. Our republic, with its system of checks and balances while not perfect, is the best man has devised to date.

Mac was as principled and honorable as any person I have ever met. Throughout his life, I could always count on him to support what was right, not what was expedient. Sadly, what an enemy couldn't snuff out, his lifelong cigarette habit did. He died of lung cancer at age seventy-six ... far too soon.

Mike and I marry

Chapter 64
Mac—The Final Destination, Arlington National Cemetery, 1994

I sat quietly on a bench in the chapel's anteroom, nervously fingering my note cards, tears streaming down my face. I was forty-seven years old. We were at Arlington National Cemetery in Virginia. Mike and I had flown back for the memorial service. It was February 1994.

"You don't have to do this, Sherry," my loving Michael said, kissing me gently on the cheek.

My sister Cathe agreed through sobs, "You don't. No one will fault you."

"Oh yes, I do," I replied, vigorously nodding my head. "Oh yes, I do."

Dad had taught me that doing the right thing isn't always the simple thing. In fact, the right thing is usually the tougher choice. You didn't just quit because something was hard. You pushed through your fear and tackled it. Dad had been my hero, my rock of Gibraltar, and my soft place to fall. There was a story I needed to tell about who this man was. Never in my life had he let me down, and I would not let him down now. He had instilled courage in me through stories and his own actions.

Someone once said, "Everyone dies twice. The first time is when your heart stops beating, and the second time is when your name is spoken for the last time." I was going to speak his name and make sure that his great-grandchildren and their great-grandchildren spoke his name as well. I was going to give a eulogy.

• • •

I learned rather abruptly that my father had finally succumbed to lung cancer, a result of his sixty years of smoking. My boss had called a sales strategy meeting in our main Los Angeles office, and I was sitting in a conference room, distracted and emotional, thinking about my father. A tap on my shoulder startled me.

"You have an important phone call," a Los Angeles assistant whispered to me. "Could you please step outside the room?" I glanced at my boss, who nodded. She knew I had been waiting for word about my father's condition.

I had flown out to Virginia two weeks earlier to see Dad and knew he wasn't doing well. A few years earlier, surgeons removed part of his lip because of cancer. He quit smoking, but too late, as the disease had already spread to his lungs. It had been heartbreaking for me to leave. I spent a few days with him at their apartment before the oncologists hospitalized him for an aggressive regimen at Georgetown Medical Center. He had elected to receive experimental treatment for lung cancer that entailed strong doses of chemotherapy and radiation, with the protocols alternating.

I stayed with him every day and talked to him, trying to keep him positive, but he wasn't very conversant and had no interest in watching the news on the television that hung on the wall at the foot of his bed or reading the newspaper. He knew his life was ending. He had resigned himself to the inevitable. This positive, *never-say-die* man had given it his best shot … and lost. His number had finally come up. He had beaten incredible odds to survive during the war, but cancer was a merciless and tenacious enemy. Maybe the doctors had been more forthcoming with him about the treatment failures, but they did not give me the answers I needed. "How much longer will he live?" I implored them outside Dad's room. "What's the prognosis?"

"It's an experimental regime. The cancer is aggressive. The treatment is aggressive. We don't know," was all they would say.

I was in such a quandary. At some point, I had to go home. I lived in California, three thousand miles away, and had taken a week off work; my family was waiting. But no one would or could tell me how long they thought he might survive. A day, two days, a week, a year? I didn't want to leave, knowing that I would never see him again, or that he might die shortly after I left. If I knew how long he had, I could stay or come back. But no one could tell me if I should stay, or for how long, because no one can predict the exact end of life.

As the week ended, I kissed him goodbye, told him how much I loved him, how much he meant to me, and what a wonderful father he was and always had been. He listened but didn't speak. I cried, and tears rolled down his cheeks as well. I left for the airport, bereft and shaken.

Back in Los Angeles, two weeks later, having stepped out of the meeting, the assistant directed me to a phone in the hallway. The clerk in our Orange County office was on the line.

"Hello, Sue?" I said to the woman I had known for five years. "This is Sherry."

"Your father died," she said matter-of-factly. No preamble. No, 'Maybe you should sit down,' or 'I'm so sorry to have to tell you this, Sherry.' Just, 'Your father died.' Her coldness struck me as much as her words. I dropped the phone and ran to the women's restroom where I cried, now consoled by my friends and coworkers.

• • •

Mike and I flew back a few weeks later for the funeral, which was held at Arlington National Cemetery. The weather was dark and cold, and rain came down in torrents. *Just as it should be,* I thought, *fitting the mood and the occasion.* The horse-drawn caissons rested in front of the small chapel, the animals immobile, seemingly oblivious to the pounding rain.

Friends and relatives filled the diminutive chapel to capacity. Dad's cousin, Bill Bradford, stepped to the podium to give the main eulogy. Brad spoke about how, as a boy, his older cousin came to live with them in Chicago and became like an older brother, a teacher, a pillar of support, a disciplinarian, and above all, a role model he could brag about his whole life. "And what a role model he was—an honor student, athlete, adventurer, scholar, and patriot." Bill listed his many accomplishments, then added, "He was a hero, a man of unswerving dedication who continued his service to his government long after the glory days of the war." Bill paused and wiped his eyes, then continued.

"Later, in our lives, when six years' difference in age didn't seem so important, we became closer, and I discovered new, more personal facets of my hero's character. He was Bara's adoring husband ... he was a devoted father ... he was about the best company in the world ... an excellent raconteur, with a great sense of humor, well read, open-minded but argumentative, and a completely dependable friend. Anyone who knew and loved Mac knew that he not only liked to teach, but he loved to lecture, tell people what to do and exactly how to do it.

"Even in parting, he remained in character. On top of all his very detailed instructions he left about things to be done by his survivors was a brief poem. It was as if Mac were at my elbow, saying, 'All right, little brother, you are going to have to say something: here are the words to use.' The poem is by William Wetmore Story:

And after you have mourned awhile,
And grief's deep rut hath worn away,
Recall my foolish jokes and smile,
For I would have my memory gay.

Think of me in the happiest mood,
And speak of me as if I were nigh.
And feel that I am with you still,
As in the days gone by."

Brad returned to his seat, and moments later, the military chaplain ushered me to the podium. I shuffled my index cards. Perspiration smeared the inked words. Then tears added to the runny mess as I glanced down at the cards, now unreadable. For some reason, I thought I had to speak without notes, like there was some funereal rule I had to adhere to. I had been anxiously memorizing my words, which made me even more nervous, sure that I would forget something. I gazed out at the sea of people gathered in the small chapel, but my eyes were on my audience of two—Mother and Chris. They sat on the right side as I faced them, in the middle, on the aisle.

"Dad was just the best father a girl could ever hope for," I began. "When we were small, he always tucked us into bed, offered a small drink of water to 'wet our whistles' so we didn't 'wet our beds,' and regaled us with the adventures of *Tarzan and Jane* before he kissed us good night. From our dad, I learned courage, discipline, order, the importance of forming good habits, working hard, and a lifelong love of reading and learning. He taught me to stand up and speak up. Integrity, honesty, and that your word is your bond were all modeled by him. He never in my life disappointed me. He was, above all else, an honorable man.

"Was he perfect? No. He could be judgmental and didn't suffer fools. He was, at his core, a teacher and liked to lecture others. But he loved a good argument, debating all things philosophical." I paused. "I never heard him raise his voice in anger. Not once. Not ever," I said, looking directly at Mother and Chris.

"Dad had the Irish gift of storytelling. He always made me laugh.

"When I visited Dad and Bara a few years ago," I said to the assembled mourners, "Bara pulled me into the kitchen and asked me to say something to him about his habit of drinking a tumbler of martinis before dinner. She was concerned that he wasn't getting the nutrition he needed, preferring his cocktails over food. She thought I would be more persuasive than she had been. Reluctantly, I agreed and approached him as he sat in his easy chair, sipping his dry martini. He put down his newspaper and looked up at me over the dark rims of his glasses, his eyes quizzical.

"'Dad,' I said, not sure how to approach the subject, 'do you think maybe a whole tumbler of martinis might be too much to drink before dinner? It worries Bara.'" He cocked his head and feigned shock as he stared at me.

"'Why, Sherry,' he said, 'I never drink unless I'm alone or with someone.'" I paused while the mourners relieved the tension of the occasion with a burst of laughter.

"Dad gave me a lifelong love of learning," I continued, "and taught me to always strive to be the best me I could be. He encouraged me to take risks. 'If you're afraid to make a mistake, you'll never make anything,' he counseled.

"Dad was an adventurer and explorer of life. After a year of college, he joined the Merchant Marine to see the world. Then, when the Japanese bombed Pearl Harbor, he joined the Army

Air Forces as a bomber pilot in WWII, flying the new B-24 bombers on missions in the Solomon Islands.

"The enemy shot him down on his first mission from Guadalcanal only days after he and the 307th BG arrived. He led his surviving crew as they paddled a raft through enemy-infested islands for three weeks before being rescued. Once back at Henderson Field, his base, like a rider thrown from his horse, he got back in the saddle and flew another fifty missions. Then, because of his prowess, the Army Air Forces chose him to train on and fly the newest bomber, the B-29, which he flew from Guam from April 1945 until the end of the war. He flew and survived an incredible eighty-three combat missions.

"As children, he took us on a grand adventure across the U.S., visiting parks and museums. He showed us the many marvels of the old-world countries in the Far East, where we lived for two years when the air force appointed him to the post of air attaché of Indochina.

"When Mother filed for divorce, it broke his heart, but he never divorced Cathe and me. We spent every weekend with him when we lived on the East Coast, and every summer when we moved with our mother and stepfather to California. I lived with him for a year while Mother was getting a divorce, and Cathe and I lived with him for another glorious year when he was with NATO, in Paris, France. Dad was a scholar who found time, in between his valuable contributions to his country, to complete two master's degrees and a PhD.

"He never missed a support payment, and he put both Cathe and me through college. He called often, wrote us letters, and made sure we visited him in person as much as possible, always insuring he was a firm presence in our lives. 'I will always be your and Cathe's father,' he promised me when I was ten years old and frantic about the impending divorce. And he was.

"When he met the lovely and devoted Bara, he took care of her and her two children, Cynthia and Eric, and treated them as his own. Some might say he was old-fashioned. He thought men should take care of the women in their lives, that it was their duty, and he was duty-bound. Even as a young man, he sent money home to his mother, a practice he continued throughout her life. And when Grandmother Allison was widowed for the second time, he brought her to live with him and Bara. Saint Bara!

"When I was older and busy with family and career, I regretted we were geographically so far apart. We kept up with letters and phone calls as best we could, but Dad lived on the East Coast in McLean, Virginia, and Mike and I lived on the West Coast in Southern California. The once-a-year visits were not nearly enough to feed my soul. I envied Cynthia and Tony, who lived in New York, a lot nearer, and could spend a good deal of time with Dad, sailing and playing golf. Their children had a close relationship with their grandfather that our children couldn't enjoy. But that was not Dad's fault. We had moved away from him. I missed not having easy access to his stories and adventures and wisdom. Both Mike and I wished we could have had dinner with him every Saturday night and discussed the politics of the day or quizzed him more on his fascinating career.

"In short, Dad was my hero—a man of honor and integrity who helped me become the person I am today. Dad was my radar when clouds rolled into my life, and I needed direction. He never let me down. I will forever miss him. I love you, Dad. You were always *'the wind beneath my wings,'* gently helping me rise and urging me to soar."

• • •

As we left the chapel and made our way outside, the seven beautiful, black horses, still motionless, waited patiently for their consignment. Soldiers sat ramrod straight on four of them, never flinching in the pounding rain. Six of the horses stood ready to pull the flag-draped casket containing the remains of our father to his final resting place in Arlington National Cemetery: Section 20, grave 6827. One horse, riderless and costumed in military finery, followed the caisson. A rider's boots were reversed in the stirrups, signifying that the warrior would never ride again.

Leaving the chapel, we trudged slowly in the rain, umbrellas raised, following the caisson to the burial plot, the clip-clop of the horses' feet barely audible in the mud and constant downpour, but each step in perfect cadence. We watched as a color guard saluted, a firing party fired shots overhead, a military band played taps, and uniformed soldiers lowered his casket into the open grave. It was a moving and fitting tribute to a great man and steadfast father.

Arlington National Cemetery

Mac received the following medals and awards during his years of service:

Two Distinguished Service Crosses, for extraordinary heroism in action against an enemy of the U.S.

Two Distinguished Flying Crosses, Heroism or extraordinary achievement while participating in aerial flight, with one bronze oak leaf.

Purple Heart, awarded for being killed or wounded in armed conflict.

Air Medal, Heroic actions or meritorious service while participating in aerial flight—one silver or four bronze oak leaf.

Presidential Unit Award—two bronze oak leaf clusters

American Campaign Medal

Asiatic-Pacific Campaign Medal- with three bronze stars

Army Commendation Medal

World War II Victory Medal

Honorable Discharge Pin

Four overseas bars.

Joint Service Commendation Medal

U.S. Air Force Commendation Medal with one bronze oak leaf cluster

National Defense Service Medal with one bronze star

Air Force Longevity Service Award Ribbon with a silver oak leaf cluster

Air Force Small Arms expert marksman ribbon

Official documents and photographs have verified all awards and attachments.

Acknowledgments

The primary sources for my dad's experiences in Guadalcanal I took from his own handwritten transcription for a speech on survival to the air force, his debrief following the rescue, other documents, war records, and his flight records. His letters home are verbatim, and to me, they show remarkable maturity, intellect, and compassion for a twenty-four-year-old young man away at war. They also show his devotion to his mother, whom he cared for throughout her life.

My secondary sources were primarily three books written by men who served with him in the 307th Bombardment Group and 13th Air Force. Up the Slot by Samuel I. Walker, who served with him as radio operator and gunner on several missions after Mac lost part of his own crew, The Long Rangers: A Diary of the 307th Bombardment Group (H) by Sam S. Britt Jr., a bomber pilot, and Missions of the Shehasta: A Story of World War II Bomber Aces by Lyman "Ace" Clark Jr., a ball turret gunner who also flew with Mac. There were many other informative books and history websites, which I have included in the bibliography.

James McCabe, the historian of the 307th Bombardment Group, was a tremendous resource in pointing me to other books and databases. He read the manuscript twice and corrected countless facts, including dates and names of men in the 307th BG Mac served with. Jim and I spent hours by phone conferring, reviewing, and editing. I am incredibly indebted to him for his time and help in this labor of love.

Matt McAvoy and Jefferson R. Blackburn-Smith did beta reads and offered valuable feedback and suggestions on the theme that enabled me to reorder events in the book and make it immeasurably better. I am so grateful for their frank suggestions and comments.

I would also like to acknowledge my friends Larry and Iris Hattersley, both retired from the U.S. Marshals Service. Larry is an aficionado of all things WWII. He helped in much of the research, offered cogent comments, and found grievous military errors, for which I am greatly appreciative. Iris, herself a published author, assisted extensively in editing and proofreading. A dynamic duo, to be sure.

My dear sister Cathe Cordova, an educator, was also a tremendous help in early editing and proofreading. Jami Carpenter, The Red Pen Girl, edited early on and was a valuable resource in editing and formatting. And my gratitude also to Joyce Mochrie, owner of One Last Look, my detailed and very patient professional copy editor and proofreader.

I thank and salute you all!

About the Author

As a daughter of an Air Force Colonel, she has lived on three continents in countries including Vietnam, France and dozens of cities in the U.S. She has written one previous book a memoir— *Bird of Passage*. A former social worker turned sales executive for an insurance company, she has been happily married to her college sweetheart for fifty years and has three grandsons.

Note from Sherry Hobbs

Word-of-mouth is crucial for any author to succeed. If you enjoyed *Mac*, please leave a review online—anywhere you are able. Even if it's just a sentence or two. It would make all the difference and would be very much appreciated.

Thanks!
Sherry Hobbs

We hope you enjoyed reading this title from:

www.blackrosewriting.com

Subscribe to our mailing list – *The Rosevine* – and receive **FREE** books, daily deals, and stay current with news about upcoming
releases and our hottest authors.
Scan the QR code below to sign up.

Already a subscriber? Please accept a sincere thank you for being a fan of Black Rose Writing authors.

View other Black Rose Writing titles at www.blackrosewriting.com/books and use promo code **PRINT** to receive a **20% discount** when purchasing.